Music of the Civil War Era

Recent Titles in
American History through Music
David J. Brinkman, Series Editor

Music of the Counterculture Era
James E. Perone

Music of the Civil War Era

Steven H. Cornelius

American History through Music
David J. Brinkman, Series Editor

GREENWOOD PRESS
Westport, Connecticut • London

Library of Congress Cataloging-in-Publication Data

Cornelius, Steven, 1952–
    Music of the Civil War era / Steven H. Cornelius.
        p.   cm.—(American history through music)
    Includes bibliographical references and index.
    ISBN 0–313–32081–0 (alk. paper)
        1. United States—History—Civil War, 1861–1865—Music and the war.   2. Music—
    United States—19th century   Social aspects.   I. Title.   II. Series.
    ML3551.4.C67   2004
    780'.973'09034—dc22   2004042531

British Library Cataloguing in Publication Data is available.

Library of Congress Catalog Card Number: 2004042531
ISBN: 0–313–32081–0

First published in 2004

Greenwood Press, 88 Post Road West, Westport, CT 06881
An imprint of Greenwood Publishing Group, Inc.
www.greenwood.com

Printed in the United States of America

For my great-great-great-uncle Casper A. Kessenich,
my grandfather Harry E. Kessenich, and my father Rupert G. Cornelius.

BEAT! BEAT! DRUMS!

Beat! beat! drums!—Blow! bugles! blow!
Through the windows—through doors—burst like a force of ruthless
    men,
Into the solemn church, and scatter the congregation;
Into the school where the scholar is studying:
Leave not the bridegroom quiet—no happiness must he have now with
    his bride;
Nor the peaceful farmer any peace, plowing his field or gathering his
    grain;
So fierce you whirr and pound, you drums—so shrill you bugles blow.

Beat! beat! drums!—Blow! bugles! blow!
Over the traffic of cities—over the rumble of wheels in the streets:
Are beds prepared for sleepers at night in the houses? No sleepers
    must sleep in those beds;
No bargainers' bargains by day—no brokers or speculators—Would
    they continue?
Would the talkers be talking? would the singer attempt to sing?
Would the lawyer rise in the court to state his case before the judge?
Then rattle quicker, heavier drums—you bugles wilder blow.

Beat! beat! drums!—Blow! bugles! blow!
Make no parley—stop for no expostulation;
Mind not the timid—mind not the weeper or prayer;
Mind not the old man beseeching the young man;
Let not the child's voice be heard, nor the mother's entreaties;
Make even the trestles to shake the dead, where they lie awaiting the
    hearses,
So strong you thump, O terrible drums—so loud you bugles blow.

—Walt Whitman, *Drum-Taps*

Contents

Series Foreword

The elements of music are well known. They include melody, rhythm, harmony, form, and texture. Music, though, has infinite variety. Exploring this variety in the music of specific time periods, such as the Colonial and Revolutionary Period, the Roaring Twenties, and the Counterculture Era, is the purpose of the "American History through Music" series. The authors of each volume describe the music in terms of its basic elements, but more importantly, focus on how the social, economic, political, technological, and religious influences shaped the music of that particular time. Each volume in the series not only describes the music of a particular era but the ways in which the music reflected societal concerns. For these purposes, music is defined inclusively; this series considers such diverse musical genres as classical, folk, jazz, rock, religious, and theater music, as each of these genres serve as both reflections of society and as illustrations of how music influences society.

Perhaps the most important conclusion that readers will draw from this series is that music does not exist independently of society. Listeners have enjoyed music throughout time for its aesthetic qualities, but music has also been used to convey emotions and ideas. It has been used to enhance patriotic rituals, and to maintain order in social and religious ceremonies. The "American History through Music" series attempts to put these and other uses of music in an historical context. For instance, how did music serve as entertainment during the Great Depression? How did the music of the Civil War contribute to the stability of the Union—and to the Confederacy? Answers to these and other questions show that music is not just a part of society; music *is* society.

The authors of "American History through Music" present essays based in sound scholarship, written for the lay reader. In addition to discussing important genres and approaches to music, each volume profiles the composers and performers whose music defines their era, describes the musical instruments and technological innovations that influenced the musical world, and provides a glossary of important terms and a bibliography of recommended readings. This information will help students and other interested readers understand the colorful and complex mosaics of musical history.

David J. Brinkman
University of Wyoming

Preface

If the Revolutionary War gave Americans the freedom to form a nation, the Civil War provided the glue that would hold it together once and for all. Sectional differences and bitterness would remain—indeed, in regional pockets they remain today—but the Union would be just that, a union of many peoples and many convictions woven together into one nation under a single flag. Those four years, during which some 620,000 men died, were arguably the most important in the nation's history, not just because they saw the nation preserved, but also because they forged from many peoples a common heritage tempered with shared experience and suffering.

We who live today are children of that experience. Ghosts of the war abound. Rebel battle flags still adorn truck windows North and South. Films, such as *Glory* and *Gettysburg*, the Ken Burns documentary *The Civil War*, and even the 1939 classic *Gone with the Wind* continue to spark the public imagination. Thousands of Civil War reenactors assemble each summer on aging, and in many cases quietly disappearing, battlefields. Characters from the era, both fictitious and real, populate our time. Captain John Carter, the hero of Edgar Rice Burroughs's early twentieth-century Martian adventure novels, was both Virginia gentleman and Confederate officer; Abraham Lincoln adorns the penny and five-dollar bill, Ulysses S. Grant is on the fifty.

My own introduction to the Civil War came in 1965 when, as an eighth grader in Madison, Wisconsin, I was assigned to create a booklet about the

Civil War for my history class. As the project got under way, I enlisted the help of my grandfather who, then in his late seventies, had won two Purple Hearts for his service in World War I. Although he had always declined to talk about experiences in France, my Civil War project sparked his interest. Soon he was telling me of Casper A. Kessenich, his grandfather's brother and my great-great-great uncle. Casper was a musician just like me. And he had enlisted in the Union army to serve as a drummer boy. Casper was killed at Shiloh at age sixteen.

So his story went anyhow, and the tale took a place in the family lore for the next quarter century. Around that point, however, my cousin took it upon himself to compile the Kessenich family genealogy. Naturally, he came across Casper who, it turned out, died in the Battle of Sabine Cross Roads, not Shiloh. A private in the 23rd Wisconsin, he was born in Oedekoven, Germany in 1835 and was in his late twenties at the time of his death. We know nothing about his musical background.

Unimpressed by tales of heroics, and pragmatic to the core, my grandfather had little patience for war-born fantasies. I am certain he believed the drummer-boy story just as he related it. Indeed, the entire family believed it. How did he get the facts all wrong? We will never know for certain, but I will venture a guess. Oral history is a fickle thing, and I suspect my grandfather, who was born in 1887 and some twenty-three years too late to ever know Casper, conflated boyhood remembrances of a martyred ancestor with the famous Civil War song "The Drummer Boy of Shiloh," a work he undoubtedly knew from his youth.

Fortunately, we who study the Civil War today have many opportunities to clarify the record. There is a vast amount of period and modern documents at our disposal. Some 90 percent of white Northern soldiers and 80 percent of their Southern counterparts were literate.[1] They read the newspapers, kept diaries, and wrote letters home. Many of their writings have been published. Others have been saved and quietly await discovery in archives across the nation.

As this book developed, I immersed myself in those documents. I read diaries, collections of letters from the front lines, and regimental histories. The diaries and letters of common soldiers offered fascinating (and often horrifying) remembrances of the war's brutality and occasional majesty. For a view closer to the top, so to speak, I read works by Confederate General John B. Gordon and Union General Joshua Lawrence Chamberlain. For wide-ranging studies of the Civil War and the time period, I turned to historians James M. McPherson, Shelby Foote, Bruce Catton, Bell Irvin Wiley, Jay Winik, and others. For a sense of the period's occasionally gothic tastes, I read the Civil War short stories of Ambrose Bierce. Tony Horwitz's lively *Confederates in the Attic* reminded me that, for some at least, skirmishes are taking place today.

Web sites proved invaluable across a broad range of topics. The "American Memory" section of the Library of Congress Web site offers a wealth of important literary documents as well as digitized sheet music and photographs. Equally useful were The Johns Hopkins University's "Lester S. Levy Collection of Sheet Music" and Duke University's "Historic American Sheet Music" sites. The "North American Slave Narratives" site at the University of North Carolina at Chapel Hill Libraries includes a superb collection of period texts that have been made digitally available.[2] These are just a few of the hundreds of useful sites maintained by public and private organizations. Thousands more (though not always rigorous in their accuracy) are maintained by individuals.

In finding my musical focus I studied the writings of George Templeton Strong, the publications of Boston and New York City critics John Sullivan Dwight and William Henry Fry, and the reminiscences of composer/pianist Louis Moreau Gottschalk. Each provided helpful insights into the time's high urban culture. For the music of African Americans I turned to Frederick Douglass, Thomas Wentworth Higginson, Charlotte L. Forten, Elizabeth Hyde Botume, William Francis Allen, and others. Modern histories on the music of the period by Richard Crawford, Charles Hamm, H. Wiley Hitchcock, Nicholas Tawa, and other musicologists helped me to both understand the period's aesthetics and comprehend the multifaceted scope of mid-nineteenth-century musical life.

Curiously, while soldier musicians' diaries, letters home, and publications were helpful, they included less discussion of music than I had expected. Even the letters of "Wisconsin's Singing Soldier" Edwin Kimberley, who directed a brigade band in Sherman's army, are surprisingly short on musical reminiscences. Yet, music (ranging from string bands to brass bands to just plain singing) was an essential part of army life. I suspect the many sounds of camp were so woven into a soldier's daily experience that they seemed hardly worthy of mention.

Not to all, thankfully. Some soldiers—such as John D. Billings, W. H.

Bentley, Francis Adams Donaldson, David Holt, Augustus Meyers, Frank Rauscher, Robert Knox Sneden, and others—discussed musical life in considerable detail.

These documents were invariably filtered through a screen of nineteenth-century morality. Soldiers' diaries often tell in gruesome detail of war's horrors: of cowards and heroes, of comrades and enemies. Yet even these most private accounts were written with posterity in mind. Surely these men cussed and hated and engaged in unsavory activities, but few wrote about it. Surely they sang vulgar songs; I found not a single example.

Almost invariably, whites of long-standing American heritage appear on the top of the social ladder, while recent immigrants sit on lower rungs. African Americans and Native Americans occupy the bottom. The speech of African Americans (and occasionally Germans and Irish) was written in dialect that separated them from the mainstream culture. These transcriptions must be understood as markers of difference, of contemporary strategies of exclusion; period writers ignored other sorts of regional accents and idiosyncrasies. I have quoted these various sources without "correcting" either spelling or dialect.

About what sort of things did people of that era sing? In contrast to today, much of the music was topical in nature. There were songs of love and nostalgia, of course, but songs also dealt with social issues and events. Indeed, so socially connected was the music that one might term this the era of "song bites," much in the same way that ours is an era of televised "sound bites." Lyricists freely glossed social issues and mined personal emotions. Composers then set those lyrics to catchy melodies for the masses to sing. Songs spoke of immigration and westward expansion, states' rights and human rights, technology and tradition, nation and home, mother and lover, life and death.

Music helped emotions soar. Some songs moved men to tears; others drove them to ferocious acts of patriotism. Many, as at the Battle of Lookout Mountain, are the tales of bands fortifying men's courage as they marched into combat. On occasion, soldiers even credited bands for helping to turn the tide of battle.

Music was used as a political weapon and tool. Southern women, complained Louis Moreau Gottschalk, liked to wrap "their children in Confederate flags, and [make] them sing . . . 'My Maryland' or 'Dixie,' for the purpose of drawing on themselves the prosecution of the government."[3] In an act rich with symbolism, President Abraham Lincoln publicly reclaimed

"Dixie" for the Union shortly after Confederate General Robert E. Lee's surrender at Appomattox.

Curiously, the most moving description of "music" that I encountered during research for this book came from neither singing nor playing, but from music's conspicuous absence. General Joshua Lawrence Chamberlain, the one-time Bowdoin College linguistics professor and hero at Gettysburg's Little Round Top, wrote of the surrender at Appomattox that:

> Before us in proud humiliation stood the embodiment of manhood: men whom neither toils and sufferings, nor the fact of death, nor disaster, nor hopelessness could bend from their resolve; standing before us now, thin, worn, and famished, but erect, and with eyes looking level into ours, waking memories that bound us together as no other bond;—was not such manhood to be welcomed back into a Union so tested and assured? . . . On our part not a sound of trumpet more, nor roll of drum; not a cheer, nor word nor whisper of vain-glorying, nor motion of man standing again at the order, but an awed stillness rather, and breath-holding, as if it were the passing of the dead![4]

Heroes and rogues, rich and poor, and ethnically diverse, Americans of the Civil War era were a remarkable lot. Their experiences bound them together, comrades and enemies alike. Armies fought with near superhuman tenacity and valor. Men died by the thousands, sometimes—as at Antietam in 1862, Gettysburg in 1863, and Cold Harbor in 1864—reaching those marks in spans just minutes long. Amidst these horrors, and after the last bullet had killed, a nation was reformed that, over time, would learn to speak and sing with a collective voice. When the guns of Fort Sumter, Gettysburg, and Petersburg were finally quieted, the dead buried, and the grief assuaged, the songs would remain. Many are still sung today.

Antebellum America

As French nobleman Alexis de Tocqueville noted in his 1835 classic work *Democracy in America*, antebellum America was a land of opportunity. Or it was, at least, for the tenacious, the lucky, and the white.[1] The most ambitious and resolute strove tirelessly to ascend the social ladder. Some, like the soldier-politician Andrew Jackson (1767–1845) and fur trader John Jacob Astor (1763–1848), attained their dreams. Most did not.

As the century progressed, white Americans moved steadily westward, displacing Native Americans, usurping their land, and often introducing slavery. Giving focus to this development was the notion of "Manifest Destiny," a political catchphrase of the 1840s suggesting that national expansion from the Atlantic to the Pacific was not only inevitable, but preordained. The idea set the United States on a collision course with Mexico in 1844 and with England (over the Oregon Territory) in 1846. Because the right to hold slaves was contested in many of the new territories, westward growth would help drive an irreconcilable wedge between North and South. The South sought to expand slavery throughout the Western Hemisphere; the North sought its limitation and eventual abolishment.

By the century's midpoint, the sinews of culture and commerce that held North to South were being stretched to breaking. Escalating this discord was the fact that North and South were following conflicting visions. The white South remained socially aristocratic, culturally homogeneous, agrarian in focus, and anti-industrial. The North followed the drumbeat of hard-driven capitalists who filled their ever-expanding factories with anonymous wage laborers, many of whom were recent immigrants.

Although South Carolina was the first state to secede from the Union (on December 20, 1860), hers was not the first attempt to fracture it. That happened almost immediately after the nation was formed when the short-lived Whiskey Rebellion of 1794 pitted the gentrified East against a frontier West. That was just the first of many internecine flare-ups. Four years later, James Madison (1751–1836) and Thomas Jefferson (1743–1826) would open the question of the legal right of states to secede from the Union when they authored the 1798–1799 Virginia and Kentucky Resolutions. Massachusetts considered secession during the War of 1812. In the decades to come, and animated by a variety of different issues, so too would Western-oriented California and Oregon, Mormon Utah, and even New York City.

In fact, while slavery was the topic that brought secession to a head, it was an issue over which few common soldiers fought—Confederate or Union. The Southern reality was that just a fraction of ordinary Confederate soldiers were slave owners. Most were small farmers swept up in the passions of the day who, as the war dragged on, increasingly saw the conflict as "a rich man's war and a poor man's fight."[2] Southern diaries and letters suggest that the notion of states' rights, not slavery, was the issue for which most of these fiercely individualistic men went to war. As the struggle developed and the death toll mounted, however, they increasingly fought for personal honor and to protect their Southern way of life.

Northern soldiers, for their part, wrote about preservation of the Union and defending it against treason. Strong as the abolition movement was in some regions, particularly New England, a large percentage of soldiers would never have enlisted had the war originally been cast in solely abolitionist terms. Letters and diaries show that Union soldiers were often highly racially prejudiced. Many felt cheated by the Emancipation Proclamation of January 1, 1863. Emancipation, they complained, was not the cause for which they had enlisted. Moreover, they worried that the law would make things worse by inspiring the Confederates to fight even harder. Union soldiers knew from the previous month's disaster at Fredericksburg and too many other battles that the Confederates fought plenty hard already.

Seen from the halcyon spring days of 1861, however, these various thoughts were not yet formed. President Abraham Lincoln's (1809–1865) initial call for troops was astoundingly unrealistic; he required only 75,000 men for a three-month enlistment. Young men stepped forward in droves, spurred on at rallies by a patriotic fervor that was excited in no small part by the sounds of choruses and marching bands. Enlistees wanted to witness the glory of combat, to "see the elephant," as the contemporary phrase went. They saw far more.

DEMOGRAPHICS

Change was rapid as the nation expanded inexorably westward. By 1840 one-third of the population would live between the Appalachians and the Mississippi River. In Ohio, the population soared from 45,000 in 1800 to more than 2.3 million by 1860. Missouri jumped from 384,000 in 1840 to 1.2 million twenty years later. Eastern states also grew, but more slowly. The population of Massachusetts rose from 738,000 in 1840 to 1,231,000 in 1860; Virginia's from 1.2 million to nearly 1.6 million during the same period. Eastern and western cities paralleled this growth. New York City's population rose from 124,000 in 1820 to 800,000 in 1860. Chicago, which benefited from the arrival of rail transportation in 1854, surged from 5,000 in 1840 to 110,000 by 1860. By 1860, nine Northern cities had populations over 100,000. The South had just one, New Orleans. Nationally, the population stood at slightly under 17 million in 1840; it had nearly doubled to more than 31 million by 1860.

Immigration fueled population growth. In the decades from 1820 to 1840, some 751,000 people came into the country. Over the next twenty years that figure more than quintupled to 4.3 million. In 1860 three-fourths of foreign-born Americans were Irish or German. The Irish tended to remain in the urban Northeast; many Germans continued west to Ohio, Indiana, Illinois, Wisconsin, and Missouri. In both of these groups, ethnic bonds remained strong. When the Civil War broke out, they would often form their own regiments. Both the Irish and Germans sustained and created distinctive music.

Not surprisingly, immigrant songs written and published in the United States often spoke of longing for home and of family and heritage left behind. Leon Rawicz Ganronski's "The Exile's Farewell to Poland" (1844) for voice and guitar is typical in its recollection of an idyllic childhood in the homeland.[3] Sometimes songs spoke of future hopes. Charles Green's "From Lovely Erin Sad I Come" (1848) featured on its front piece a solitary and loosely garbed young woman seated under the protection of a tree. She plays a Celtic harp. She is alone but content:

> From lovely Erin sad I come,
> Across the rolling sea;
> In stranger land to seek a home,
> A home of liberty.

Such hopes were often dashed. Fretted the protagonist in Hannah F. Gould and Dr. Hook's 1852 song " 'The Dying Exile' (Respectfully Inscribed to the Sons of Hungary)":

> Who will stand when I shall pillow
> In the earth this aching head,
> Pensive by the drooping willow
> O'er my cold and lowly bed!
> There will be no tender mother,
> Aged sire nor constant friend;
> There will be no sister, brother,
> O'er my lonely grave to bend!

INDUSTRY

Spurring immigration was the promise of economic opportunity. The subsequent march westward was stimulated by a revolution in transportation and the hope that economic self-sufficiency could be attained through farming, cattle, land, or gold. It sometimes was. By the 1840s, farmers were increasingly moving from subsistence to market-based agriculture. Instead of simply providing for their families, farmers grew cash crops to ship to the urban East and, in the case of cotton, even Europe.

This change was made possible by improved transportation that made shipping both faster and cheaper. Here three factors came into play: the building of the Northeast's canal system, the development and proliferation of the steamboat, and the development of the steam locomotive. There were some 3,300 miles of rail track in 1840, 30,000 in 1860. The vast majority was in the industrial North.

All of these developments inspired music. Workers sang as they moved

along the canals; publishers printed songs that caught the poetic imagina-
tions and comic fancies of customers often far removed. Examples are
P. Morris's tongue-in-cheek "The Raging Canal" (1844) and L.V.H. Crosby's
minstrel song, "I'm Sailin' on de Old Canal" (1845):

> De earth did quake and de breakers roar,
> When she came on board and left de shore;
> De boat did dance wid joy to see,
> My coloured gal sail off wid me.

Composers published amateur piano pieces based on colorful or dramatic
marine themes, for example, J. Long's "The Empire Quickstep" (1844), dedicated to that ship's captain. The disastrous January 1854 sinking of the S.S.
San Francisco motivated Oscar Comettant's programmatic composition,
"Wreck of the San Francisco," which portrayed the various legs of the ship's
voyage from the "Farewell to Land" to "The Gale" that sunk her.

Trains inspired solo piano pieces with animated names, such as Theodore
von la Hache's "Locomotive Polka" (1849) and Adolf Baumbach's "Metro-
politan Rail Road Galop" (1857). Composers almost invariably imitated the
various sounds of the trains, from the rising tone of the whistle to the flexed
power of the engine. The front piece of Jas. N. Beck's "Fast Line Gallop"
(1853) further suggests the ways in which the railroad stimulated contemporary notions of progress. Illustrated is a map of rail lines connecting towns
from the Atlantic seaboard to the Mississippi.

Some railroad songs, like George Holman's "Wake Up, Jake" (1862), were
in blackface minstrel style. Typical of minstrel characters, Jake is a blur of
contradictions. He is clever, but lazy; knows Milton, but speaks English
poorly. Jake dismisses Byron as "witty," prefers everyday subjects, and looks
to lend his own talents towards immortalizing the tangibly gritty muscularity
of the "Iron City" (Pittsburgh).

> Oh, Jake has been to college,
> And says he am a Poet,
> And while the track am good and strong,
> He says he means to go it.
> Dat Milton went to "paradise,"
> And Byron he was witty,
> But Jake he means to 'mortalize,
> Dat same ole Iron City.

The relative shortfall in Southern rail mileage mirrored its technological pace in general. By 1850, the South had one-third of the nation's population but only one-tenth of the nation's manufacturing capability. In fact, the South had less than one-third the manufacturing capacity of Massachusetts alone.

What the South did have was cotton, whose economic ascendancy had been guaranteed by Eli Whitney's 1793 invention of the cotton gin. Cotton was antebellum America's premiere cash crop, and its production drove virtually all aspects of the Southern economy. Some 3,000 bales were exported in 1790, 4.5 million bales in 1860. The economics of cotton transformed the South by spurring farm development into the prime climates and soils of Alabama, Mississippi, Louisiana, and eastern Texas. Because cotton production remained labor intensive, its production further reinforced the institution of slavery.

"Cotton is king," proclaimed South Carolina Senator James H. Hammond during a March 4, 1858, Senate speech. The analogy quickly became a Southern rallying point. George P. Morris (1802–1864) and Delia W. Jones later anthropomorphized the aristocratic crop in their song, "Old Cotton is King!" (1862):

> Old Cotton is King, boys, aha!
> With his locks so fleecy and white.
> He shines among kings like a star!
> And his is the sceptre of right, boys, of right,
> And his is the sceptre of right.

John Hill Hewitt's (1801–1890) "Dixie, the Land of King Cotton" appeared in the finale of his 1863 operetta *The Vivandiere*:

> Oh, Dixie! the Land of King Cotton,
> The home of the brave and the free;
> A nation by Freedom begotten,
> The terror of despots to be.

Perhaps, but Northerners generally saw such notions as just so much bluster. H. T. Merrill responded to Morris and Jones with "Corn is King!" (1862), an ode to a Northern cash crop. With each ensuing chorus Merrill unleashed a new assault:

> Old King Cotton's dead and buried,
> Brave young Corn is King
>
> Massa Cotton's dead foreber,
> Massa young Corn am King
>
> Pallid Cotton's dead and buried,
> Yellow Corn is King
>
> Tyrant King Cotton's dead and buried,
> Honest Corn is King

For their part, Southerners paid scant attention to Merrill or any Northerner. Indeed, the notion of King Cotton survived well into the twentieth century.

LITERATURE

Cheaper paper and the development of steam-driven presses occasioned the rise of print media. Newspapers expanded their circulation and began to wield significant political power. Modern news reporting was introduced with two highly influential newspapers, James Gordon Bennett's (1795–1872) *New York Herald* and Horace Greeley's (1811–1872) *New York Tribune*. The music criticism of Bostonian John Sullivan Dwight (1813–1893) and New Yorker William Henry Fry (1813–1864) would be some of the nation's earliest and most memorable.

Literature also rose in importance. Immensely popular were sentimental novels and poetry written by, and often for, women. Scenes of domestic music making are woven throughout Louisa May Alcott's (1832–1888) Civil War–period novel *Little Women* (1869). Emily Dickinson (1830–1886) often invoked music to enhance the delicate quality of her subjects. Most influential at the time was Connecticut-born Harriet Beecher Stowe (1811–1896), whose sentimental and politically incendiary abolitionist novel *Uncle Tom's Cabin* (1852) is peppered with song. The saintly slave Uncle Tom rejoiced in singing Methodist hymns; other African-American characters sang what Stowe called "those unmeaning songs, common among slaves":

> Mas'r see'd me cotch a coon,
> High boys, high!
> He laughed to split—d'ye see the moon,

Ho! ho! ho! boys, ho!
Ho! yo! hi—e! oh![4]

Also using music as a means to raise Northern abolitionist sentiments was ex-slave Frederick Douglass (1817–1895), whose powerful autobiography, *Narrative of the Life of Frederick Douglass*, was published in 1845. His newspaper, *North Star* (later *Frederick Douglass' Paper*), was published from 1847 to 1863.

Other writers developing American themes, characters, and voices included Washington Irving (1783–1859); Nathaniel Hawthorne (1804–1864), whose *The Scarlet Letter* (1850) showed the righteous character of the New England consciousness; and Herman Melville (1819–1891), whose inward-looking *Moby Dick* (1851) explored regions of the human soul just beginning to be noticed. Henry Thoreau (1817–1862) contributed *Walden* in 1854. Walt Whitman's (1819–1892) loose non-metrical verse and sensual language redefined the rules of poetry.

Occasionally, authors wrote about Native Americans. For the white man, the red man was an enigma—cast on the one hand as a heathen savage, idealized on the other for his bravery and honor. The former attitude is most starkly represented by the Indian Removal Act (1830) and the subsequent forced migration known as the "Trail of Tears" (1838). The latter attitude is most famously encountered in James Fenimore Cooper's (1789–1851) *Leatherstocking Tales* and Henry Wadsworth Longfellow's (1807–1882) twenty-two canto epic poem "The Song of Hiawatha" (1855). The poem glorifies a culture that by then had but a tenuous cultural hold east of the Mississippi River.

Should you ask where Nawadaha
Found these songs so wild and wayward,
Found these legends and traditions,
I should answer, I should tell you,
"In the bird's-nests of the forest,
In the lodges of the beaver,
In the hoofprint of the bison,
In the eyry of the eagle!"

Longfellow presented certain truths: then as now, for example, a Native American might receive songs from nature. But the words mostly present the distant imaginings and longings of the white man. Fantasy or not, however, these ideas had tremendous power. Longfellow's poem inspired numerous songs and piano pieces, including: Ch. C. Converse's "The Death of Minnehaha" (1856) and C. L. Peticolas's "Hiawatha Polka" (1856). Robert Stoepel's *Hiawatha: A Romantic Symphony* would be premiered on January 8, 1859, at the Boston Theatre.

British novelist Charles Dickens (1812–1870) toured America as far west as St. Louis in 1841–1842 and returned in 1867–1868. So popular were his works with American readers that book titles and characters were sometimes used as hooks for selling piano sheet music. Examples included F.A.S.'s oddly optimistic "Bleak House Polka" (1852) and C. L. Peticolas's "Little Dorrit Schottisch" (1856).

Particularly important to understanding mid-nineteenth-century popular song texts were the ideas of Ralph Waldo Emerson (1803–1882) and Edgar Allan Poe (1809–1849). The transcendentalist Emerson maintained that knowledge transcends intellect, that intuition and emotional awareness provide knowledge just as useful as schooled modes of learning. Poe, who "would much rather have written the best *song* of a nation than its noblest *epic*," saw the best lyrics as accomplishing this ideal by eliciting "sensations which bewilder while they enthrall."[5]

To Poe, the era's greatest song poet was New York journalist George P. Morris, who wrote sentimental poems that combined images of an Arcadian past with those of idealized romantic love. Morris and others of the period's judicious Romanticists found an intangible "just out of reach" type of satisfaction by either peering back into a nostalgic past or looking forward into a gossamer future. Wrote Morris in "Open Thy Lattice, Love," which was set by eighteen-year-old Stephen Collins Foster (1826–1864) and published in 1844:

> Open thy lattice, love listen to me!
> In the voyage of life, love our pilot will be!
> He will sit at the helm wherever we rove,
> And steer by the load-star he kindled above

Picture the scene. As did Romeo to Juliet, the man stands without and calls to his love sheltered within (and symbolically, to an idealized inner self). He offers not physical passion, but a vision of love's purity.

Foster used this formula time and again, as with "Jeanie with the Light

Brown Hair" (1854) and "Beautiful Dreamer" (1862, published posthumously in 1864). In each, the protagonist "dreams" rather than acts or touches:

> I dream of Jeanie with the light brown hair,
> Borne, like a vapor, on the summer air;

> Beautiful dreamer, wake unto me,
> Starlight and dewdrops are waiting for thee;
> Sounds of the rude world heard in the day,
> Lull'd by the moonlight have all pass'd away!
> Beautiful dreamer, queen of my song,
> List while I woo thee with soft melody;
> Gone are the cares of life's busy throng,
> Beautiful dreamer, awake unto me!

Grandiloquent as these lyrics might seem to us today, they were deeply affecting to the period's listeners. These myriad chronicles of disembodied passion brought listeners of both sexes to tears.

This was a remarkable situation. Men, who would never show "feminine" emotions in response to their own personally trying circumstances, were free to do so during a song recital. Tears were acceptable because the memories and/or hopes being expressed were experienced communally as human universals. Thus, such a response confirmed one's breadth of humanity, not weakness of character. Lincoln himself embodied these affects. Although firm enough to push America's bloodiest war to its conclusion, he was also "cultured" enough to weep. Ward Lamon recalled the song "Twenty Years Ago," relating that "Many a time have I seen [Lincoln] in tears while I was rendering in my poor way that homely melody."[6] Lincoln neither played an instrument nor read music.

MUSICAL HERITAGE

Nineteenth-century American music drew from rich streams of culture: European, African, and Native American. Each was complex in its diversity. Before colonization, each had formed a musical world whole within itself. As the nineteenth century progressed, African and European music sometimes converged to form styles both new and uniquely American. The music of Native Americans, generally like the culture itself, remained distinctly separate from the other two.

Our understanding of these streams varies. Music by those of European heritage, the period's dominant culture, was woven into the nation's social institutions and economy at large. Musical offerings ranged in genres from opera to minstrel shows to folksongs, a sampling broad enough to satisfy urban dilettantes and sinewy frontiersmen, rank amateurs and accomplished professionals. The activities of white Americans were well documented by contemporary writers and historians. In contrast, accounts of nineteenth-century Native American music barely exist; those that do are often biased and highly derogatory. Nineteenth-century African-American musical traditions are better documented, but often they too are deeply skewed by cultural prejudice.

Early immigrants from Europe were mostly English, but there were also sizeable populations of Germans and Moravians. They arrived in the New World with little material wealth or power, but were steeled by deep religious and moral convictions. Along with their social institutions, they brought a simple musical language that befitted a generally humble social class. That music quickly took root. By the 1720s, New England singing school instructors were traveling down the East Coast as far as the Carolinas. Within two generations, the rough-hewn melodies of William Billings (1746–1800), Daniel Read (1757–1836), and others would coalesce into the beginnings of a national vocal style.

As urban centers developed, so did interest in art music. Foreign-language opera saw its first flowering in French New Orleans in 1796 with Frenchman André Modeste Grétry's one-act comedy *Silvain* (1770). That city was America's most important opera center until the Civil War. By comparison, New York City was but a distant second and did not stage a foreign-language opera until the 1825 arrival of Manuel García's Italian Opera Company. By the middle of the century, American-composed art music was beginning to emerge from a state of quiet gestation. Though mostly forgotten today, composers such as Anthony Philip Heinrich (1781–1861), William Henry Fry, Lowell Mason (1792–1872), George Frederick Bristow (1825–1898), William Mason (1829–1908), and others wrote occasionally colorful scores. Louis Moreau Gottschalk (1829–1869) would be the first American art music composer whose work would hold a significant place in the standard repertoire.

If most mid-century American art music composers were still some decades away from carving out a lasting voice, the institutions in which those voices would eventually be heard were already being founded. Boston's Handel and Haydn Society, which continues to play an important role in that city's musical life, was established in 1815 by forty-eight-year-old German immigrant Gottlieb Graupner. The New York Philharmonic Society was founded in 1842. Concert bands also rose in popularity beginning in the early 1840s; there would be thousands by 1860.

Folk music and popular songs came to the New World from the British Isles. These sounds were sometimes preserved in their original forms, but most often were set to new lyrics, and even instruments, that reflected specifically American experiences. Some of these melodies were incorporated into American ballad operas that combined spoken dialect and song. Of the many tunes brought over, British composer John Stafford Smith's "To Anacreon in Heav'n" (1780) would have the most celebrated fate. The melody was set to several different sets of lyrics, the most famous being Francis Scott Key's "The Star-Spangled Banner," written in 1814 and inspired by American resistance during the British bombardment of Fort McHenry. Though it would not officially become the national anthem until 1931, the song would be a Union staple throughout the Civil War. The melody, if not the lyrics, remained popular in the South. Virginian George Tucker set the tune to pro-Confederacy words in March 1861, titling the song "The Southern Cross":

> Oh! Say can you see, through the gloom and the storm,
> More bright for the darkness, that pure constellation!
> Like the symbol of love and redemption its form,
> As it points to the heaven of hope for the nation.
> Now radiant each star, as the beacon afar,
> Giving promise of peace, or assurance in war,
> 'Tis the CROSS OF THE SOUTH, which shall ever remain
> To light us to freedom and glory again!

The history of African American music begins with the arrival of the first slaves and free Africans to St. Augustine, Florida in 1565. The importation of slaves was made illegal in 1807, but the slave trade continued surreptitiously into the 1850s.[7] At the time of the Civil War, there were approximately four million slaves in the South and nearly 490,000 freedmen in the North and South.

The vast majority of these people were born in the United States, but their music remained infused with a sensibility that invariably reflected African social values and collective experiences. New World songs and ballads presented moral lessons; work songs helped organize the rhythms of group labor. Spirituals adapted Christian images of God and the Devil, oppression and salvation, but personalized the content to reflect the realities of life under the lash. European-style drums, when drums were allowed at all, replaced African types. Violins and banjos, often crudely made with pine boards or gourds, gradually replaced African-style one-stringed fiddles and a wide variety of plucked lutes. Flutes were common, so too were percussion idiophones made of scrap iron, sheep ribs, and jawbones.

Slowly, but inexorably, these various African-American innovations impacted broader American culture. The era's blackface minstrel shows were jagged imitations of African-American musical life. Today's gospel, blues, and jazz traditions are direct descendants.

Some 180,000 African Americans served in the Union military. Even more might have served in the Confederacy had that government acted sooner. On March 13, 1865, the Confederate Congress passed a bill that allowed slaves to fight in exchange from their freedom. The war was over before more than a handful of these units could be raised, however.

Some 20,000 Native Americans participated in the Civil War, though these peoples would seem to have had little incentive to help the white man, North or South. In the Union army, Native Americans were sometimes grouped with African Americans. For example, Connecticut Pequot and New York Tuscarora Indians served alongside each other and African Americans in the 31st U.S. Colored Infantry. Other Union soldiers included the Seneca, Oneida, and Menominee. Southern-based Union volunteers included the Carolinas, Pamunkey, and Lumbee. Confederate volunteers included Cherokee, Creek, Choctaw, Chickasaw, Osage, Seminole, and Catawba. The most prominent Native American on the Union side was Lieutenant Colonel Ely Samuel Parker (ca. 1828–1895), a Seneca chief who served on the staff of General Ulysses S. Grant (1822–1885) and later became Commissioner of the Bureau of Indian Affairs. The most successful Confederate commander was the Cherokee Stand Watie (1806–1871), who rose to the rank of brigadier general. The tenacious Watie was the last Confederate general to surrender.

While the Civil War raged in the East, the centuries-old war to subjugate the Native American continued mostly quietly in the West. One of the most villainous massacres in American history occurred on November 29, 1864, at Sand Creek, Colorado. There a column of 700 men under the command of Colonel John M. Chivington attacked without provocation a Cheyenne camp of 600, mostly women and children. Not wanting to fight, the Cheyenne tried to surrender as they huddled under what they hoped would be the security of the American flag. They were shot down; 105 women and children and 28 men were killed. Soldiers later mutilated many of the bodies. One musical memory, a death chant, survives from that horror:

> Medicine Calf Beckwourth, riding beside Colonel Chivington, saw White Antelope approaching, "He came running out to meet the command," Beckwourth later testified, "holding up his hands and saying 'Stop! stop!' He spoke it in as plain English as I can. He stopped and folded his arms until shot down." Survivors among the Cheyennes said that White Antelope sang the death song before he died:
>
> Nothing lives long
> Only the earth and the mountains.[8]

There are few other Native American musical examples from the period. Mention can be found of an Onondaga brass band assigned to the 2nd New York Artillery, death chants being sung by men caught in the Petersburg Crater, spiritual preparations before combat, and even an Indian version of the Rebel yell. Detailed accounts are not available.

THE MUSIC INDUSTRY

American music of the mid-nineteenth century flourished in a variety of directions simultaneously. Then, as today, money was a driving force. Presenters and performers had to be able to sell their material to diverse and often highly opinionated audiences.

The impresario P. T. Barnum (1810–1891) understood this when he brought the "Swedish Nightingale" Jenny Lind (1820–1887) to America in 1850. Barnum invested a small fortune to get Lind to sign a contract. Then, he set out to promote her as the world's greatest singer. The campaign was phenomenally successful. Thirty thousand people were on hand when Lind's steamship landed in New York; in Boston a ticket to her concert was auctioned off for $625, a small fortune in those times.[9] Lind stayed for two years, during which she sang everything from arias by Italian opera composer Vincenzo Bellini to sentimental favorites like "Home, Sweet Home."

During the Civil War, American virtuoso Louis Moreau Gottschalk fared less well financially, but understood that he too was a commodity. Writing from New York City in early 1862 after six years abroad, Gottschalk noted that:

> My impresarios, Strakosch and Grau, having discovered that my first concert in New York on my return from Europe in 1853 took place on February 11, decided to postpone my reappearance for some days so that it might take place on February 11, 1862—a memorable coincidence, of which the public (whom it did not interest the least in the world) was informed through all the newspapers.
>
> A question by many of my friends: "Why do you say such things in your advertisements? Why don't you strike out such ambitious epithets in your placards?" Alas! Are you ignorant that the artist is merchandise that the impresario has purchased, the value of which he enhances as he chooses? You might as well reproach certain pseudo gold-mine companies for announcing dividends that they never will pay as to render an artist responsible for the lures of his contractor. A poor old Negress becomes, in the hands of the Jupiter of museums (Barnum), Washington's nurse. Why, then, do you think you should be astonished at the magnificent titles that are coupled with my name?[10]

Money was not always music's driving factor, of course. The Hutchinson family singers performed regularly from their debut on Thanksgiving Day in 1839 until after the Civil War. Yes, they were financially successful, but always their interest was social change. They sang for temperance, women's rights, and most prominently, for abolition. They worked alongside many of the era's most important reformers (including Harriet Beecher Stowe and Susan B. Anthony) and performed for three presidents. The Hutchinsons, wrote Frederick Douglass, "brought to the various causes that they served, the divinest gift that heaven has bestowed upon man, the gift of music—the superb talent to touch the hearts and stir the souls of men to noble ends, even when such hearts were encased with the hardest pride and selfishness."[11]

Popular theater of the day was inexpensive enough that most everyone could afford it and broad enough in content that most everyone, whatever his education, could enjoy it. Theaters were also the scenes of rowdy spectacles. Audiences would boo and cheer. If thoroughly displeased, they might even throw things at the actors and musicians. When the stage was out of range, they sometimes aimed at each other. On a number of occasions, the turmoil spilled out onto the streets. The most notorious of these events took place in 1849 in New York City when thirty-one people died after the salt-of-the-earth fans of American actor Edwin Forrest clashed with those of upper-crust British actor William Macready.

As troubling as this and other fracases may have been, they also mark defining moments in American entertainment. Such encounters were, as historian Robert C. Toll has noted, "parts of a fundamental struggle between aristocrats and 'middling' Americans" in which the nation and its values would be defined.[12] To characterize that struggle—as did John Sullivan Dwight, William Henry Fry, and other spokesmen firmly in the fine arts camp—as simply one of high versus low, good versus bad, pure versus coarse, was certainly naïve, perhaps disingenuous. Whatever the genre— opera or a minstrel show, virtuoso piano playing or a small-town brass band—an act's ability to engage its audience determined who was heard when and where. Successful performers were those whose music reflected the values, aspirations, and also prejudices of their public.

MUSIC PUBLISHING, SOUTH AND NORTH

As the 1800s progressed and economic conditions improved for a growing middle class, so did interest in domestic music making. Pianos became more common in parlors as families and friends gathered around the instrument for an evening's entertainment. Accordingly, sheet music publication increased steadily from about 600 pieces in the late 1820s to about 1,600 annually in the early 1840s to about 5,000 annually in the early 1850s.[13] Successes were spotty, however. Most publications would make little or no money. One in a thousand, however, might make its publisher rich, if not necessarily the composer.

The onset of war stimulated music publishing as composers set quickly unfolding events to music. As with other industries, the economic and material circumstances that governed music publishing houses mirrored the relative strengths of the Northern and Southern economies. In the North, where raw materials were in good supply, publishers thrived. In the South, however, a growing shortage of both paper and ink made for increasing difficulties as the war progressed. This, coupled with mounting financial hardships exacerbated by spiraling inflation, made for a relatively expensive, but low-quality retail product. With Northern occupation of Southern cities, printers were forced to move their shops elsewhere if they were to continue in business at all.

The South

Initially, the Civil War was a boon for Southern music publishers. Because secession broke legal ties. Union copyright laws were no longer valid and profit margins increased. More important still, the Confederacy required its own songs, ones that could symbolize and motivate the new nation. Companies old and new quickly stepped up. Southern firms would publish some 648 pieces during the war.

America's oldest music publisher was the Siegling Music Company, founded in 1819 and located in Charleston, South Carolina. Another long-established company was the New Orleans–based E. Johns & Co. (established in 1837), later sold to W. T. Mayo, and finally to Philip P. Werlein in 1854. Werlein would be the first Southern firm to publish a version—unauthorized though it was—of Daniel Decatur Emmett's (1815–1904) "I Wish I Was in Dixie's Land." New Orleans's other major music publisher was Vermont native and music teacher Armand Edward Blackmar, who moved to New Orleans in 1860 and, with his brother Henry Clay Blackmar, published "The Bonnie Blue Flag" and "Maryland! My Maryland!"[14]

With the April 28, 1862, fall of New Orleans and the city's subsequent occupation by the Union army under General Benjamin Butler (1818–1893), Confederate music publishing in New Orleans effectively came to an end. Werlein's store was shut down and most of his inventory confiscated.[15] The Blackmars abandoned New Orleans and set up shop in Augusta, Georgia, where business was generally strong. By war's end, Blackmar & Bro. had published some 232 compositions, more than any other Southern firm. On April 10, 1865, one day after the surrender of General Robert E. Lee (1807–1870) at Appomattox but before the news had reached Augusta, the Blackmars sold their entire Augusta inventory to John Hill Hewitt. Hewitt could not have timed the purchase more poorly. With the loss of the war, demand for Confederate music collapsed. And so did Southern publishing.[16]

Perhaps the most adventurous Southern publisher was the Macon, Georgia-based firm of Schreiner & Son, established in 1860 and controlled by John Schreiner and his son Hermann. For the Schreiners, who initially were operating only at the level of retail sheet music sales, the Union occupation of New Orleans meant that they could no longer obtain their inventory. Undeterred, the enterprising Hermann used this bit of adversity to expand into the printing side of the business. He soon set out northward to Cincinnati where he purchased musical type. His return south, however, proved to be more difficult. Schreiner was captured and temporarily held as a possible spy by Confederate forces under the command of General Braxton Bragg (1817–1876). Delayed but safe, Schreiner eventually made his way home where he and his father set up printing facilities. Shortly afterwards, they expanded their business with a second base in Savannah.[17] During the war, the Schreiners would publish 121 works.

Smaller still was the Richmond-based publishing house of George Dunn & Company. During the war, Dunn would publish some thirty-two compositions with Julian A. Selby and approximately twenty-four more on his own. As the war progressed, Southern publishers increasingly struggled. Paper and ink became scarce, inflation soared. By war's end, the paper was so thin as to be semi-transparent. A piece of music in 1861 cost thirty-five cents; by 1865 the price could be as high as three dollars.

The North

As prolific as the South's publishing industry may have been, its output fell far short of the North's. Thanks to its staff composers, the most successful Civil War–period music publisher was the Chicago firm of Root & Cady, founded in 1858 by Ebenezer Towner Root and Chauncy Marvin Cady. The firm took just three days to respond to the Confederate's April 1861 attack at Fort Sumter when it published "The First Gun Is Fired! May God Protect the Right," a song written by Ebenezer's brother, George Frederick Root (1820–1895). By May 23, five war-related songs had already been published. Three were written by G. F. Root, including "God Bless Our Brave Young Volunteers" and "Forward, Boys, Forward." The company would publish some eighty war-related compositions over the next four years. Larger scale undertakings included the monthly magazine *The Song Messenger of the Northwest* and *The Silver Lute*, which was not only the first music book to be published in Chicago, but was soon adopted by the city's school board for use in the public schools.[18]

In composers G. F. Root and Henry Clay Work (1832–1884), the firm of Root & Cady had the strongest one-two punch of any publisher of the war. Root would write many of the conflict's most successful songs. Work was only slightly less successful. His first published song, the 1862 minstrel-styled "Kingdom Coming (Year of Jubilo)" became enormously popular in both the North and South. So were "Come Home, Father" (1864) and "Marching through Georgia" (1865). An April 1864 story in *The Song Messenger* stated that Root & Cady had issued 258,000 pieces of sheet music and 100,000 music books in that year alone. By the end of the year, paper consumption reached nearly one ton per week.[19]

The postwar era would not prove so kind to Root & Cady. By G. F. Root's account, the publisher lost upwards of a quarter million dollars worth of inventory in sheet music, books, and musical instruments during the Great Chicago Fire of October 1871.[20] The firm would be bankrupt within twelve months.

Another important publisher was the Boston-based firm of Oliver Ditson & Co., whose wartime publications included "The Battle Hymn of the Republic," "Tenting on the Old Camp Ground," and Luther O. Emerson's setting of James Sloan Gibbons's poem "We Are Coming Father Abra'am." Ditson's experience in the publishing business dated back to 1826, he formed his own company by 1835. The Civil War–era version of the firm was established in 1857 when Ditson teamed up with John C. Haynes. In 1864, Ditson gave financial support to start the Chicago-based firm of Lyon & Healy. This he did in order to gain distribution in the region. After the war, Ditson expanded his firm dramatically through acquisition. By the early 1870s half of the nation's titles in print were under his control. By 1900, the company would boast a catalogue of some 100,000 pieces.[21]

PIANO MUSIC

Paralleling the mid-century growth of sheet music was the rise of the piano as an essential fixture in the middle-class home. Nineteenth-century Americans loved the piano, and with the exception of a drop during the Civil

War itself, sales grew briskly throughout the century. Some 9,000 pianos were built and sold in 1851; approximately 21,000 in 1860, that is, one for every 1,500 Americans.[22] Already by the 1850s, publishers could hardly print enough amateur-level material to meet demand. An 1867 Ditson catalogue listed 33,000 compositions in print.[23]

There were many reasons for the instrument's extraordinary popularity. First, it was relatively easy to learn. Second, it was adaptable to many needs, an ideal parlor instrument capable of sounding delicate melodic lines, accompanying singers, or imitating the rich breadth of an orchestra. It could be played by one, two, and even three people. Finally, it was an elegant piece of furniture and a symbol of financial success, a suitable monument around which to gather family and friends.

The instrument first arrived in North America in the 1760s, nearly six decades after its Italian invention. American manufacture began soon after. Bostonian Alpheus Babcock established the lasting credibility of the American-built piano in 1825 when he advanced the design of an iron frame. Another Bostonian, Jonas Chickering, developed a single-piece iron frame in 1843. The idea was a great success. By the early 1850s the Chickering Piano Company was producing over 1,000 pianos annually. So strong was their product that in 1857 the famed Swiss virtuoso Sigismond Thalberg (1812–1871) switched to Chickering.[24]

Chickering's biggest competition came from the Steinway Piano Company, established in New York City in 1853. A third prominent manufacturer was the Baltimore-based William Knabe & Company, which by 1860 controlled the sales throughout the South. This strength turned into a liability during the war, when the company nearly went bankrupt. The business was saved when son Ernest Knabe found new markets in the North and West. Both Chickering and Steinway designs won honors at the 1867 Paris Exposition. Both also established concert halls to serve as centerpieces for their instruments: Chickering in Boston and New York, Steinway in New York.

Satisfying this huge market with music required many composers. Demand was high, musical quality generally low. Few composers were particularly gifted. One of the era's better writers, and almost certainly the most prolific, was German-born Charles Grobe (ca. 1817–1879), who published nearly 2,000 piano works between 1841 and 1879. His *New Method for the Pianoforte* (1859) remained popular for nearly three decades. Grobe generally wrote along well-worn lines and tended to follow one of two formulas. Pieces either consisted of variations on well-known songs or they had a programmatic flavor. An example of the former is "Brilliant Variations on the Star-Spangled Banner" (1854). His programmatic work included "Boarding-School Life: Its Lights and Shades, A Descriptive Potpourri for the Piano Forte" (1858), which is undoubtedly as curious a musical topic as one might ever hope to find.

The Civil War provided new subjects for Grobe's saws. The increased interest in patriotic fare led him to compose "Major Anderson's Grand March" (1861), "Maryland My Maryland with Brilliant Variations for the Piano" (1863), and similar titles. He composed instrumental responses to popular songs, such as, "Hope on—hope ever! Brilliant Variations on Henry Tucker's Beautiful Song When This Cruel War Is Over" (1863) and "Bonnie Blue Flag with Brilliant Variations" (1863). The war also provided endless possibilities for programmatic "battle" pieces, like the rousing and peripatetic "The Battle of Roanoke Island: Story of an Eyewitness" (1862). With crashing chords, a constant array of changing themes, and no musical depth to speak of, the music follows the battle from first preparations to "General Burnside's address to his soldiers" to the general fight (a combination of imitation bugle calls and discordant harmonies) and through to the "Burial of the Dead" finale, a brief slow march in C minor. Adding drama (and presumably boosting sales) was the cover page, which featured a stirring illustration of the sea-land battle. Similar covers illustrated "Battle of Port Royal" (1861), "Battle of New Orleans" (1862), and "Battle of Fort Donelson" (1862), which had both an illustration and a descriptive map. The fact that Grobe published no programmatic accounts of later battles suggests that the battle concept had a limited shelf life and eventually failed to spark public interest. Evidently a friend to North and South, Grobe published instrumental versions of both sides' popular songs.

Other composers followed similar strategies. Adolphus Brown's 1862 " 'Potomac Artillery Grand March' (Dedicated 'To the Southern Artillerists')" was little more than a motley assortment of bugle calls and the sorts of scale patterns one might expect to find in an étude book. British-born and New York City–based Richard Hoffman (1831–1909) wrote a lively caprice on "Dixie" titled "Dixiana" (1861). Mason M. Bunow published his rhythmic "Signal Corps Schottisch" (1863) in Augusta with Blackmar & Bro. Thomas Green ("Blind Tom") Bethune (1849–1909), a child prodigy who was born a slave in Georgia, published "The Battle of Manassas" (1866), a lively musical collage that includes "The Girl I Left Behind Me," "Dixie," "Yankee Doodle," and other popular melodies.

Composers also wrote works to honor war heroes. In 1861, Septimus Winner (1827–1902) published "Col. Ellsworth's Funeral March." That same year, Confederate President Jefferson Davis (1808–1889) was the subject of three piano works: C. F. Yagle's "Jefferson Davis Grand March," Mrs. Flora Byrne's "President Jefferson Davis Grand March," and P. Rivinac's "Our First President's Quickstep." The following year, C. Orloff published the "Ashby Galop" ("Dedicated to Gen. Turner Ashby, C.S.A."). In 1863, both Charles Young and Hermann Schreiner wrote and published piano pieces titled "Stonewall Jackson's Grand March."

Packaging was all important. Titles and attractive title pages probably induced as many sales as did the music itself. Thomas Caulfield's 1860 "Grand Succession March" ("Composed for & dedicated to the Charleston Delegation") featured a remarkable multicolor picture of a palm tree overlooking a seacoast with ships sailing below. A snake wraps itself around the tree trunk; a red five-pointed star dominates a sky contrasting deep blue with billowing white clouds. Few publishers went to this sort of expense, of course, but many publications had gray-toned pictures or elegant graphic designs.

Get past the cover pages, however, and there is often little to distinguish one piece from another. Piano music was mass-produced for undiscriminating masses, mostly beginner and intermediate level pianists. Accessibility was the goal. There were few technical or intellectual challenges. Tunes were almost invariably in eight-bar phrases; themes often outlined basic harmonies. Keys were generally uncomplicated (rarely more than three sharps or flats); rhythms undemanding.

Some of the music seems so absurd that we can only wonder what composer and publisher might have been thinking. Consider John Prosinger's bizarrely jovial "Pickets Charge March," published in 1863 and "Dedicated to the Northern Army of Virginia." From the title page on, Prosinger seems to have gotten most everything wrong. Pickett's name is misspelled; the grammar incorrect; the army misidentified. Even the season was wrong (if the title page is to be believed): fall instead of early summer. The title's letters are shaped from live oak branches bearing fully mature leaves and acorns. Most damning of all, this happy-go-lucky music in F major seems more appropriate for a carnival than the slaughter pen that was the third day at Gettysburg. What to make of all this? One can only assume that here, as with many of the period's publications, catchy titles were arbitrarily slapped on any music otherwise ready for publication.

More serious fare was also available. Oliver Ditson offered J. S. Bach's monumental collection *The Well Tempered Clavier*, as well as sonatas of Mozart and Beethoven, Chopin waltzes, and other European material. Theodore Moelling's "Retour de Printemps" (Return of Spring), a "Polka Brilliant," shows a difficulty level and rhythmic flexibility reminiscent of Chopin. Opera transcriptions were widely available as piano solos or with vocal accompaniment. There was also a significant market for piano four-hand literature. Titles ranged from James Bellak's regionally aimed "Ypsilanti Galop" to popular dances to opera transcriptions. New York–based William Hall & Son published Gottschalk's "Ojos Criollos (Les yeux créoles), Danse cubaine, Caprice brillant á quatre mains pour le piano" in 1860.

Music in Everyday Life

POPULAR SONGS OF THE WAR

Civil War–related vocal music was both specific and general in its content. Often, pieces echoed the passions and concerns of the moment. Lyricists responded to unfolding events with newspaper quickness. They composed for an honored war hero or recent battle, a call for volunteers or impending draft. Consequently, sales of event-inspired music tended to quickly spike then drop as subsequent events unfolded. Conceived with a longer market window were songs about broader ideas of love and family, honor and nation. Across the war's duration, composers generally shifted the focus of their songs. The early years tended to be nationalistic; the middle years spoke of death and loss; the final years looked towards homecomings.

Two Unofficial War Anthems: One for the North, One for the South

Two of the Civil War's most famous songs—"I Wish I Was in Dixie's Land" in the South and "John Brown's Body" in the North—seemed ideally suited to the psychology of their respective populations. Both songs became popular around 1859, and both were set to a variety of lyrics. Each suggests something of the opposing characters of the industrial, abolitionist North and the agricultural, slower-paced, slave-holding South. Curiously, the melody of the North's "John Brown's Body" has Southern roots; "Dixie" was born in the North. It is possible that both songs were lifted in part or whole from already existent folk versions.

Although both are easy to sing, their melodic and rhythmic flavor could hardly be more different. "John Brown's Body" (also called "Glory, Hallelujah!" and later "The Battle Hymn of the Republic") is exactly one octave in range and is built around the first inversion of the tonic chord. The melody is strongly centered on the most stable degrees of the major scale. The marchlike rhythm seems to demand that every emotion, just like a soldier's every step, must be controlled and contained if fear and other potential character flaws are to be overcome.

In contrast, "Dixie"—as it was most commonly known—conveys lightness and joy rather than firm resolve. The song is built on an up-tempo two-beat rhythm upon which the melody tumbles along with the ease of cascading water. Here too, the simple harmonic language is built solidly around stable tones, but the melody has a slightly wider melodic range and uses more scale tones. The rhythmic character brings a sense of emotional relaxation that differs markedly from the stoic tension of "The Battle Hymn of the Republic."

"John Brown's Body"

Some scholars attribute the melody of "John Brown's Body" to South Carolinian William Steffe, contending that it was popular at prewar religious revivals where it was set to the words, "Say brothers, will you meet us on Canaan's happy shore?" In her short, chatty, and anecdote-filled book, *Glory, Hallelujah!* Katherine Little Bakeless insists that the song should be attributed to Maine composer Thomas Brigham Bishop. Yet, she also cites a conflicting story of African-American girls in Georgia dancing gravely to the melody as it was played in 1864 by one of the bands attached to the army of General William Tecumseh Sherman (1820–1891). These girls, says Bakeless, had evidently long known the tune as a wedding dance.[1] A commonly told account contends that the song was first sung with the "John Brown's Body" text by the 12th Massachusetts Regiment "to taunt a fellow-soldier named John Brown."[2] Perhaps this is true, but soldier Brown was almost certainly merely a convenient peg for a song about the other John Brown

(1800–1859), the abolitionist and religious zealot who was hung after attempting in 1859 to take over the federal arsenal at Harper's Ferry, Virginia.

This latter Brown merits a brief discussion, for he was one of the most influential men of his time. The Harper's Ferry event was the culmination of the troubled life of a violent and deeply troubled fanatic. Three years earlier Brown had extracted biblical-style retribution in Kansas. There, in response to the May 1856 pro-slavery raid on Lawrence, he and his followers abducted five pro-slavery settlers and executed them by using a broadsword to crush in their skulls. For Brown, that event was just a warm-up. At Harper's Ferry he hoped that, by distributing firearms stolen during the attack, he could engender a full-blown slave revolt.

Nothing of the sort happened. Instead, U.S. Marines led by Colonel Robert E. Lee and Lieutenant J.E.B. Stuart (1833–1864) quickly subdued Brown and his eighteen attackers. Nevertheless, Brown succeeded in failure; his actions caught the North's imagination and his influence soared. Prior to his execution, Brown succeeded in casting himself as a martyr for the cause of freedom. Church bells across the North marked the hour of his death and congregations held vigils. Not surprisingly, such actions infuriated Southerners. North–South relations chilled to the breaking point. Thus began a stormy twelve-month countdown to Lincoln's election, and with it, the inevitability of Southern secession.

The "John Brown" song became universally known in the following six years. Yankees, and occasionally Confederates, sang the melody with a seemingly endless variety of lyrics. Best known were:

> John Brown's body lies a-mold'ring in the grave,
> John Brown's body lies a-mold'ring in the grave,
> John Brown's body lies a-mold'ring in the grave,
> His soul is marching on.

Other versions included:

> He's gone to be a soldier in the army of the Lord,
> He's gone to be a soldier in the army of the Lord,
> He's gone to be a soldier in the army of the Lord,
> But his soul goes marching on.
>
> John Brown's knapsack is strapped upon his back,
> John Brown's knapsack is strapped upon his back,

John Brown's knapsack is strapped upon his back,
His soul is marching on.

Brave McClellan is our Leader now,
Brave McClellan is our Leader now,
Brave McClellan is our Leader now,
With him we're marching on!

Focusing southward was:

We'll hang Jeff Davis on a sour apple tree,
We'll hang Jeff Davis on a sour apple tree,
We'll hang Jeff Davis on a sour apple tree,
As we go marching on.

Abolitionist Edna Dean Proctor (1829–1923) wrote the following for publication in the *Liberator*:

John Brown died on a scaffold for the slave;
Dark was the hour when we dug his hallowed grave;
No God avenges the life he gladly gave—
Freedom reigns today![3]

The melody was equally popular with African Americans. Indeed, historian Eileen Southern calls it the "unofficial theme song of black soldiers."[4] The song supposedly brought tears to the eyes of African-American women when the 54th Massachusetts band played the melody as the regiment marched down Boston's State Street en route to Battery Wharf from which it would embark for South Carolina. Colonel Thomas Wentworth Higginson (1823–1911) of the 1st South Carolina Volunteers wrote that his men marched singing, "We'll beat Beauregard on de clare battlefield."[5] Higginson also records them singing, presumably to the "John Brown Song" melody:

All true children gwine in de wilderness
Gwine in de wilderness, Gwine in de wilderness,
True believers gwine in de wilderness
To take away de sins ob de world
(*Hoigh!*)[6]

The 1st Arkansas Colored Regiment sang the following:

> Oh! We're de bully soldiers ob de "First ob Arkansas,"
> We are fightin' for de Union, we are fightin' for de law,
> We can hit a Rebel furder den a white man eber saw,
> As we go marchin' on.[7]

The song was also popular with German-American troops. A version of the song sung by the Blenker Division of the Army of the Potomac goes as such:

> Wir sind Deutsche und wir kämpfen
> Für die Freiheit der Union
> Fest im Glauben an die Einheit
> So wie "48" schon
> Yankee-Doodle auf den Lippen
> Ist Gerechtigkeit der Lohn
> Für das Banner der Union!
>
> [Chorus:]
> Auf, für Lincoln und die Freiheit,
> Auf, für Lincoln und die Freiheit,
> Auf, für Lincoln und die Freiheit
> Für das Banner der Union!
>
> We are Germans and we're fighting
> For the Freedom of the Union
> True in faith for the Union
> As we were in "48"
> Yankee-Doodle on our lips
> And justice is our reward
> For the banner of the Union!
>
> [Chorus:]
> Rally for Lincoln and for Liberty
> Rally for Lincoln and for Liberty
> Rally for Lincoln and for Liberty
> For the Banner of the Union![8]

Abolitionist Julia Ward Howe was responsible for the setting we know as "Battle Hymn of the Republic." She wrote the words after hearing soldiers

singing the John Brown lyrics in Washington in December 1861. Her poem
was published in the February 1862 edition of the *Atlantic Monthly*:

> Mine eyes have seen the glory of the coming of the Lord:
> He is trampling out the vintage where the grapes of wrath are stored;
> He hath loosed the fateful lightning of His terrible swift sword:
> His truth is marching on.
>
> I have seen Him in the watch-fires of a hundred circling camps,
> They have builded Him an altar in the evening dews and damps;
> I can read His righteous sentence by the dim and flaring lamps:
> His day is marching on.
>
> I have read a fiery gospel writ in burnish'd rows of steel:
> "As ye deal with my condemners, So with you my grace shall deal;
> Let the Hero, born of woman, crush the serpent with his heel,
> Since God is marching on."
>
> He has sounded from the trumpet that shall never call retreat;
> He is sifting out the hearts of men before His judgment seat:
> Oh, be swift, my soul, to answer Him! be jubilant, my feet!
> Our God is marching on.
>
> In the beauty of the lilies Christ was born across the sea,
> With a glory in his bosom that transfigures you and me:
> As he died to make men holy, let us die to make men free,
> While God is marching on.[9]

Poets and soldiers would continue to set new lyrics throughout the war.
None, however, matched the steely power of Howe's apocalyptic vision.

"Dixie's Land"

   The North had John Brown, the South had "I Wish I Was in Dixie's Land."
Indeed, "Dixie" (or somewhat more formally "Dixie's Land") was so popular
that many have called it the South's unofficial national anthem.[10] Emmett
wrote "Dixie" in New York City for a stage performance by Bryant's Minstrels. Necessity, not inspiration, was responsible for the song's genesis. Remembered Emmett:

> Like most everything else I ever did, it was written because it had
> to be done. One Saturday night, in 1859, as I was leaving Bryant's

Theater, where I was playing, Bryant called after me, "I want a walk-'round for Monday, Dan."[11]

Bryant got his showstopper. Soon the Confederacy would have its "anthem." "Dixie's" lyrics befit its minstrel origin. Emmett wrote six stanzas in all, each separated by the chorus. Best known is the stanza and chorus below:

> I wish I was in de land ob cotton,
> Old times dar am not forgotten,
> Look away! Look away! Look away! Dixie land.
> In Dixie land whar I was born in
> Early on one frosty mornin'
> Look away! Look away! Look away! Dixie land.
>
> [Chorus:]
> Den I wish I was in Dixie, Hooray! Hooray!
> In Dixie Land I'll take my stand,
> To lib and die in Dixie,
> Away, away, away down south in Dixie.
> Away, away, away down south in Dixie.

This is not the song's first stanza, which, printed below, was suppressed before the first New York performance. Bryant's wife, it seems, feared that the public might be offended by the flippant attitude towards religious mythology:[12]

> Dis worl' was made is jiss six days,
> An' finished up in various ways,
> Look away! Look away! Look away! Dixie land.
> Dey den made Dixie trim and nice,
> But Adam called it "paradise,"
> Look away! Look away! Look away! Dixie land.

Stanzas three through six are as follows:

> Old Missus marry Will-de-weaber,
> Willium was a gay deceaber;
> Look away! Look away! Look away! Dixie Land.
> But when he put his arms around 'er

He smiled as fierce as a forty-pounder,
Look away! Look away! Look away! Dixie Land.

[Chorus]

His face was sharp as a butcher's cleaber,
But dat did not seem to greab 'er;
Look away! Look away! Look away! Dixie Land.
Old Missus acted the foolish part,
And died for a man dat broke her heart,
Look away! Look away! Look away! Dixie Land.

[Chorus]

Now here's a health to the next old Missus,
And all the gals dat want to kiss us;
Look away! Look away! Look away! Dixie Land.
But if you want to drive 'way sorrow,
Come and hear dis song to-morrow,
Look away! Look away! Look away! Dixie Land.

[Chorus]

Dar's buckwheat cakes an' Injun batter,
Makes you fat or a little fatter;
Look away! Look away! Look away! Dixie Land.
Den hoe it down and scratch your grabble,
To Dixie's land I'm bound to trabble,
Look away! Look away! Look away! Dixie Land.

"Dixie" was an immediate success and soon began to appear with new sets of lyrics. Parodies abounded. The melody was used as a campaign song in the 1860 elections. The song was inserted into a New Orleans production of the show *Pocahontas* where it powered the routine of a forty-member, female, Zouave, military-style drill team.[13] New versions were published regularly throughout the war. In the process, the song's composer was often ignored. New Orleans publisher P. P. Werlein, for example, issued a version of the song with no mention of Emmett, only the aphoristic statement that the song was the same as had been "Sung by Mrs. John Wood" in her performances with the *Pocahontas* Zouaves.[14]

"Dixie" gave little pleasure to Emmett, an ardent Unionist. Related journalist T. Allston Brown in regard to a wartime encounter with Emmett and friends in a lower Manhattan bar:

> While I was dramatic editor of the *New York Clipper*, in 1861, Tom Kingsland of Dodsworth's Band, was proprietor of a famous bar and lunch room in Broome Street, much frequented by actors, newspaper men, minstrels, etc. D. T. Morgan, having come back from the army, in the winter, dropped in at Kingsland's.
>
> Sitting at the several tables and all, apparently, having a good time, were about twenty jovial fellows and among them, Dan Bryant. I was soon at a table with him, Nelse Seymour, Dan Emmett and others.
>
> Morgan told Emmett that, at night, he could hear the Confederate bands playing Dixie; and that they seemed to have adopted it down South, as their national air. Emmett replied warmly:
>
> "Yes: and if I had known to what use they were going to put my song, I will be damned if I'd have written it!"[15]

Of course, Emmett had no control over how his music would be used or, as we will soon see, how it would be published. Brown continued:

> I asked him [Emmett] how he came by the idea. He tipped back in his chair, moved closer to my side and, speaking very low, said he supposed me too young to have heard a song which his mother (or grandmother) sang to him in his merry young days. He said it was called "Come, Philander!" He was more than taken aback when I told him that my mother had put me to sleep many times, with that same song. Then I repeated the first two lines to him: all I could remember:
>
> "Come Philander, leet's be marchin',
> Every one for his true love sarchin!—"
>
> "Yes: that's it!" cried Emmett. "I based the first part of Dixieland upon that song of my childhood days."[16]

That childhood was spent in Mount Vernon, Ohio, were Emmett was born. And there another piece of the "Dixie" puzzle might possibly fit into place. Historians Howard and Judith Sacks believe that Emmett learned the song, in part or whole, from the Snowdons, one of Mount Vernon's first African-American families.[17] The argument is plausible, for Emmett and the Snowdons spent an abundance of musical time together. Whether or not "Dixie" was ever part of that mix will never be known, but at the very least, Emmett must have learned much about the stylistic nature of African-American music from those frequent encounters.

It is no criticism of Emmett to point out these many possible sources for "Dixie." Indeed, composers have always used other people's ideas as essential building blocks from which to construct their own innovations. Dozens of others built on Emmett's ideas. Some, at least in the Civil War South when Northern copyright laws were not binding, even took credit for writing the song itself. By Emmett's death in 1904 some thirty-seven composers had claimed authorship.

At least thirty-nine different instrumental and vocal arrangements were published between 1860 and 1866. The Daughters of the Confederacy collected twenty-two different Southern versions.[18] Many retained the minstrel flavor. Some, such as H. S. Stanton's "Dixie War Song," used a more formal tone:

> Hear ye not the sounds of battle,
> Sabres clash and muskets rattle?
> To arms! to arms! to arms in Dixie!
> Hostile footsteps on our border,
> Hostile columns tread in order,
> To arms! to arms! to arms in Dixie!
>
> [Chorus:]
> Oh, fly to arms in Dixie!
> To arms! to arms!
> From Dixie's land we'll route the band,
> That comes to conquer Dixie,
> To arms! to arms! and route the foe from Dixie.
> To arms! to arms! and route the foe from Dixie.

Some Southern versions, such as "The Bayou City Guards' Dixie," poked fun at Lincoln for his inept handling of affairs early on in the war:

> You've heard of Abe, the gay deceiver,
> Who sent to Sumter to relieve her;
> Look away! Look away! Look away! Dixie land.
> But Beauregard said, "Save your bacon!

Sumter's ours and must be taken!"
Look away! Look away! Look away! Dixie land.

The version titled "I Wish I Was in Richmond" showed no inclination for humor:

We'll meet old Abe with armies brave,
And whip the lying scoundrel knave.
Look away, look away, look away to Richmond town;
As he pleads for terms and whiskey,
We'll give him hell to the tune of Dixie.
Look away, look away, look away to Richmond town.

Some versions, rather than looking for problems northward, found plenty to criticize right at home. "The Officers of Dixie," for example, complained of the difficult life led by the common Southern soldier as compared to that of their gold-laced officers. There is a certain seditious excitement to the lyrics as the complaints grow from the first line's "whisper" to the shout of the chorus:

Let me whisper in your ear, sir,
Something that the South should hear, sir,
Of the war, of the war, of the war in Dixie;
A growing curse, a burning shame, sir,
In the chorus I will name, sir,
Of the war, of the war, of the war in Dixie.

[Chorus:]
The officers of Dixie, alone, alone!
The honors share, the honors wear
Throughout the land of Dixie!
'Tis so, 'tis so, throughout the land of Dixie!

The South may have usurped "Dixie" for its own, but even so, the song remained popular in the North, especially when set to new lyrics. "Dixie Unionized" (1861) proclaimed, "O! I'm glad I live in a land of freedom / Where we have no slaves nor do we need them" while "Dixie for the Union" (1861) opened with the lines, "On! ye patriots to the battle, / Hear Fort

Moultrie's cannon rattle." "Michigan Dixie" framed the infamy of Southern secession against images of the American Revolution:

> Away down South where grows the cotton,
> Seventy-six seems quite forgotten;
> Far away, far away, far away, Dixie land
> And men with rebel shout and thunder
> Tear our good old flag asunder;
> Far away, far away, far away, Dixie land.

The problem with this argument, however, was that it was untrue. From the Southern viewpoint, at least, the Revolutionary War was precisely the model for the current struggle. The Confederacy wanted freedom from its Northern oppressor just as the colonies had once wanted freedom from England. Men on both sides traced their lineage to 1776. Henry (Light-Horse Harry) Lee (1756–1818), for example, had been a signer of the Declaration of Independence, a cavalry officer, and hero of the Revolutionary War. His fifth child was Robert E. Lee.

Other widely sung Northern versions of "Dixie" skipped on philosophy and went straight to the insults:

> Away down South in the land of traitors,
> Rattlesnakes and alligators,
> Right away, come away, right away, come away.
> Where cotton's king and men are chattels,
> Union boys will win the battles,
> Right away, come away, right away, come away.

Or the less imaginative:

> Away down South in the land of traitors,
> Rebel hearts and Union haters;
> Look away, look away, look away, to the traitor's land.

"Dixie," with its many sets of lyrics, remained immensely popular with soldiers and civilians both North and South throughout the Civil War. It also inspired other songs that used the Dixie image, including: "Dixie Polka" (1860), "We Are Marching Down to Dixie's Land" (1862), "Southern Dixie" (1863), "It's All Up in Dixie" (1863), "Hard Times in Dixie" (1864), "Dixie

Doodle" (1865), "Dixie's Nurse" (1865), and many others. In the South, "Dixie" seemed appropriate for almost every occasion. It was played at the inauguration of Jefferson Davis and was probably the most popular marching, battle, and camp song for the Confederate army.

Interestingly, Union bands played "Dixie" as well, including on the occasion of their entry to the Confederate capital of Richmond in April 1865. It was also a favorite of Lincoln's. Speaking to a crowd of people at the White House on April 10, 1865, just one day after Lee surrendered the Army of Northern Virginia at Appomattox Court House, Lincoln said:

> I have always thought "Dixie" one of the best tunes I have ever heard. Our adversaries over the way attempted to appropriate it, but I insisted yesterday that we had fairly captured it. I presented the question to the Attorney General, and he gave his legal opinion that it is our lawful prize. I now request the band favor me with its performance.[19]

The band did and the crowd cheered. Clearly, Lincoln understood the political power of music. He took the South's most popular song and held it up as an ideal of the spirit of partnership that was part of his long-developed plan to reunify and reconcile North and South. That spirit would be shaken to its foundations four days later when Lincoln was assassinated by actor John Wilkes Booth.

The Early Years: Nation and Honor

Southern secession was all but assured with Lincoln's election. South Carolina, with a pro-secession legislature convention vote of 169 to 0, would be the first to go. Fireworks marked the event and people danced in the streets. Dancing, of course, demanded music. So, soon enough, would marching and fighting, dying and mourning.

Composer George O. Robinson responded to South Carolina's secession with "The Palmetto State Song," which he "Respectfully dedicated to the signers of the Ordinance of Secession unanimously passed in convention at Charleston, S. C., Dec. 20th, 1860." The text of "The Palmetto State Song" begins and ends with notions of liberty. The use of the word "freemen" in the last line invokes the Southern position that the North wanted to enslave

the South by imposing its economic system and lifestyles both southward
and westward:

> All hail to the dawn of this glor'ous morning,
> The genius of liberty lights from the skies,
> Points to the Palmetto, our banner adorning,
> And bids us at once from our slumbers to rise!
>
> Shall we bend to the power that threatens our peace,
> Or stand for our country till being shall cease?
> Then beneath the Palmetto, the pride of our story,
> Like freemen we'll stand, or we'll perish in glory.

These were heady times, and the South overflowed with optimism. By February 1, six more states had followed South Carolina out of the Union. Within three months of Lincoln's election, the Confederate States of America had drafted a constitution and set up temporary government in Montgomery, Alabama. Yet, while white Southerners rejected Northern dominance, few "fire-eaters," as pro-secessionists had long been called, considered the amount of blood that might be spilled in the event of war.

"The Bonnie Blue Flag," one of the South's great marching songs, was also written shortly after South Carolina's exit. The melody was the traditional Irish air "The Irish Jaunting Car"; English-born vaudevillian Harry Macarthy, also known as the "Arkansas Comedian," provided the words. The song became a great success. It may have been sung at the South Carolina convention and was probably sung on January 9, 1861, at the Mississippi Secession Convention. Its popularity surged after Macarthy sang it for soldiers in New Orleans the following September.[20] Verses were added, dropped, and modified as the war progressed. A look at the version below reveals that the order of secession listed in the third verse is not correct. Perhaps the song was simply giving optimistic voice to deeds still to be accomplished; perhaps Macarthy was taking poetic license. At any rate, Mississippi followed South Carolina in secession. After this, and in quick order, came Florida, Alabama, Georgia, and Louisiana:

> We are a band of brothers, and native to the soil,
> Fighting for our Liberty with treasure, blood and toil;
> And when our rights were threatened, the cry rose near and far,
> Hurrah for the Bonnie Blue Flag, that bears a Single Star!

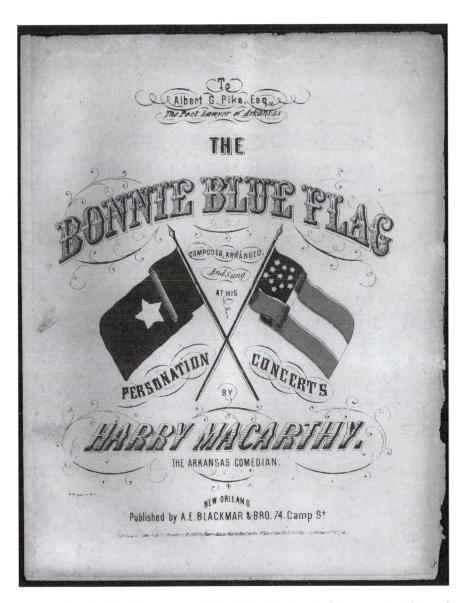

"The Bonnie Blue Flag." Photo courtesy Duke University's Rare Book, Manuscript, and Special Collections Library.

[Chorus:]
Hurrah! Hurrah! for Southern Rights, Hurrah!
Hurrah for the Bonnie Blue Flag that bears a Single Star!

As long as the Union was faithful to her trust,
Like friends and like brothers both kind were we and just;
But now, when Northern treachery attempts our rights to mar,
We hoist on high the Bonnie Blue Flag, that bears a single star.

[Chorus]

First, gallant South Carolina nobly made the stand;
Then came Alabama who took her by the hand;
Next, quickly Mississippi, Georgia, and Florida,
All raised on high the Bonnie Blue Flag, that bears a Single Star!

[Chorus]

Ye men of valor, gather round the Banner of the Right,
Texas and Louisiana, join us in the fight;
Davis, our loved President, and Stephens, Statesman rare,
Now rally round the Bonnie Blue Flag, that bears a Single Star!

[Chorus]

And here's to brave Virginia! The Old Dominion State,
With the young Confederacy at length has linked her fate
Impelled by her example, now other States prepare
To hoist on high the Bonnie Blue Flag, that bears a Single Star!

[Chorus]

Then cheer, boys, cheer, raise the joyous shout,
For Arkansas and North Carolina now have both gone out;
And let another rousing cheer for Tennessee be given,
The single star of the Bonnie Blue Flag has grown to be eleven.

[Chorus]

Then here's to our Confederacy, strong are we and brave,
Like patriots of old we'll fight our heritage to save;
And rather than submit to shame, to die we would prefer,
So cheer for the Bonnie Blue Flag, that bears a single star.

"The Bonnie Blue Flag" was just the first of numerous Southern songs focused on the flag. Others included "The Flag of Secession" (sung to the melody of "The Star-Spangled Banner," no date), "The Flag of the Free Eleven" (1861), "The Stars of Our Banner" (1861), "The Flag of the South" (1861), "The Confederate Flag" (1861), "Hurrah for Our Flag!" and even the anti-flag song "Farewell Forever to the Star-Spangled Banner" (no date). Among all of these, "The Bonnie Blue Flag" remained the best loved.

Not surprisingly, the song's text was reviled in the North. The Union's often ineffectual but politically connected General Butler found it particularly loathsome. When Butler's army occupied New Orleans, he arrested the song's publisher, A. E. Blackmar, fined him $500, and ordered the destruction of all existing copies. As if that were not enough, Butler threatened a $25 fine to anyone caught singing, playing, or even whistling the melody.[21]

Northern parodies of the song appeared as well. Lyricist Mrs. C. Sterett published the pro-Union "Reply to the Bonnie Blue Flag" in 1862:

> We are a band of Patriots who each leave home and friend,
> Our noble Constitution and Banner to defend,
> Our Capital was threatened, and the cry rose near and far,
> To protect our Country's glorious Flag that glitters with many a star.

The South got off the war's first shots and claimed the first military victory at the April 12 to 13 siege of Fort Sumter, itself a chivalric sort of affair in which no one was killed by enemy fire. The first actual war song, however, was G. F. Root's "The First Gun Is Fired! May God Protect the Right," which was published in Chicago just days after the Union surrendered the fort:

> The first gun is fired!
> May God protect the right!
> Let the free-born sons of the North arise
> In pow'r's avenging night;
> Shall the glorious Union our fathers made
> By ruthless hands be sunder'd?
> And we of freedom's sacred right
> By trait'rous foes be plunder'd?

"The First Gun Is Fired!" was the first of many songs that would make Root one of the most important composers of the war. He succeeded in part because his writing was accessible, and in part because many of his melodies were truly memorable. Most importantly, he wrote for the masses.

Others followed this strategy. The Confederate song "Maryland! My Maryland" was born in response to a violent encounter on the streets of Baltimore. On April 15, 1861, and with the secession of Virginia just two days away, Lincoln responded to the Confederate attack on Fort Sumter by issuing a call for 75,000 troops. Those men would soon be desperately needed to protect Washington, which was highly vulnerable in its location just across the Potomac River. Pennsylvania troops arrived in the capital without incident on April 18. The 6th Massachusetts Regiment, the first fully equipped unit to reach Washington, was not so fortunate. On April 19 the regiment marched its way across Baltimore from the east side rail station in order to board a train for Washington. On the way it was attacked by a pro-Confederate mob. The situation quickly developed into a minor battle. By the time the melee was over, four soldiers and twelve civilians, the first fighting casualties of the war, were dead. Scores were wounded. The event provided a rather inglorious beginning for musicians in combat who, in the midst of the chaos, had abandoned their instruments and run for their lives.[22]

The incident highlighted the political volatility of the border states. Maryland—as well as the other slave states of Delaware, Kentucky, and Missouri—would remain in the Union, but their populations would remain divided. There would be considerable pressure, both internal and from fellow slave states, to secede.

The Baltimore incident stirred Confederate sympathizers. Upon hearing of the event, James Ryder Randall (1839–1908), a native Marylander then based in New Orleans, wrote the poem "My Maryland," which he published in the New Orleans *Delta*. The poem quickly made its way northward where sisters Jennie and Hetty Cary of Baltimore noticed that by adding "My Maryland!" twice to each stanza, the poem fit perfectly to the old German folk tune "Lauriger Horatius" ("Oh, Tannenbaum"). Below are Randall's first, second, and ninth verses with the Cary sisters' additions in brackets:

> The despot's heel is on thy shore,
> Maryland[, my Maryland]!
> His torch is at thy temple door,
> Maryland[, my Maryland]!
> Avenge the patriotic gore
> That flecked the streets of Baltimore,

And be the battle queen of yore,
Maryland! My Maryland!

Hark to an exiled son's appeal,
Maryland[, my Maryland]!
My mother State! to thee I kneel,
Maryland[, my Maryland]!
For life and death, for woe and weal,
Thy peerless chivalry reveal,
And gird they beauteous limbs with steel,
Maryland! My Maryland!

I hear the distant thunder-hum,
Maryland[, my Maryland]!
The Old Line's bugle, fife, and drum,
Maryland[, my Maryland]!
She is not dead, nor deaf, nor dumb,
Huzza! she spurns the Northern scum!
She breathes! she burns! she'll come! she'll come!
Maryland! My Maryland!

Maryland's refusal to secede notwithstanding, the song remained a Southern favorite throughout the war. It was designated Maryland's state song in 1939 and remains so today.

Northerners also took up the issue of Maryland's allegiance. While not so well known or documented, a number of pro-Union versions of the song circulated. The example below retains, but subtly alters and softens, the original's elevated language. The Confederate "traitor" replaces the Union "despot." The word "foot" replaces the crushing violence implied by "heel." A secular appeal to honor replaces the original's biblical connotation of barbarians preparing to burn the temple.

The traitor's foot is on thy soil,
Maryland, my Maryland!
Let not his touch thy honor spoil,
Maryland, my Maryland!
Wipe out the unpatriotic gore
That flecked the streets of Baltimore,
And be the loyal state of yore,
Maryland, my Maryland!

Written in the vernacular is the following:

> The Rebel feet are on our shore,
> Maryland, my Maryland!
> I smell 'em half a mile or more,
> Maryland, my Maryland!
> Their shockless hordes are at my door,
> Their drunken generals on my floor,
> What now can sweeten Baltimore?
> Maryland, my Maryland!

One lyricist, identified only as "H" on the 1864 sheet music, replaced Maryland with Abraham for the song "Abraham, Our Abraham!":

> From California's sea-girt shores
> Abraham, our Abraham.
> To where the great Atlantic roars
> Abraham, our Abraham,
> The people cry with one accord,
> Death! death to all the rebel horde!
> Let Freedom conquer by the sword,
> Abraham our Abraham.

As the war unfolded, songs North and South staked out anew the longstanding American tradition of liberty or death. Nation was emphasized over individual, duty over personal desire. Songs invoked rousing notions of treachery and sedition, freedom and honor. Almost invariably, lyrics proclaimed combat a glorious calling. In fact, composers jumped on these ideas even before the war began. Wrote T.H.W. and William Dressler in the song "Close the Ranks—Firmly" (1860):

> Close the ranks firmly, as onward we go,
> Victory now and forever
> Down with the traitor, the ingrate and foe,
> Who endeavors the seeds of disunion to sow,
> Or this glorious Republic to sever.

War dead were honored with songs. Chicago bandmaster A. J. Vaas wrote his "Ellsworth Requiem" (1861) to mark the death of Colonel Elmer Ephraim Ellsworth (1837–1861), the first Union officer to be killed in the war. Thomas

Davis and Gustavus Geary eulogized another Union fallen with "The Death of Sarsfield. A Lyric for the Brigade" (1862).

Death was glorious. Indeed, Alfred Delaney's "Dirge" (1863) assured listeners that death with honor was no death at all:

> O! it is great for our Country to die,
> Whose ranks are contending
> Bright is the wreath of our fame
> Glory awaits us for aye;
> Glory that never is dim,
> Shining on with a light never ending
> Glory that never shall die.

Southern lyrics were equally bracing. William M. Johnston and A. E. Blackmar's "God and Our Rights" (1861) spoke of "marching ranks of fearless men." Theodore von la Hache's "The Free Market" (1861) asserted that "Our patriot boys on tented fields, / Are eager for the fight." Weapons shone; death was venerated. Such was the message of James Pierpont's "We Conquer or Die" (1861):

> The war drum is beating prepare for the fight,
> The stern bigot Northman exults in his might
> Gird on your bright weapons your foemen are nigh,
> And this be our watchword, "We conquer or die!"

The South also fought for justice, as evidenced by "God Will Defend the Right" (1861) by "a Lady of Richmond":

> Sons of the South arise,
> Rise in your matchless might,
> Your war cry echo in the skies,
> "God will defend the right."

John Hill Hewitt drew from the lasting success of his still popular ballad "The Minstrel's Return'd from the War" by refitting the melody with new lyrics. The original "Minstrel" harked back to a romanticized chivalric past. In that song, the minstrel went off to war, came home, and then was called again to duty, to not return.

"Southern Song of Freedom" (no date) looked to a happier conclusion:

A nation has sprung into life
Beneath the bright Cross of the South;
And now a loud call to the strife
Rings out from the shrill bugle's mouth.
They gather from morass and mountain,
They gather from prairie and mart,
To drink, at young Liberty's fountain,
The nectar that kindles the heart.
Then hail to the land of the pine!
The home of the noble and free
A palmetto wreath we'll entwine
Round the altar of young Liberty!

Sheet music covers were often dramatic. C. C. Flint and A. J. Higgins's "Down with the Traitors' Serpent Flag" (1861) featured a color picture of a Union soldier with plumed hat standing on the enemy's flag, itself covering an abandoned drum. In one hand he carries his own banner, which waves in the breeze. In his other hand he holds an unsheathed sword. The ground is barren. Two cannon balls, presumably symbolizing the emasculated foe, lie there. The lyrics are as confident as the picture:

Sons of the bright and glorious land
Where freedom first did find a home.
Arouse and with consenting hand
Consign the traitors to their doom.

The flags of winners flew proudly; those of losers were trampled underfoot. Northerners had their flag songs as well. They were encouraged to "All Hail to the Flag of Freedom." The flag was the nation and the nation was honor. Girded by these ideals, men found that war held little terror. Or such was the idea, at least. Proclaimed G. Simcoe Lee and Charles G. Degenhard in "Every Star Thirty-Four" (1861):

Tho' oceans of blood shall encrimsom the land
In the cause—tho' the *cost* we may sadly deplore—
Untarnished thy glory forever must stand
Undimed in their luster thy stars—Thirty Four

The North's most esteemed flag song was George Root's "The Battle Cry of Freedom" (1862), composed for a Chicago war rally in response to Lincoln's call for an additional 300,000 volunteers. So inspiring were tune and lyrics that more than once the song was credited for turning the tide of battle:

> Yes, we'll rally round the flag, boys,
> We'll rally once again,
> Shouting the battle cry of Freedom;
> We will rally from the hillside,
> We'll gather from the plain,
> Shouting the battle cry of Freedom.
>
> [Chorus:]
> The Union forever,
> Hurrah! boys, hurrah!
> Down with the traitors,
> Up with the stars;
> While we rally round the flag, boys,
> Rally once again,
> Shouting the battle cry of Freedom.
>
> We are springing to the call
> Of our brothers gone before,
> Shouting the battle cry of Freedom;
> And we'll fill our vacant ranks with
> A million free men more,
> Shouting the battle cry of Freedom.
>
> [Chorus]
>
> We will welcome to our numbers
> The loyal, true and brave,
> Shouting the battle cry of Freedom;
> And although they may be poor,
> Not a man shall be a slave,
> Shouting the battle cry of Freedom.
>
> [Chorus]
>
> So we're springing to the call
> From the East and from the West,
> Shouting the battle cry of Freedom;
> And we'll hurl the rebel crew
> From the land that we love best,
> Shouting the battle cry of Freedom.
>
> [Chorus]

The song proved a perfect fit with Root's notion of topical music written to be easily digested in a single hearing. Upon learning of Lincoln's request for troops, said Root:

> Immediately a song started in my mind, words and music to-gether: "Yes, we'll rally round the flag, boys, we'll rally once again, Shouting the battle-cry of freedom!"
>
> I thought it out that afternoon, and wrote it the next morning at the store. The ink was hardly dry when the Lumbard brothers—the great singers of the war—came in for something to sing at a war meeting that was to be holden immediately in the court-house square just opposite. They went through the new song once, and then hastened to the steps of the court-house, followed by a crowd that had gathered while the practice was going on. Then Jule's magnificent voice gave out the song, and Frank's trumpet tones led the refrain "The Union forever, hurrah, boys, hurrah!" and at the fourth verse a thousand voices were joining in the [chorus]. From there the song went into the army, and the testimony in regard to its use in the camp and on the march, and even on the field of battle, from soldiers and officers, up to generals, and even to the good President himself, made me thankful that if I could not shoulder a musket in defense of my country I could serve her in this way."

The song invariably found its way to soldiers' lips, often in the most des-perate of situations. A battered Iowa regiment at Vicksburg sang it as they struggled to regroup. A soldier in the 45th Pennsylvania began singing it during the Wilderness Campaign of 1864 as his regiment was on the verge of defeat. "Soon the entire brigade was singing the defiant chorus," wrote William Wiley.[24] 3rd Michigan Infantryman David Crotty had a similar ex-perience during the same conflict:

> A wounded soldier, as he is borne to the rear on a stretcher, caught sight of my tattered banner, and begun the song "Rally Round the Flag, Boys." Every man took up the words and went in with re-newed vigor. . . . [Later] some of our lines commence to fall back, and a huge rebel asks me to surrender my colors, but these I never intend to let go out of my hands til I have no life in me to carry them.[25]

Another remembrance, recorded decades after the war was over, illustrates the power that this and other patriotic songs had on soldiers' spirits. In his autobiography, Root cites a story published in *The Century* some twenty-five years after the war had finished and titled, "Union War Songs and Confederate Officers":

> A day or two after Lee's surrender in April 1865, I left our ship at Dutch Gap, in the James river, for a run up to Richmond, where I was joined by the ship's surgeon, the paymaster and one of the junior officers. After "doing" Richmond pretty thoroughly we went in the evening to my rooms for dinner. Dinner being over, and the events of the day recounted, the doctor, who was a fine player, opened the piano, saying: "Boys, we've got our old quartet here; let's have a sing." As the house opposite was occupied by paroled Confederate officers no patriotic songs were sung. Soon the lady of the house handed me this note:
>
> "Compliments of General—and staff. Will the gentlemen kindly allow us to come over and hear them sing?"
>
> Of course we consented, and they came. As the General entered the room, I recognized instantly the face and figure of one who stood second only to Lee or Jackson in the whole Confederacy. After introductions and the usual interchange of civilities we sang for them glee and college songs, until at last the General said:
>
> "Excuse me, gentlemen; you sing delightfully; but what we want to hear is your army songs." Then we gave them the army songs with unction—the "Battle Hymn of the Republic," "John Brown's Body," "We're Coming, Father Abraham," "Tramp, Tramp, Tramp, the Boys are Marching," through the whole catalogue to the "Star-Spangled Banner"—to which many a foot beat time as if it had never stepped to any but the "music of the Union"—and closed our concert with "Rally Round the Flag, Boys."
>
> When the applause had subsided, a tall, fine-looking fellow, in a major's uniform, exclaimed: "Gentlemen, if we'd had your songs we'd have whipped you out of your boots! Who couldn't have marched or fought with such songs? We had nothing, absolutely nothing, except a bastard 'Marseillaise,' the 'Bonny Blue Flag' and 'Dixie,' which were nothing but jigs. 'Maryland, My Maryland' was a splendid song, but the old 'Lauriger Horatius' was about as inspiring as the 'Dead March in Saul,' while every one of the Yankee songs is full of marching and fighting spirit." Then turning to the

General, he said: "I shall never forget the first time I heard 'Rally Round the Flag.' 'Twas a nasty night during the 'Seven Days' Fight,' and if I remember rightly it was raining. I was on picket, when, just before 'taps,' some fellow on the other side struck up that song and others joined in the chorus until it seemed to me the whole Yankee army was singing. Tom B , who was with me, sung out, 'Good heavens, Cap, what are those fellows made of, anyway? Here we've licked 'em six days running, and now on the eve of the seventh they're singing, 'Rally Round the Flag.' I am not naturally superstitious, but I tell you that song sounded to me like the 'knell of doom,' and my heart went down into my boots; and though I've tried to do my duty, it has been an uphill fight with me ever since that night."

The little company of Union singers and Confederate auditors, after a pleasant and interesting interchange of stories of army experiences, then separated, and as the General shook hands at parting, he said to me: "Well, the time may come when we can all sing the 'Star-Spangled Banner' again." I have not seen him since.[26]

"The Battle Cry of Freedom" spurred imitations, like Mrs. E. A. Souder and John Darcie's "Come Rally Boys Around Our Flag" (1862). Indeed, so popular was Root's song that J. C. Schreiner & Son published a Confederate song by William H. Barnes and Hermann Schreiner with the exact same title. Also sung in the South was Root's melody with the following lyrics:

> We are marching to the field, boys,
> We're going to the fight,
> Shouting the Battle Cry of Freedom!
> And we bear the Heavenly cross,
> For our cause is in the right,
> Shouting the Battle Cry of Freedom!
>
> Our rights forever!
> Hurrah boys hurrah!
> Down with the tyrants, raise the Southern star,
> And we'll rally round the flag, boys
> We'll Rally once again
> Shouting the Battle Cry of Freedom!

"The Battle Cry of Freedom" was not the only famous verse to come from Lincoln's 1862 call for troops. There was also the poem "We Are Coming, Father Abraham," which first appeared anonymously in New York's *Evening Post* on July 16 and has been attributed to New York City–based Quaker abolitionist and economist James Sloan Gibbons, though some editions of the sheet music list William Cullen Bryant as lyricist. The poem was set by at least six composers, including Stephen Foster and Patrick Gilmore (1829–1892). Most popular was the setting by L. O. Emerson, of which an estimated two million copies were sold by war's end. The poem stated:

> We are coming Father Abra'am,
> Three hundred thousand more,
> From Mississippi's winding stream
> And from New England's shore;
> We leave our plows and workshops,
> Our wives and children dear,
> With hearts too full for utterance,
> With but a silent tear;
> We dare not look behind us,
> But steadfastly before.
> We are coming, Father Abra'am,
> Three hundred thousand more!

There were a number of parodies. One version doubted (correctly, it turned out) that 300,000 would be enough and doubled the size of the request. Emmett poked fun at "Father Abra'am's" greenback dollars (the new national currency) in his 1863 song "Greenbacks!" writing that "Wall Street is but a small plantation, / Too small to ever rule the nation." E. Bowers and Charles Glover drew on the original in their song "How Are You Green-Backs!" (1863):

> We're coming, Father Abram, One hundred thousand more,
> Five hundred presses printing us from morn till night is o'er;
> Like magic, you will see us start and scatter thro' the land
> To pay the soldiers or release the border contraband,

Both "greenback" songs were performed by Bryant's Minstrels.

Many of the men who enlisted in the army soon came to regret their

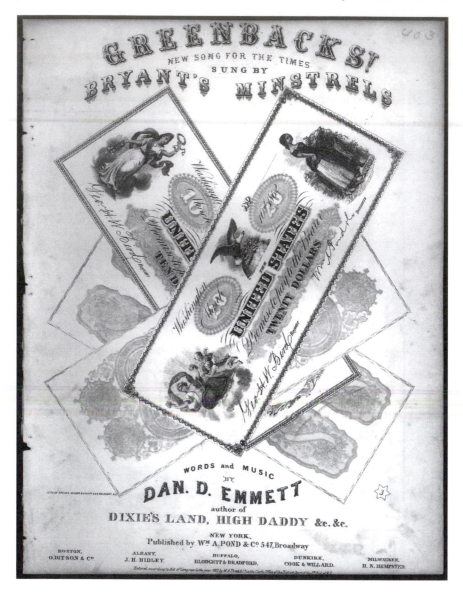

"Greenbacks!" Photo courtesy Duke University's Rare Book, Manuscript, and Special Collections Library.

decision. That story is told in Henry Work's deflating comic song "Grafted into the Army" (1862). Like a scion inserted upon a stock, Jimmy too has been grafted. The cover illustration is perhaps more interesting than the song itself. Featured are two pictures, one above the other. On top is a

mother in bonnet and apron holding up "the [tiny] trousers he used to wear."
Below stands the pathetic Jimmy on guard duty in front of a picket fence.
One of the pickets has fallen off, and there in the gap he stands, as if he
too is just one more piece of wood plugging a hole. In the background are
the flowing stylized tents of the army camp. Each sports an American flag.
Floral arrangements frame each portrait.

> Our Jimmy has gone for to live in a tent,
> They have grafted him into the army
> He finally pucker'd up courage and went,
> When they grafted him into the army.

The common soldier was sometimes little more than cannon fodder, but the
general was destined for a grander fate. Early in the war, they were often
the subjects of rousing music. General Pierre Beauregard (1818–1893) inspired both songs and piano pieces, including, "Salut 'a Beauregard" (1862,
by S. C. of C.S.A.), in which the incendiary chorus proclaimed that, "As with
cannon, mortar, and petard, / We saluted the North with a Beauregard!"
Generals J.E.B. Stuart and Thomas "Stonewall" Jackson (1824–1863) were
also frequent subjects. Charles Nordendorf dedicated his "Southern Troop-
ers" (no date) "To Genl. J.E.B. Stuart and his gallant soldiers." The song
"Riding a Raid" (1863), sung to the Scottish melody "Bonnie Dundee,"
honored Stuart's guarding action in the days leading up to the battle of
Antietam:

> 'Tis old Stonewall the Rebel that leans on his sword,
> And while we are mounting prays low to the Lord:
> "Now each cavalier that loves honor and right,
> Let him follow the feather of Stuart tonight."
>
> [Chorus]
>
> Come tighten your girth and slacken your rein;
> Come buckle your blanket and holster again;
> Try the click of your trigger and balance your blade,
> For he must ride sure that goes riding a raid.

In fact, many songs, piano works, and marches were inspired by, and dedicated to, hero generals. One of the best-known songs among Southerners
was "Stonewall Jackson's Way" (1862), inspired by a poem by John W. Palmer:

> We see him now; the queer slouched hat
> Cocked o'er his eye askew;
> The shrewd, dry smile; the speech so pat,
> So clam, so blunt, so true!
> The 'cute old Elder knows him well:
> Says he, "That's Banks—he's fond of shell;
> Lord save his soul! We'll give him—"
> Well! That's Stonewall Jackson's way.

Other songs dedicated to Jackson include Hewitt's "The Stonewall Quick-step" (1862), Charles Nordendorf's "The Stonewall Brigade" (1863), J. W. Randolph's "The Stonewall Banner" (1863), and Jules C. Meininger's " 'Stonewall' Jackson's Last Words" (1865). Jefferson Davis was the subject of surprisingly few songs. Perhaps this was due to the South's paper shortage and spiraling inflation. More likely, however, is that the cheerless Davis simply did not elicit musical responses in comparison to the South's more colorful figures.

In the North, the most musically honored general was the hapless George B. McClellan (1826–1885), who remained an immensely popular figure with both the public and his soldiers despite his organizational incompetence and repeated thrashings on the battlefield. "Give us back our old Commander, / Little Mac, the people's pride," begins the first verse and chorus of Septimus Winner's "Give Us Back Our Old Commander" (1862). H. Coyle's remarkable "General McClellan's Farewell" (1863) relives the moment when Mc-Clellan relinquished his command of the Army of the Potomac to General Ambrose E. Burnside (1824–1881). Coyle suggests that the very army was ready to mutiny, should McClellan but say the word:

> They watched their leader's words with awe,
> Should they lay down their arms?
> But in his eye they quickly saw
> What silenced their alarms
> Calmly he laid his laurels down,
> His heart was rent and sore;
> He loved the hands which twined that crown,
> But loved his country more.

Ulysses S. Grant was the subject of dozens of pieces in his later life. Few were written during the war, however. Perhaps this was because he ascended to prominence relatively late in the conflict and his subsequent campaigns

were too bloody to inspire song. Or perhaps the stoop-shoulder general simply lacked the requisite flair. Despite the title, the tone of J. M. Darling's
"Grant's the Man" (1864) was hardly confident:

> Our country has a leader now,
> That's gallant, true, and brave;
> Though many a one we've had before,
> Has proved himself a knave,
> And honesty's been laid aside,
> While scrambling after pelf,
> As one by one we've found them out,
> And laid them on the shelf.

Anti-War Songs

Not all publications stirred martial passions. Some were pacifist. Living in
a border state, Kentucky-based journalist and untutored musician Will
Shakespeare Hays (1837–1907) found himself caught along the line on which
the nation was about to divide. He hoped it would not. A Unionist, Hays
also wrote songs sympathetic to the South. In his "Let Us Have Peace" (1861)
he implored:

> America! Beloved land!
> Once beautiful and bright.
> Oh! Why should friendship turn to hate,
> Why should brothers fight?

Hays's ideas would resonate in both the North and South. His collected sheet
music sales ultimately reached upwards to the level of twenty million copies.

Though the situation would sometimes prove awkward, many pacifist
songs became popular within the armies themselves. One such song was
Henry S. Washburn and George Root's "The Vacant Chair," which in both
physical imagery and emotional affect seems to hearken back to Henry Russell's "The Old Arm Chair." The song was published in the Worcester *Spy*
around Thanksgiving of 1861. It was apparently written in honor of Lieutenant John William Grout of the 15th Massachusetts Infantry:[27]

> We will meet but we will miss him,
> There will be his vacant chair;
> We will linger to caress him

While we breathe our evening prayer;
When a year ago we gathered,
Joy was in his mild blue eye,
But a golden chord is severed,
And our hopes in ruin lie.

We will meet, but we will miss him,
There will be his vacant chair,
We will linger to caress him
While we breathe our evening prayer.

There were other anti-war songs, some of which achieved lasting fame. One was Hewitt's "All Quiet Along the Potomac To-night" (1862), the most adept of many settings of Mrs. Ethel Lynn Eliot Beers's poignant five-stanza anti-war poem "The Picket Guard," published in the November 30, 1861, edition of *Harper's Weekly Magazine*. The poem appeared in a Southern newspaper the following year and was subsequently claimed, almost certainly falsely, to have been written by Confederate cavalry officer Major Lamar Fontaine. The words echoed the thoughts and experiences of the lowly foot soldier:

All quiet along the Potomac, they say,
Except here and there a stray picket
Is shot, as he walks on his beat, to and fro,
By a rifleman hid in the thicket.
'Tis nothing, a private or two now and then
Will not count in the news of the battle;
Not an officer lost, only one of the men
Moaning out all alone the death rattle.

All quiet along the Potomac to-night,
Where the soldiers lie peacefully dreaming,
Their tents in the rays of the clear autumn moon,
O'er the light of the watch fires, are gleaming;
A tremulous sigh, as the gentle night wind,
Through the forest leaves softly is creeping,
While stars up above, with their glittering eyes,
Keep guard for the army is sleeping.

There's only the sound of the lone sentry's tread,
As he tramps from the rock to the fountain,
And thinks of the two in the low trundle bed,
Far away in the cot on the mountain.

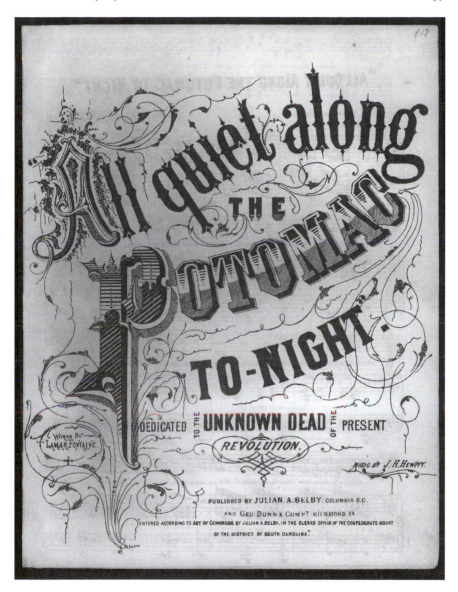

"All Quiet Along the Potomac To-night." Photo courtesy Duke University's Rare Book, Manuscript, and Special Collections Library.

His musket falls slack, and his face, dark and grim,
Grows gentle with memories tender,
As he mutters a prayer for the children asleep,
For their mother, may Heaven defend her.

The moon seems to shine just as brightly as then,
That night when the love yet unspoken
Leaped up to his lips when low-murmured vows,
Were pledged to be ever unbroken.
Then drawing his sleeve roughly over his eye
He dashes off tears that are welling,
And gathers his gun closer up to its place
As if to keep down the heart-swelling.

He passes the fountain, the blasted pine tree
The footstep is lagging and weary;
Yet onward he goes, through the broad belt of light,
Toward the shades of the forest so dreary.
Hark! Was it the night wind that rustled the leaves,
Was it moonlight so wondrously flashing?
It looks like a rifle—"Ah! Mary, good-bye!"
And the lifeblood is ebbing and splashing.

All quiet along the Potomac tonight,
No sound save the rush of the river;
While soft falls the dew on the face of the dead—
The picket's off duty forever.

Northern composers H. Coyle, W.H. Goodwin, J. Dayton, and David A. Warden all set the poem. Hewitt's version, however, with its simple, straightforward, declamatory style in which the melody so clearly supports the lyrics, was the most successful and most remembered.[28]

Equally affecting was Walter Kittredge's "Tenting on the Old Camp Ground" (1862). Due to poor health, the New Hampshire native never served in the army. Still, he was able to neatly capture the mood of lonely men far from home. The lyrics are particularly effective in their inexorable progress, verse by verse, from loneliness to death:

We're tenting to-night on the old camp ground,
Give us a song to cheer
Our weary hearts, a song of home,
And friends we love so dear.

[Chorus:]
Many are the hearts that are weary to-night,
Wishing for the war to cease,
Many are the hearts looking for the right,

To see the dawn of peace.
Tenting to-night, tenting to-night,
Tenting on the old camp ground.

We've been tenting to-night on the old camp ground,
Thinking of days gone by,
Of the loved ones at home that gave us the hand,
And the tear that said "Good-by!"

[Chorus]

We are tired of war on the old camp ground,
Many are dead and gone,
Of the brave and true who've left their homes,
Others been wounded long.

[Chorus]

We've been fighting to-day on the old camp ground,
Many are lying near;
Some are dead, and some are dying,
Many are in tears.

Many are the hearts that are weary to-night,
Wishing for the war to cease,
Many are the hearts looking for the right,
To see the dawn of peace.
Dying to-night, dying to-night,
Dying on the old camp ground.

Kittredge's early attempts to sell the song to a publisher came to naught. Eventually, he brought it to the Hutchinson family singers who presented the music in a series of Massachusetts concerts. With Asa Hutchinson's support, the song was published by Oliver Ditson & Co. It would remain a favorite long after the war's conclusion.[29]

Sung from the perspective of the lover left at home, was Charles Carroll Sawyer and Henry Tucker's "Weeping, Sad and Lonely; or, When This Cruel War Is Over" (1862). The song was first published in Georgia and achieved immense popularity both North and South in army camps and domestic parlors.[30] There is little to recommend the plain tune in terms of inventiveness, yet the pathos-filled lyrics had a most powerful effect. Indeed, the song created such longing for home that some regiment commanders prohibited their soldiers from singing it:

Dearest love, do you remember, when we last did meet,
How you told me that you loved me, kneeling at my feet?
Oh, how proud you stood before me in your suit of blue,
When you vowed to me and country ever to be true.

[Chorus:]
Weeping sad and lonely,
Hopes and fears how vain!
When this cruel war is over,
Praying that we meet again.

When the summer breeze is sighing mournfully along;
Or when autumn leaves are falling, sadly breathes the song.
Oft in dreams I see thee lying on the battle plain,
Lonely, wounded, even dying, calling but in vain.

[Chorus]

But our country called you, darling, angels cheer your way;
While our nation's sons are fighting, we can only pray.
Nobly strike for God and liberty, let all nations see
How we love the starry banner, emblem of the free.

Hugely popular during the war and in the decades that followed was Will Hays's heartrending "The Drummer Boy of Shiloh" (1862). The song elicits a wide range of emotions. War's senselessness is brought into relief by the fact that the victim is no warrior, but a mere child, a drummer. The men around him, hardened combat veterans all, cry and pray for both the boy and themselves. How many lives have they taken? When will they kill again? For the moment, at least, all that is forgotten. The child's suffering has restored their own humanity.

A number of candidates have been put forward for the honor of being Shiloh's drummer boy, including: Jesse Nelson, who was killed at Shiloh; Johnny Clem of the 22nd Michigan Infantry, who earned the title "Johnny Shiloh" and later the "Drummer Boy of Chickamauga"; and Edward H. Hagar of the 61st Illinois Infantry, who later died of wounds suffered at Shiloh. The subject, however, may also have been Confederate. In fact, Hays quite probably had no particular boy in mind. That, of course, makes the song no less moving. Drummer boys, some who were not yet even teenagers, were well loved by the adult soldiers with whom they lived and served. Hays's song tells of one boy's sad story:

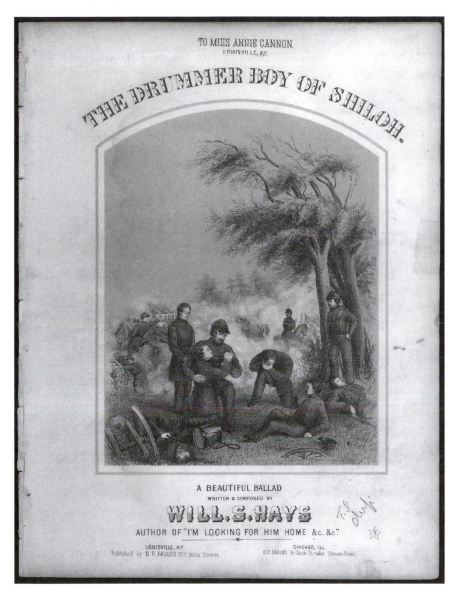

"The Drummer Boy of Shiloh." Photo courtesy Duke University's Rare Book, Manuscript, and Special Collections Library.

On Shiloh's dark and bloody ground
The dead and wounded lay,
Amongst them was a drummer boy
Who beat the drums that day.

A wounded soldier held him up
His drum was by his side;
He clasped his hands, then raised his eyes
And prayed before he died.
He clasped his hands, then raised his eyes
And prayed before he died.

Look down upon the battlefield,
Oh, Thou our Heavenly Friend!
Have mercy on our sinful souls!
The soldiers cried, "Amen!"
For gathered 'round a little group,
Each brave man knelt and cried.
They listened to the drummer boy
Who prayed before he died.
They listened to the drummer boy
Who prayed before he died.

"The Drummer Boy of Shiloh" was just one of many ballads composed on the theme of child drummers. Others included Albert Fleming's "Drummer Boy of Antietam," J. C. Koch and L. Grube's "The Dying Drummer Boy," Henry Work's "Little Major" (1862), S. Wesley Martin's "Little Harry, the Drummer Boy," P. De Geer's "The Drummer Boy of Vicksburg," and George Cooper and Stephen Foster's "For the Dear Old Flag I Die" (1862). Such songs of innocents following—and often dying for—their beliefs were obviously designed to tug at the heartstrings. They constituted another subject area for pacifist songs.

Related to anti-war songs were those about the draft, which began in the South in April 1862 and in the North with the March 3, 1863, Enrollment Act of Conscription. A later act (February 1864) required all Confederate men between the ages of seventeen and fifty to serve. North and South, the draft was highly unpopular and unfair, especially to the poor. Union wealthy could buy their way out with a "commutation" fee; Southern landowners were exempted at the rate of one white man per twenty slaves. Tension broke into violence during the New York City draft riots on July 13–16, 1863, when some 50,000 demonstrators took to the streets. Federal troops were called in to quell the violence. Ednor Rossiter and B. Frank Walters's 1863 song "Come In out of the Draft" ("Respectfully Dedicated to all Disconsolate Conscripts") was a response to the Union conscription act. It was marketed as a comic song, but is more sad than funny:

> As it was rather warm, I thought the other day,
> I'd find some cooler place, the summer months to stay;
> I had not long been gone, when a paper to me came,
> And in a list of conscripts I chanced to see my name.
> I showed it to my friends, and at me they all laugh'd;
> They said, "How are you conscript?—come in out of the draft."

Septimus Winner's "He's Gone to the Arms of Abraham" (1863) spoke directly to the North, but addressed Southern concerns as well:

> My true love is a soldier
> In the army now today,
> It was the cruel war that made him
> Have to go away;
> The "draft" it was that took him,
> And it was a "heavy blow,"
> It took him for a Conscript,
> But he didn't want to go.
>
> [Chorus:]
> He's gone—He's gone—As meek as any lamb,
> They took him, yes, they took him, to the Arms of Abraham.
>
> Oh should he meet a rebel,
> A pointin' with his gun,
> I hope he may have courage
> To "take care of number one."
> If I were him, I'd offer
> The fellow but a dram;
> For what's the use of dying
> Just for Jeff or Abraham?

The Middle Years: Songs of Mother and Family

As the fighting dragged on and intensified, even pro-war songs offered less emphasis on masculinity, less subjugation of self for country. War brought suffering; families were torn apart. Lyrics reflected that reality by focusing on particularly emotional scenarios. Jennie Caulfield and Hermann Knake's "Blue-Eyed Soldier Boy" (1862) portrayed a widowed mother worrying about her son. Death often followed worry, as in M. A. Geuville and Frederick Buckley's "Break It Gently to My Mother" (1863). M. L. Hofford and J. C. Beckel's "Dead on the Battle Field" (1862) confronted war's horror while holding desperately to the increasingly stale notion that death in combat was a glorious end:

> Dead upon the battlefield
> The bravest of the brave
> In the foremost ranks he nobly fought
> And found a soldier's grave.
> His country mourns his loss
> A nation o'er him weeps.
> But glory guilds the honored name
> Our fond remembrance keeps.

Motherhood symbolized fidelity and innocence, hearth and home. Motherhood balanced masculine images of valor and duty, nation and flag. As the horrors and suffering of the war became better understood, images of nation were replaced with nurturing, even mystical, images of mother. The graphic lyrics in J. Dayton's "The Dying Volunteer" (1863) portray a man lying on the battlefield:

> My mother's form is with me now,
> Her wail is in my ear;
> And drop by drop as flows my blood,
> So drops from her the tear.

Such pathos would become commonplace as writers wove together images of death and motherhood with songs like E. Bowers and Henry Tucker's "Dear Mother I've Come Home to Die" (1863), and A. J. Higgins's "The Dying Mother's Advice to Her Volunteer Son" (1863):

> Dry up those manly tears you shed,
> Your dying mother, kiss;
> You leave for scenes of strife and blood—

And I for endless bliss.
One more embrace before we part.
A last and long adieu,
Whatever be thy fate, my son,
Be to thy Country—True.

Lyricist George Cooper collaborated with the ailing Stephen Foster on a number of war-related songs. Written in a distant third person was "The Soldier's Home" (1863), in which the father, after a brief stay at home with wife and children, is called back to the war. He does not return:

But hark! the drum; it loudly beats upon the ear of night,
It calls to arms! wake! comrade wake! and rally for the fight!
The soldier's joy is over now for 'mid the battle's roar;
'Mid clanging steel and hissing ball he sleeps forevermore.

"My Boy Is Coming from the War" (1863) is particularly disturbing, for here the upbeat tempo suggests the conclusion will be far happier than it is. The mother speaks until the brutal final verse, at which point, as if ripped from the song by anguish, her voice is replaced by a narrator:

My boy is coming from the war,
He's coming home to me,
O! how I long to see his face,
And hear his voice of glee.
Of all the days that ever dawned
This is the brightest day,
For sad and lonely was my heart
When Harry went away.

[Chorus:]
My boy is coming from the war
He's coming home to me,
O! how I long to see his face,
And hear his voice of glee.

My boy is coming from the war,
I've waited for him long,
I miss the music of his laugh,
His light and happy song;

But now I'll clasp him in my arms
And ever by my side,
He'll linger while my life glides on
To quiet eventide.

[Chorus]

My boy is coming from the war
The mother fondly said,
While on the gory battle plain
Her boy was lying dead!
His comrades came with lightsome steps
And sound of martial drums,
But now that Mother sadly waits
For one who'll never come!

A curious twist on the notion of sacrifice can be found in Henry Bedlow's "The Conscript Mother's Song" (1863). The music's cover shows mother stealing an anxious look at a young soldier marching past. Her son? The soldier seems to look at the house, not at the mother. He has become a man. She holds a small portrait. A large one of a bearded man is on the wall above her. Son and husband? We assume so. The plodding lyrics are more lugubrious still:

Away with all sighing! away with all tears!
My boy shall behold, not my grief, but my pride;
Shall I taint his young manhood with womanish fears,
When the flag of his country is scorn'd and defied?
I will arm him, and bless him, and send him away,
Tho' my heart break with grief when he goes from my sight;
And bid him not falter and blanch in the fray,
But fight to the death for the Truth and the Right!
I must teach my brave lad what it is to be true
To the Red and the White and the Stars in the Blue.

Hugely popular was G. F. Root's far more digestible "Just Before the Battle, Mother" (1864):

Just before the battle, Mother,
I am thinking most of you.

> While upon the field we're watching,
> With the enemy in view.
> Comrades brave are 'round me lying,
> Filled with thoughts of home and God;
> For well they know that on the morrow,
> Some will sleep beneath the sod.
>
> [Chorus:]
> Farewell, Mother, you may never
> Press me to your breast again;
> But, oh, you'll not forget me, Mother,
> If I'm numbered with the slain.

Root followed the popularity of this song with the sequel "Just After the Battle" in which the young soldier, after fighting bravely with his comrades, lies wounded on the field among the dead and the dying. He seems to talk to his mother as he awaits the dawn. Will he survive? Probably not, for the young man's "night is drear with pain" and Civil War survival rates were dreadfully low. Still, at least the young soldier (and one assumes mother as well) is able to take consolation in the fact that the battle has been won.

Southern publications also focused on a mother's love. Having survived his first battle, a young soldier surveys the carnage and wonders, "Mother! Can This the Glory Be?" (1862, by Stephen Glove). A soldier asks for comfort in M. Keller's "Mother, Oh! Sing Me to Rest" (no date) while in Mrs. M. W. Stratton and Joseph Hart Denck's "Keep Me Awake Mother" (1863), a boy fights against unconsciousness and the death that is sure to follow:

> Forward! Oh forward! time stays not his flight,
> I'm older and wiser and sadder tonight,
> Mother dear mother I see thee no more,
> But watch me oh watch me again as of yore,

It is impossible to know whether the soldiers themselves, many who were still in their teens, found these sorts of sentiments invigorating or debilitating. Perhaps both. In C. C. Sawyer and C. F. Thompson's "Who Will Care for Mother Now" (1863), a dying soldier sees a glorious afterlife for himself but worries for the woman he leaves behind:

> Soon with angels I'll be marching,
> With bright laurels on my brow;
> I have for my country fallen!
> Who will care for Mother now?

In times of trial another woman might stand in for mother, as in Elmer Ruan Coates's "Be My Mother 'till I Die" (1863) in which the dying soldiers asks, "Ladies, someone be my mother, / Then 'twill seem that I am home." When lovers replaced mothers in song texts, they could stand in for mother and country both, as with the protagonist in C. D. Benson's "Lucilla, the Maid of Shiloh!" (1864), who showed a fervor reminiscent of Joan of Arc:

> Aurora shed her crimson blushes,
> O'er Shiloh's bleak and dreary hills,
> A maiden fair to battle rushes,
> Resolved to share her lover's ills,
> In buoyant steps she onward presses,
> With bold defiance, proud disdain,
> Advancing in a march triumphant,
> She marks her pathway with the slain.

Rare were songs of soldiers and their children. Septimus Winner, publishing under the pseudonym Alice Hawthorne, wrote "Down upon the Rappahannock" (1863), in which a mother tries to prepare her children for terrible news:

> Ask me not my child, my darling,
> When thy father will be here;
> For upon that fated river,
> Many hearts may sigh in vain—
> Dream of home and friends forever
> But shall not return again.

In James G. Clark's "The Children of the Battle Field" (1864), a soldier dies with a photo of his children pressed to his breast. The sheet music cover shows three young and forlorn children stiffly posed like miniature adults. The lyrics read:

And none more nobly won the name,
Of Champion of the Free,
Than he who pressed the little frame
That held his children three;
And none were braver in the strife
Than he who breathed the prayer:
O! Father, shield the soldier's wife,
And for his children care.

Boys and men died not only on the battlefield but also in the prisons, where disease and starvation were rampant. The most successful of the prison songs was George Root's "Tramp! Tramp! Tramp! (The Prisoner's Hope)" (1864). Written from the prisoner's perspective, the song opens with a desolate inmate trying to hold back his tears while, "Thinking Mother dear, of you." Each verse raises new hopes, until the final one:

So within the prison cell,
We are waiting for the day
That shall come to open wide the iron door,
And the hollow eye grows bright,
And the poor heart almost gay,
As we think of seeing home and friends once more.

A relatively early song about a soldier's homecoming was the optimistic contribution, "When Johnny Comes Marching Home" (1863), written by Patrick Gilmore, though originally published under the pseudonym Louis Lambert. The bracing tune may have been taken from the Irish melody, "Johnny, I Hardly Knew Ye":

When Johnny comes marching home again,
Hurrah, hurrah!
We'll give him a hearty welcome then,
Hurrah, hurrah!
The men will cheer, the boys will shout,
The ladies, they will all turn out,
And we'll all feel gay when Johnny comes marching home.

With this song too, there were seemingly endless variations on the lyrics. A San Francisco–based minstrel supplied the following chorus:

And if they lost a leg, the girls won't run,
For half a man is better than none,
And we'll all feel gay when Johnny comes marching home.

The line that concludes each stanza was often changed from "And we'll all feel gay when Johnny comes marching home" to "And we'll all drink stone blind, Johnny fill up the bowl."

Democrat and New York City theater owner Tony Pastor (1873–1908) contributed the following:

The Union cause is going ahead,
Ahead! Ahead!
The Rebel cause will soon be dead,
Be dead! Be dead!
Their game is up and their hope is fled,
And we'll make them pay for the blood they shed,
We'll all drink to Uncle Sam,
Johnny fill up the bowl!

The melody was also adopted during the 1864 presidential campaign. The "widow-maker" was Lincoln. Little Mac was General George B. McClellan:

The widow-maker soon must cave,
Hurrah, Hurrah,
We'll plant him in some nigger's grave,
Hurrah, Hurrah.

Torn from your farm, your ship, your raft,
Conscript. How do you like the draft,
And we'll stop that too,
When little Mac takes the helm.

The Campaign of 1864

The hotly contested presidential campaign of 1864 pitted the Republican Lincoln against the Democrat McClellan, who had been a popular commander, but ineffective fighter. Overly cautious and invariably a step behind his enemy, McClellan was removed from command by Lincoln in 1862 after

failures to coordinate attacks and exploit advantages during first the Peninsula Campaign and later that year at Antietam. The candidates' dislike for
one another was legendary.

Lincoln ran on a platform that would continue the war until the South
capitulated. McClellan's Democrats, though not McClellan himself, sought
to end the fighting immediately and negotiate a settlement. Northern peace
sentiment was becoming increasingly common as the war ground on and
the public grew ever more tired of death. In fact, the electorate might have
gone for McClellan had not Sherman achieved a decisive Union victory in
the first days of September with the capture of Atlanta.

Both campaigns had songs that attacked the opposition. Stephen Foster's
vulgar "Little Mac! Little Mac! You're the Very Man" derided not only Lincoln
but also abolitionists Horace Greeley and Charles Sumner:

> Democrats, Democrats, do it up brown
> Lincoln and his Niggerheads wont go down
> Greeley and Sumner and all that crew,
> We must beat Lincoln and Johnson too.

J. William Pope's pro-Lincoln "Uncle Sam's Menagerie" framed McClellan
as little more than a toy soldier:

> I'll have that man of wondrous fame,
> George B. [McClellan], George B.
> George Blunder I would call his name,
> Would ye? Would ye?
> Before Yorktown he beat his drums,
> But was afraid of wooden guns;
> But still, upon a dress parade,
> He was a splendid man.

As for the anti-abolition rhetoric, pro-Lincoln songs often faced the issue
head-on, such as in John Adams and Mrs. Parkhurst's "Come Rally, Freemen Rally":

> Come, rally freemen, rally!
> We'll whip the copperheads,
> Hurrah boys! hurrah boys!

And plant our noble banner
Where Afric's sons have bled.

In the "Campaign Song for Abraham Lincoln," H. M. Higgins more subtly juxtaposed the words "traitor" and "freedom":

Come all ye true hearted, let this be your cry:
Our chieftain must conquer, the traitor shall die!
'Neath freedom's proud banner we'll march to the field,
Now press them with vigor, the traitors shall yield.

Pastiche songs published on broadsides were effective attention-getters and inexpensive to distribute. Both candidates used the melody of "The Battle Cry of Freedom." The pro-Lincoln "Rally Round the Cause Boys" (by "Our Ned") was abolitionist in flavor:

Now, we'll rally round the cause boys, we'll rally in our might,
Singing the holy cause of freemen;
We will battle for our Union, the sacred cause of right,
Singing the holy cause of freemen.

"Shouting our Battle-Cry, 'McClellan,' " in contrast, built on the general's popularity with the soldiers:

McClellan is our watchword, hurrah! boys, hurrah!
So down with the Joker, and up with Little Mac;
While we rally 'round the polls, and vote the hero in,
Shouting our battle-cry—"McClellan!"

The tune "Wait for the Wagon" had been set by Democrats and Republicans alike in the presidential elections of 1856 and 1860. John A. McSorley's "McClellan Campaign Song" was anti-abolitionist in character:

Come all you gallant democrats, and listen for a while,
'Twill ruffle nigger-lovers, but cause you all to smile,
They'd sacrifice all principles, and over us they'd ride,
While worshipping the nigger, they'd let the Union slide.

Hurrah for the Union, hurrah for the Union.
Hurrah for the Union, and the gallant little Mac.

A pro-Lincoln setting of the melody called for voters to stay the course for four more years:

> Stick to the Wagon
> The Old Union Wagon,
> The triumphant Wagon,
> Abe Lincoln's bound to ride;
> Hurrah boys for Lincoln,
> Hurrah boys for Lincoln,
> Hurrah boys for Lincoln,
> Little Mac is played.

While the preceding broadsides used music with patriotic or humorous associations, another "McClellan Campaign Song" (by "Our Ned") was set to the melody of "Who Will Care for Mother Now" and "Respectfully dedicated to the McClellan Glee Clubs and 'White Boys' of the United States":

> Why are we so strong and sanguine—
> See our banners waving high:
> All around the sky is brightening.
> "Mac" will give us victory!
> He will guide our noble vessel,
> Soon this "cruel war" will cease:
> Now, we've got our "Old Commander,"
> We'll soon have a glorious peace.
> Soon our country'll be united.
> To McClellan we will bow;
> We have promised him our ballots,
> Who will care for Abra'm now?

The Late Years: Songs of Victory and Defeat, Home and Reconciliation

As the war passed its nadir in the fall of 1864, and the hope of peace emerged, songs again shifted their focus. Union songs spoke of homecomings and victories with works like William T. Rogers's "Coming Home from the Old Camp Ground" (1865), S.H.M. Byers and A. E. Wimmerstedt's "The Boys in Blue Are Coming Home" (1865), J. G. Huntting's "The Boys Are

Marching Home" (1865), and George A. Meitzke's "Charleston Is Ours!" (1865). Loved in the North and hated in the South was Henry Work's "Marching Through Georgia" (1865). The song recounts the details of one of the most audacious and destructive campaigns of the war when, after the Battle of Atlanta, Sherman split his army. He sent 60,000 men northward under the leadership of General George H. Thomas. With a remaining army of 62,000, Sherman cut away from his supply lines and lived off the land as his men marched the 285 miles to Savannah. Sherman promised that he would "make Georgia howl," and he did. With his foragers destroying most everything in their sixty-mile-wide path, Sherman sought to break the psychological backbone of the South.[31]

While Work's song seems to provide a historical accounting, the text gets some of the facts wrong. Sherman's army was bigger; the distance to travel shorter. Putting such details aside, however, Work does capture the upbeat attitude of the soldiers. After so much hard fighting in the previous years, many saw the campaign as an extended picnic—"the most gigantic pleasure excursion ever planned," one officer is famously reported to have said.[32] Georgia's rich farmland provided the pickings.

The song's chorus refers to the year of jubilee. In fact, thousands of newly freed slaves followed along at the rear of the Union army. As for the Union men mentioned in the third verse, their tears might not have been as joyful as Work suggests. Union sympathizers were treated little or no differently than anyone else. As for the fourth stanza comment about never reaching the coast, amazingly enough, Confederate President Jefferson Davis had expressed exactly that sentiment in speeches as the march was going forward. Davis must have been dreaming. With only a few thousand Georgia militia and 3,500 Confederate cavalry in the way, there was nothing to stop Sherman's war machine. The army moved at a pace of about twelve miles daily:

> Ring the good ol' bugle, boys, we'll sing another song,
> Sing it with a spirit that will start the world along,
> Sing it like we used to sing it 50,000 strong
> While we were marching through Georgia.

> [Chorus:]
> Hurrah, hurrah, we bring the jubilee!
> Hurrah, hurrah, the flag that makes you free!
> So we sang the chorus from Atlanta to the sea
> While we were marching through Georgia!

How the darkies shouted when they heard the joyful sound!
How the turkeys gobbled which our commissary found!
How the sweet potatoes even started from the ground
While we were marching through Georgia!

[Chorus]

Yes, and there were Union men who wept with joyful tears
When they saw the honored flag they had not seen for years.
Hardly could they be restrained from breaking forth in cheers
While we were marching through Georgia!

[Chorus]

"Sherman's dashing Yankee boys will never reach the coast!"
So the saucy rebels said, and 'twas a handsome boast,
Had they not forgot, alas, to reckon with the host
While we were marching through Georgia!

[Chorus]

So we made a thoroughfare for freedom and her train,
Sixty miles in latitude, 300 to the main.
Treason fled before us, for resistance was in vain
While we were marching through Georgia!

Of all the songs written during the Civil War, "Marching Through Georgia" remained—in the North, that is—one of the most popular in the decades to come. Work's colleague George Root thoughtfully noted that the reason for the song's postwar popularity may have been due to its unusual outlook. While most of the popular war songs talked about either "going in" to combat or its bloody consequences, "Marching Through Georgia" was "retrospective." The song was "a glorious remembrance of coming triumphantly out, and so has been more appropriate to soldiers' and other gatherings ever since."[33]

Composers also wrote to express public rage. Such was the case with Eastburn and M. E.'s fascinating and vindictive "Dixie's Nurse" (1865), which addressed cotton-importing England's longstanding Southern sympathies. The score's cover page gives a preview of what will be found inside. Featured is a rendering of an obese and helmeted maiden—a sort of Valkyrie figure gone to seed. With short chubby fingers she grasps a three-pronged trident in one hand and in the other what may be a cask lid, though the planks are crossed so as to form the design of a Union Jack. The lyrics are equally abusive:

> Way down in South Car'lina State,
> In Uncle Sam's domains;
> A naughty child called Dixie lived,
> Who lacked sufficient brains.
> He had been fed on PUBLIC PAP,
> 'Till he had saucy grown;
> So thought he'd start a Government
> And have it all his own.
>
> [Chorus:]
> And all that marks the fatal spot
> Where little Dixie fell,
> Is bonnet, boots, a pair of spurs,
> Hoop-Skirt and Balmoral[34]
>
> Britania was quite jealous of
> Her neighbor Uncle Sam;
> So full of wicked thoughts did she,
> The head of Dixie cram,
> She nursed him well, until she thought,
> He large enough had grown,
> To try the hard experiment
> Of standing all alone.

Union writers also went after Jefferson Davis. The sheet music front piece for Amos Patton's "How Do You Like It Jefferson D?" (1864) shows an African-American soldier relaxing. He complacently watches the Devil hold Davis by the pants and roast him over a fire. In another action indicative of African-American empowerment, the song's protagonist speaks to Davis without dialect, directly and forcefully:

> Oh, how do you like it as far as you've got?
> Jefferson D! Jefferson D!
> Are you glad you began it, or d'ye wish you had not?
> Jefferson D! Jefferson D!
> People say (tho' of course I don't know that its so,)
> That your spirits are getting decidedly low,

And you're sick and discourag'd, and I don't know what;
But say tho', do you like it as far as you've got?

Oh Ho! Jefferson D! Things look rather shaky, now,
'Twixt you and me!
Oh Ho! Jefferson D! Things look rather shaky,
'Twixt you and me!

After Union forces captured Davis outside Irwinsville, Georgia, on May 10,
1865, several Northern songs focused on the rumor that he was wearing
women's clothing when apprehended. The story was false, but held a grain
of truth. Davis, who had been on the run since abandoning Richmond over
a month earlier, was fleeing southward with his family and a small body-
guard. Union soldiers overran the camp in the predawn darkness. In
his rush to escape, Davis evidently grabbed his wife's cloak instead of his
own.[35]

Whatever his attire, Davis was no coward. Details were unimportant, however. The North wanted revenge for four years of war. Emasculating Davis,
and by extension Southern manhood at large, must have held a special joy.
"Jeff in Petticoats," by lyricist George Cooper and composer Henry Tucker,
was typical:

Now when he saw the game was up,
He started for the woods,
His bandbox hung upon his arm
Quite full of fancy goods:
Said Jeff, "They'll never take me now;
I'm sure I'll not be seen,"
"They'll never think to look for me
Beneath my crinoline."

Jeff took with him, the people say,
A mine of golden coin,
Which he from banks and other places,
Managed to purloin:
But though he ran, like every thief,
He had to drop the spoons,
And maybe that's the reason why
He dropped his pantaloons!

J. W. Turner's "The Sour Apple Tree; or, Jeff Davis' Last Ditch." Photo courtesy Duke University's Rare Book, Manuscript, and Special Collections Library.

Additional songs, all written within weeks of his capture, included lyricist Charles Haynes and composer James E. Haynes's "Jeff Davis in Crinoline," E. L. Kurtz's "A Confederate Transposed to a Petticoat," J. W. Turner's "The Sour Apple Tree; or, Jeff Davis' Last Ditch," and Henry Schroeder's "Oh,

Jeff, Oh, Jeff, How Are You Now?" In "Jeff's Last Proclamation" (no composer listed), Davis forecasts a disagreeable future:

> The yankees have got me and soon I shall be
> In petticoats hung to that sour apple tree.

Davis was imprisoned in Virginia's Fortress Monroe and indicted on treason charges in 1866. Union jailers showed little mercy. Evidently from spite alone, Davis was put in irons inside his locked cell with a twenty-four-hour guard. The humiliating ordeal devastated his already fragile health. As word of Davis's weakening condition leaked out, Northern sentiment slowly began to soften in his favor. Reflecting the change in public opinion was the Rev. J. Barker and Alfred Schmidt's "Jefferson Davis in Prison" (1867):

> The orb of thy fame to its zenith uprisen
> Thy firm spirit yet stands unhurt in the flame;
> And vain are the capture, the shackles, the prison,
> For freedmen look upwards, still shouting thy name.

Davis was finally released in May 1867 on a $100,000 bond signed by Horace Greeley and others. His case never went to trial.

Lincoln's assassination prompted an outpouring of poetry, song, and instrumental music. George Root set text by L. M. Dawn in the song, "Farewell Father, Friend and Guardian" (1865):

> All our land is draped in mourning,
> Hearts are bowed and strong men weep;
> For our loved, our noble leader,
> Sleeps his last, his dreamless sleep,
> Gone forever, gone forever,
> Fallen by a traitor's hand;
> Tho' preserv'd, his dearest treasure,
> Our redeem'd beloved land.
>
> Farewell father, friend and guardian,
> Thou hast joined the martyr band;
> But thy glorious work remaineth,
> Our redeemed, beloved land.

Other songs, all written in 1865, included: "A Nation Mourns Her Martyr'd Son" by Alice Hawthorne (Septimus Winner), as well as M. B. Ladd's "We Mourn Our Fallen Chieftain," H. S. Thompson's "A Nation Mourns Her Chief," and George Cooper and J. R. Thomas's "Our Noble Chief Has Passed Away." Dozens of funeral marches were written.

Songs painted various aspects of the assassination, often setting up the scenario with explanations on the coversheet. J. W. Turner's "Live But One Moment!" recalled words the First Lady supposedly said to Lincoln at his death:

> "Live but one moment!"
> Speak but once more!
> Speak to the children,
> One word I implore!
> O breathe but one accent
> To cheer this sad heart
> "Live but one moment"
> E'er we must part!

In the song "The Savior of Our Country" (1865), O. Wheelock and James W. Porter sent Lincoln to a heavenly reunion with his son Willie, who had died three years earlier at the age of eleven:

> Father! when on earth you fell
> Father! was my Mother well?
> When I fell your Mother cried!
> Then unconsciously I died.
> Glory forms our sunlight here!
> Astral Lamps our Chandelier!
> Rode your [sic] here among the stars,
> In the train of silver cars!
>
> [Chorus:]
> Willie! on the earth look back!
> Father! tis a speck of black!
> Robed in Mourning as you see!
> Mourns the Earth for you and me!

John Wilkes Booth was invariably demonized. Guilt and righteous vengeance were the themes in another J. W. Turner song, "The Assassin's Vision"

(1865). The music, stated the coversheet, was "suggested on seeing the representation of the assassin Booth wildly fleeing through the forest on his horse, startled by the apparition of his victim appearing in the trees & around him":

> The assassin rode on with trembling and fear,
> And mournfully murmur'd the breeze;
> Before him! around him! all vivid and drear,
> The vision appeared in the trees

Confederate songs generally became more subdued as the war ground to an end. Songs spoke with quiet pride of fighting no more, of going home and beginning life anew, as in Charles Lever and Edward O. Eaton's "When the Battle Is Over" (1865) and G. M. Wickliffe's "We're Coming Again to the Dear Ones at Home!" (1865). Some songs spoke of bygones and moving on, like Clarence J. Prentice and Charles L. Ward's "Why Can We Not Be Brothers, or, We Know That We Were Rebels" (1865):

> We know that we were rebels,
> And we don't deny the name,
> We speak of that which we have done
> With grief, but not with shame.

Others honored the past and the dead, like Mrs. C. A. Ball and Charlie L. Ward's "The Faded Gray Jacket, or, Fold It Up Carefully" (1866):

> Fold it up carefully, and lay it aside,
> Tenderly touch it, look on it with pride—
> For dear must it be to our hearts ever more,
> The Jacket of gray our loved soldier boy wore.

Soon, composers both North and South would turn away from the war altogether. Enough had been written about death and suffering. A new and lighter era was about to dawn.

SINGING SOLDIERS

"The men who wore the blue, and the butternut Rebs who opposed them, more than American fighters of any period, deserve to be called singing soldiers," observed historian Bell Irvin Wiley.[36] He was right. In camp, soldiers played games, told stories, and made music with violins and guitars, fifes and bugles, drums and bones, any instruments they might have made or brought with them from home. Brass bands often roamed about serenading officers or enlisted men. Sometimes the soldiers danced, or presented theatrical performances. Minstrel songs were popular, so were sentimental ballads. More extravagant staged endeavors were especially popular during the long nights that made up the dreary months of winter camp.

On the march, soldiers sang to keep spirits up and feet moving. For those unfortunate enough to be taken prisoner, music not only offered relief from depression, but offered a vehicle for soldiers to join together in acts of solidarity and defiance. When it came to stiffening resolve or engendering patriotic fervor, song was also effective in combat, its effects not only exhilarating to those doing the singing, but occasionally debilitating to those on the other side. Nearly two decades after the war, Carlton McCarthy, a Confederate soldier in the Army of Northern Virginia, included Northern music, along with enlistment bounties (as high as $300) and regular monthly salary, as a potent force against which he and his Southern compatriots had to contend:

> The Confederate soldier fought . . . the "Stars and Stripes," the "Star-Spangled Banner," "Hail Columbia," "Tramp, Tramp, Tramp," "John Brown's Body," "Rally Round the Flag," and all the fury and fanaticism which skilled minds could create,—opposing this grand array with the modest and homely refrain of "Dixie," supported by a mild solution of "Maryland, My Maryland."[37]

Throughout the war, publishers did their best to keep soldiers well supplied with songs. Aware that soldiers knew and could remember many melodies but might forget a song's words, publishers printed songsters. Often adorned with colorful names like the South's *Bonnie Blue Flag Song Book* (1861) or the North's *The Frisky Irish Songster*, these collections were popular on both sides of the Mason-Dixon Line and provided the soldiers with hundreds of songs. Southern songsters included *The Southern Flag Song Book* (1861), *Hopkins' New Orleans 5 Cent Song-Book* (1861), *The Dixie Land Songster* (1863), *Virginia Songster* (1863), *Stonewall Song Book* (1864), *The Army Songster* (1864), *The Punch Songster* (1864), *Jack Morgan Songster* (1864), *The Beauregard Songster* (1864), *The Rebel Songster* (1864), *Songs of Love and Liberty* (1864), *Southern Songster* (1864), and *The Gen. Lee Songster* (1865). Northern songsters included the *Stars and Stripes Songster* (1861), *Beadle's Dime Union Song Book* (1861), *The Flag of Our Union Songster* (1861), *Beadle's Dime Napsack Songster* (1862), *The Camp Fire Songster, Tony Pastor's New Union Song Book* (1862), *The Little Mac Songster* (1862), *Nat Austin's New Comic and Sentimental Song Book, The Patriotic Glee Book* (1863), *Fred May's Comic Irish Songster, Shoddy Songster, Camp Fire Companion, Dawley's Ten-Penny Song Books, Union League Melodies, Bugle Call* (1863), *The American Union Songster, War Songs for Freemen* (1863), *John Brown Songster, The Union Right or Wrong Songster* (1863), *Bob Hart's Plantation Songster* (1862), *Christy's New Songster and Black Joker* (1863), *The Campfire Songster* (1864), and *The Yankee Doodle Songster.*

Songs in Camp

Yankees and Confederates shared many of the same songs. John Howard Payne and Henry Rowley Bishop's "Home, Sweet Home" (1823), for example, was popular with all soldiers and one of the most sung of the war. Its simple melody and nostalgic lyrics ("Mid pleasures and palaces though I may roam, / Be it every so humble, there's no place like home") brought solace to soldiers everywhere.

Much of the repertory originated in the British Isles. Hugely popular was Scotland's most beloved sentimental ballad, "Annie Laurie" (also known as "Maxwelton Braes"), based on a poem by William Douglas and written in the late 1600s. As was common with music passed along by oral tradition, there were many variants of both the melody and lyrics. Here, rich in dialect, is one common rendering of the first verse:

> Maxwelton braes are bonnie,
> Where early fa's the dew,

And 'twas there that Annie Laurie
Gie'd me her promise true.
Gie'd me her promise true
Which ne'er forgot will be;
And for bonnie Annie Laurie
I'd lay me donne and die.[38]

Also in fashion was the agonizing love ballad "Kathleen Mavourneen," written between 1835 and 1838 by English composer and cellist Frederick Nicholls Crouch (1808–1896), who immigrated to the United States in 1849 and served throughout the war as a trumpet player in the Richmond Howitzers:

Kathleen, mavourneen, the grey dawn is breaking,
The horn of the hunter is heard on the hill.
The lark from her light wing the bright dew is shaking,
Kathleen, mavourneen, what! Slumbering still?

Oh, hast thou forgotten how soon we must sever?
Oh, hast thou forgotten this day we must part?
It may be for years, and it may be forever,
Then why art thou silent, thou voice of my heart?
It may be for years and it may be forever,
Then why art thou silent, Kathleen, mavourneen?[39]

Nearly forty years after its composition, John Hill Hewitt's "The Minstrel's Return'd from the War" would be widely sung by Civil War soldiers. John Beatty of the 3rd Ohio Volunteer Infantry recalled the song in a diary entry on September 23, 1861:

What a glorious scene! The sky filled with stars; the rising moon; two mountain walls so high, apparently, that one might step from them into heaven; the rapid river, the thousand white tents dotting the valley, the campfires, the shadowy forms of soldiers; in short, just enough of heaven and earth visible to put one's fancy on a gallop. The boys are in groups about their fires. The voice of the troubadour is heard. It is a pleasant song that he sings, and I catch part of it.

The minstrel's returned from the war,
With spirits as buoyant as air,[40]

Beatty was a Romantic and deeply bitten by the grandeur of camp life. Describing the evening of October 6, 1861, he wrote:

> I never looked upon a wilder or more interesting scene. The valley is blazing with campfires; the men flit around them like shadows. Now some indomitable spirit, determined that neither rain nor weather shall get him down, strikes up:
>
> Oh! Say can you see by the dawn's early light,
> What so proudly we hailed at the twilight's last gleaming,
> Whose broad stripes and bright stars, through the perilous fight,
> O'er the ramparts we watched were so gallantly streaming?
>
> A hundred voices join in, and the very mountains, which loom up in the firelight like great walls, whose tops are lost in the darkness, resound with a rude melody befitting so wild a night and so wild a scene. But the songs are not all patriotic. Love and fun make contribution also, and a voice, which may be that of the invincible Irishman, Corporal Casey, sings:
>
> 'Twas a windy night, about two o'clock in the morning,
> An Irish lad, so tight, all the wind and the weather scorning,
> At Judy Callaghan's door, sitting upon the paling,
> His love tale he did pour, and this is part of his wailing:
> Only say you'll be mistress Brallaghan;
> Don't say nay, charming Judy Callaghan.
>
> A score of voices pick up the chorus, and the hills and mountains seem to join the corporal's appeal to the charming Judy:
>
> Only say you'll be mistress Brallaghan;
> Don't say nay, charming Judy Callaghan.[41]

Were such broad scenes of music making commonplace in camps? One assumes so. Wrote John Billings in language more matter of fact:

> When this slight matter of the proper thing for the army to do was disposed of, some one would start a song, and then for an hour at least "John Brown's Body," "Marching Along," "Red, White, and Blue," "Rally 'round the Flag," and other popular and familiar songs would ring out on the clear evening air, following along in quick succession, and sung with great earnestness and enthusiasm as the chorus was increased by additions from neighboring camp-fires, until tired Nature began to assert herself, when one by one the company would withdraw, each going to his hut

for two or three hours' rest, if possible, to partially prepare him
for the toils of the morrow.[42]

Not all nights were so idyllic, of course. The following March 20, as the
army prepared to march to Murfreesboro, Beatty recorded that he and his
comrades:

> Turned out at four o'clock in the morning, got breakfast, struck
> our tents, and were ready to march at six; but the brigade being
> now ordered to take the rear, we stood uncovered in a drenching
> rain three hours for the division and transportation to pass. All
> were thoroughly wet and benumbed with cold, but as if to show
> contempt for the weather the Third sang with great unction:

> There is a land of pure delight,
>   Where saints immortal reign;
> Infinite day excludes the night,
>   And pleasures banish pain.
> There everlasting spring abides,
>   And never withering flowers;
> Death, like a narrow sea, divides
>   This heavenly land from ours.[43]

Themes of unfulfilled love, separation, and death—all common topics before
the war—remained popular with soldiers. Additional ballads of this sort included poet Thomas Dunn English and Nelson Kness's "Ben Bolt" (1848),"
George Root's "The Hazel Dell" (1853), and Henry Webster and J. P. Webster's "Lorena." Particularly well-liked in the South was "Juanita," by British
women's rights advocate Caroline Elizabeth Sarah Norton (1808–1877).

More buoyant was "The Girl I Left Behind Me," a long-established import
from the British Isles that became widely popular both on the stage and as
a square dance tune. With its easy-going text and lively melody, it had been
played and sung by American soldiers on the march since the Revolutionary
War.[44] The *Forget Me Not Songster* of 1842 included the following lyrics:

> I'm lonesome since I crossed the hills
> And o'er the moor that's sedgy,
> With heavy thought my mind is filled
> Since I patted Naegy.
> Whene'r I turn to view the place,

> The tears doth fall and blind me,
> When I think of the charming grace
> Of the girl I left behind me

The song's imagery inspired the Civil War–period printing of multicolored letterhead stationery featuring a girl bidding farewell to a soldier dressed in Zouave-style uniform. A symbol of both nation and home, the girl wears a blue blouse adorned with white stars and a dress of red and white stripes. The following text, not from a song version that I have found elsewhere, is included alongside the picture:

> "The Girl I Left Behind Me"
>
> "He turn'd and left the spot—O! do not deem him weak—
> For dountless was the soldier's heart, though tears were on his cheek:
> Go, watch the foremost rank, in danger's dark career;
> Be sure the hand most daring then has wiped away a tear."

This melody was also set by John F. Poole to lyrics in a quasi-German-American dialect and published as a broadside titled "I Goes to Fight mit Sigel." German officer Franz Sigel (1824–1902) had fought with the rebellious forces in the Prussian Revolution of 1848–1849. Upon defeat, he went into exile in the United States where he became a Union general during the Civil War. His troops were thrashed and humiliated in August 1861 at Wilson's Creek, Missouri, but redeemed themselves in 1862 at the Battle of Pea Ridge, Arkansas:

> I've come shust now to tells you how,
> I goes mit regimentals,
> To "schlauch" dem voes of Liberty,
> Like dem old Continentals,
> Vot fights mit England long ago,
> To save der Yankee Eagle;
> Und now I gets my sojer clothes;
> I'm going to fight mit Sigel.
>
> [Chorus:]
> Yaw! daus is drue, I shpeaks mit you,
> I'm going to fight mit Sigel.

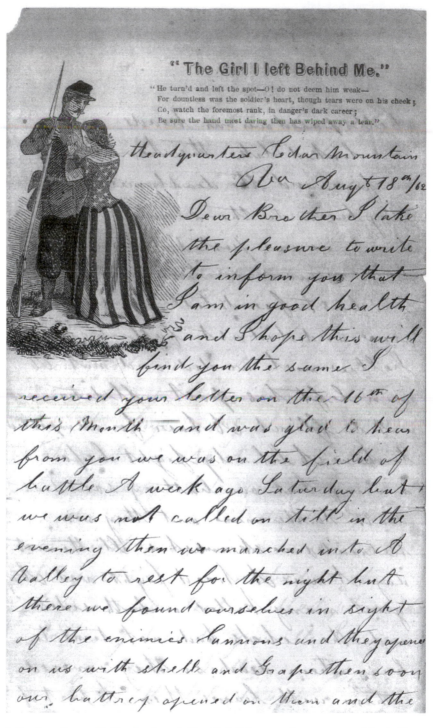

"**The Girl I left Behind Me.**"

"He turn'd and left the spot—O! do not deem him weak—
For dauntless was the soldier's heart, though tears were on his cheek;
Go, watch the foremost rank, in danger's dark career;
Be sure the hand most daring then has wiped away a tear."

Headquarters Cedar Mountain
Va Augt 18th /62
Dear Brother I take
the pleasure to write
to inform you that
I am in good health
and I hope this will
find you the same I
received your letter on the 16th of
this Month and was glad to hear
from you we was on the field of
battle A week ago Saturday but
we was not called on till in the
evening then we marched into A
Valley to rest for the night but
there we found ourselves in sight
of the enimies Cannons and they opened
on us with shell and Grape then soon
our battery opened on them and the

Letter from George H. Bloodough, 97th New York Volunteers. Image courtesy John A. Kingsley.

Ven I comes from der Deutsche Countree,
I vorks somedimes at baking;
Den I keeps a lager beer saloon,
Und den I goes shoe-making;
But now I was a sojer been
To save der Yankee Eagle,
To schlauch dem tam secession volks,
I goes to fight mit Sigel.

More recently composed songs with the same folklike directness that reached immense popularity were "Listen to the Mocking Bird" from 1855 and "Der Deitcher's Dog" ("Where, Oh Where Has My Little Dog Gone") from 1864. The melody of the former was written by the African-American street musician Richard Milburn (1817–unknown) and set to words by Alice Hawthorne (Septimus Winner). Over the next fifty years the song would sell some twenty million copies. Winner wrote both melody and words to "Der Deitcher's Dog."

Abraham Lincoln was particularly fond of "Listen to the Mocking Bird," a song he found "as sincere as the laughter of a little girl at play." "Mocking Bird" was also a favorite of Union General Philip Kearney, who often gave out whiskey to his band when they played it, which was frequent, at least "as long as the musician can see his instrument":[45]

I'm dreaming now of Hallie,
my sweet Hallie,
my sweet Hallie,
I'm dreaming now of my Hallie,
for the thought of her is one that never dies;

[Chorus:]
Listen to the mocking bird,
Listen to the mocking bird,
The mocking bird still singing o'er her grave,
Listen to the mocking bird,
Listen to the mocking bird,
Still singing where the weeping willows wave.

The song was also popular on the march. Wrote Augustus Meyers during the Peninsula Campaign of 1862:

In the morning, while on the march, when the sun was shining, and we were in good spirits, some regiment would start up a song. I particularly remember that my regiment marched directly behind the "Duryee Zouaves" one morning when one of their fine singers started "The Mocking Bird," and presently the entire regiment, twice as large as ours, took up the chorus. It was beautiful, and it has ever since remained one of my favorite sings.[46]

Death and its attendant sorrows (from disease as often as combat) were the soldiers' constant companions. Nevertheless, both in camp and on the march, there was almost always room for levity. A great many songs were of a fully upbeat nature. One of the silliest, but no worse for marching because of that, was "Goober Peas," a cheery homage to the lowly peanut. The song was written by A. E. Blackmar but published under a pair of pseudonyms. P. Nutt was the credited composer; A. Pender the lyricist:

Sittin' by the roadside on a summer's day,
Chattin' with my messmates, passing time away,
Lying in the shadows, underneath the trees—
Goodness, how delicious, eating goober peas!

[Chorus:]
Peas! Peas! Peas! Peas! Eating goober peas!
Goodness, how delicious, eating goober peas!

When a horseman passes, the soldiers have a rule
To cry out at their loudest "Mister, here's your mule!"
But still another pleasure enchantinger than these
Is wearing out your grinders, eating goober peas!

[Chorus]

Just before the battle, the General hears a row;
He says "The Yanks are coming, I hear their rifles now"!
He turns around in wonder, and what do you think he sees?
The Georgia Militia, eating goober peas!

[Chorus]

I think my song had lasted almost long enough!
The subject's interesting, but rhymes are mighty rough!
I wish this war was over, when free from rags and fleas,
We'd kiss our wives and sweethearts and gobble goober peas!

Widely popular with both armies was R. B. Buckley's snappy mid-century song, "Wait for the Wagon":

> Will you come with me, my Phyllis dear
> To yon blue mountain free?
> Where the blossoms smell the sweetest
> Come rove along with me.
> It's every Sunday morning
> When I am by your side
> We'll jump into the wagon
> And all take a ride.
>
> [Chorus:]
> Wait for the wagon,
> Wait for the wagon,
> Wait for the wagon,
> And we'll all take a ride.

The melody was used in any number of situations and set to a nearly endless variety of lyrics. A Unionist named "E. F." used the melody to make his frustration known after General George G. Meade and his Army of the Potomac (citing lack of supplies) failed to pursue and potentially destroy Lee's army, which had stalled along the Potomac River following its retreat from Gettysburg:

> You must wait for the wagons,
> The real army wagons,
> The fat contract wagons,
> Bought in the red-tape way.

Northern anti-abolitionists, and there were many, used the tune to set a song titled "Fight for the Nigger":

> Fight for the nigger,
> The sweet-scented nigger,
> The wooly-headed nigger
> And the Abolition crew.

Also popular were Northern and Southern versions called "The Old Union Wagon" and "The Southern Wagon" respectively. The songs' choruses frame the conflicting stances:

"The Old Union Wagon"

Hurrah for the wagon,
The old Union wagon,
We'll stick to our wagon
And all take a ride.

"The Southern Wagon"

So wait for the wagon!
The dissolution wagon!
The South is the wagon,
And we'll all take a ride.

To ease the boredom from lack of activity during the winter months, soldiers often set up theaters within their camps. Confederate private John O. Casler of the Stonewall Brigade described one such undertaking during the winter of 1864:

> Directly after we went into winter quarters, near Orange Court House, the Louisiana brigade and our brigade joined together and built a large log house, covered it with clapboards, erected a stage, organized a theatrical troupe of negro minstrels and gave performances nearly every night to a crowded audience. "Admission one dollar—net proceeds to be given to widows and orphans of Confederate soldiers."
>
> Noble T. Johnson, of the 5th Virginia, was one of the end men, handled the bones, and was one of the most comical characters I ever saw. He could keep the house in a roar of applause all the time. Miller, of the 1st Louisiana, was banjoist, and a splendid performer. They would write some of their own plays, suitable to the times and occasion.
>
> One splendid piece was called the "Medical Board"—a burlesque on the surgeons. The characters were a number of surgeons sitting around a table playing cards, with a bottle of brandy on the table, which was passed around quite frequently, until one doctor inquired how they came to get such good brandy.
>
> "Oh! this is some that was sent down from Augusta County for the sick soldiers, but the poor devils don't need it, so we'll drink it."
>
> Then a courier would come in and inform them that there was a soldier outside badly wounded.

"Bring him in! bring him in!" said the chief surgeon. When brought in an examination would take place with the result that his arm would have to be amputated. Then the poor fellow wanted to know if when that was done he could not have a furlough.

"Oh! no," replied the surgeon. A further examination developed that his leg would have to be amputated.

"Then can I have a furlough?" said the soldier.

"By no means," replied the surgeon, "for you can drive an ambulance when you get well."

It was finally determined by the medical board, as he was wounded in the head, that his head would have to come off.

"Then," says the soldier, "I know I can have a furlough."

"No, indeed," replied the surgeon, "we are so scarce of men that your body will have to be set up in the breastworks to fool the enemy."

Many such pieces as the foregoing were acted-burlesques on the officers, quartermasters and commissaries, or whatever was interesting and amusing. Taking it all together we had splendid performances. I have never seen better since the war, as we had amongst us professional actors and musicians; and the theatre became a great place of resort to while away the dull winter nights.[47]

Such salt-of-the-earth fare must have delighted the plain-speaking Casler who—in a time when more lofty-gazing men recorded their war experiences through a filter of romance and honor—spoke freely of his own less than glamorous army adventures that included being absent without leave and robbing the dead.

Less formalized offerings often included amateur string players and other instrumentalists who performed folk music and minstrel songs:

There was probably not a regiment in the service that did not boast at least one violinist, one banjoist, and a bone player in its ranks. ... One or all of them could be heard in operation, either inside or in a company street, most any pleasant evening. However unskilled the artists, they were sure to be the center of an interested audience. The usual medley of comic songs and Negro melodie comprise the greater part of the entertainment, and, if the space admitted, a jig or clog dance was stepped out on a hard-tack box or other crude platform. Sometimes a real Negro was brought in to enliven the occasion by patting and dancing "Juba," or singing his quaint music.[48]

Fiddle players appear to have been consummate entertainers and enjoyed great popularity:

> The first stroke of his bow never failed to be cheered enthusias-
> tically by the regiment. After playing an hour or two he invariably
> closed with "O Lord Gals one Friday," which he would play, sing
> and dance at the same time. He was afterwards wounded . . . in
> the right arm just above the wrist resulting in a permanent de-
> flection of the arm at that point; and being asked whether he could
> still use the bow replied: "Why, yes; my arm now has exactly the
> right crook for the business."[49]

The war's most famous music aficionado was General J.E.B. Stuart, the Confederacy's dashing cavalry officer who participated in all of the Army of Virginia's major battles from 1st Manassas until his death on May 11, 1864, at age thirty-one. Flamboyant in dress, Stuart wore a peacock-plumed hat and either a flower or ribbon in his red-lined gray coat. He was equally audacious in battle. His standing order to his men was to gallop toward the enemy but, should retreat ever be necessary, to do so at no more than a trot. Many are the tales of Stuart's singing or whistling as he rode forward at the head of the column while leading his men into combat.

So great was Stuart's love for music and dance, and the sundry enjoyments that such entertainments might scare up, that he made special efforts to recruit singers and instrumentalists into his command. Stuart kept a string band on hand. Minstrel player and banjoist Sam Sweeney, the younger brother of famous minstrel singer Joe Sweeney, served as his personal musician. Stuart's biracial servant Bob played the bones. Stuart even named one of his horses "My Maryland" after the James Ryder Randall poem. Wrote Raphael Palacios of Stuart:

> So there was always music. Sweeney on the banjo, Mulatto Bob
> on the bones, a couple of fiddlers, Negro singers and dancers, the
> ventriloquist, and others who caught Stuart's eye. Sweeney rode
> behind Stuart on the outpost day and night. Stuart often sang and
> Sweeney plucked the strings behind him: "Her Bright Smile

Sam Sweeney playing the banjo. The scene depicted probably was at Stuart's Confederate Hospital near Culpeper. Image courtesy Appomattox Court House National Historical Park.

Haunts Me Still," "The Corn Top's Ripe," "Lorena" and "Jine the Cavalry."[50]

Stuart's musical tastes were broad and included not only the minstrel songs of the day, but also parlor songs from the past three decades, traditional songs of the British Isles and American South, African-American songs, and even opera arias. There were multiple sets of lyrics for many of these melodies.

Equally developed, it would seem, was Stuart's gallantry when it came to women. A soldier describes an evening during which Stuart had detained two women after they were caught trying to evade his pickets. Stuart decided to call in Bob and some other entertainers:

> Stuart turns round with a laugh and calls for a breakdown. The
> dilapidated African advances, dropping his hat first at the door.
> Bob strikes up a jig upon his guitar, the ventriloquist claps, and

the great performance of the breakdown commences, first upon the heeltap, then upon the toe. His antics are grand and indescribable. He leaps, he whirls, he twists and untwists his legs until the crowd at the door grows wild with admiration. The guitar continues to soar and Stuart's laughter mingles with it. The dancer's eyes roll gorgeously, his steps grow more rapid, he executes unheard-of figures. Finally a frenzy seems to seize him; the mirth grows fast and furious; the young lady laughs outright and seems about to clap her hands. Even the elder relaxes into an unmistakable smile; and as the dancer disappears with a bound through the door, the guitar stops playing, and Stuart's laughter rings out gay and jovial, the grim lips open and she says, "You rebels *do* seem to enjoy yourselves!"[51]

As the danger level increased, so, evidently, did Stuart's lust for music. "I have often seen him busy arranging for some of his most brilliant cavalry movements, and after all was prepared, come out of his tent, call for Sweeney and the banjo and perhaps for some of the men to dance for him, and then, to our amazement, order everybody to mount and be off. . . . The gayer he was the more likely it was we were to move soon."[52]

To the tune "The Old Gray Mare" Stuart and his soldiers often sang:

> If you want to have a good time,
> Join in the cavalry,
> Join in the cavalry

The song underwent other transformations as well. During the spring 1863 Confederate victory at Chancellorsville, General James Longstreet recalled that "Stuart's ringing voice could be heard high, high above the thunder of artillery and the ceaseless roar of musketry singing 'Old Joe Hooker, won't you come out the wilderness?' "[53]

The Union's General William Tecumseh Sherman was hardly dashing, but he too is strongly associated with music, though this was not of his own doing. Edwin Kimberley, who was attached to Sherman's command as leader of the regimental band of the 3rd Wisconsin Infantry, wrote to his parents on April 7, 1865, after receiving news of the fall of Richmond:

> Last night according to previous notice we repaired to Sherman's
> Headquarters for a Serenade. A new song—composed by [illegible]

is in my possession, entitled "Sherman's March to the Sea." After
some rehearsing I was the first one to sing it before our old hero
Billy S. and his entire Staff after which I sang another and received
a very high compliment from Sherman. After playing several
pieces the crack Band of the Army made its appearance (namely
33rd Massachusetts) and played several pieces—after all this we
played another piece and returned to camp assured we had done
honor to ourselves, at least.[54]

There were at least two songs with the title "Sherman's March to the Sea."
There may have been more. The best known was written by lyricist Lieutenant Samuel Hawkins M. Byers and composer Lieutenant J. C. Rockwell.
Byers wrote the words while being held in a prison camp in Columbia, South
Carolina, and after he had heard about Sherman's march to Savannah.[55] It
is possible that this is the version that Kimberley sang that night. The lyrics
recount the army's movement southward from Tennessee to Atlanta and
then on to Savannah:

> Our camp-fires shone bright on the mountain
> That frown'd on the river below,
> As we stood by our guns in the morning
> And eagerly watched for the foe.
> When a rider came out from the darkness
> That hung over mountain and tree,
> And shouted, "boys, up and be ready
> For Sherman will march to the sea."

Regimental Music

Just as there were songs written about specific campaigns and people, so
too there were songs composed specifically for individual regiments. "Give
Us a Flag" is one example. A member of Company A of Robert Gould Shaw's
African American 54th Massachusetts Volunteer Infantry wrote it in 1863:

> Fremont told us, when this war was first begun,
> How to save this Union, and the way it should be done,
> But Kentucky swore so hard, and old Abe he had his fears,
> So that's what's the matter with the Colored Volunteers.

[Chorus:]
Give us a flag all free without a slave,
We will fight to defend it as our fathers did so brave
Onward boys, onward, it's the year of jubilee,
God bless America, the land of liberty.

Little Mack went to Richmond with three hundred thousand brave—
Said keep back the negroes and the Union he would save;
But Mack he was defeated, and the Union now in tears,
Is calling for the help of the Colored Volunteers.

[Chorus]

Old Jeff he says he'll hang us if we dare to meet him armed—
It's a very big thing, but we are not at all alarmed:
He has first got to catch us before the way is clear,
And that's what's the matter with the Colored Volunteers.

That same year the tireless former slave, abolitionist, and women's right advocate Sojourner Truth wrote "The Valiant Soldiers" for the 1st Michigan Colored Regiment. The words were set to the melody of "John Brown's Body":

We are valiant soldiers who've enlisted for the war;
We are fighting for the Union, we are fighting for the law;
We can shoot a rebel farther than a white man ever saw,
As we go marching on.

[Chorus:]
Glory, glory, hallelujah!
Glory, glory, hallelujah!
Glory, glory, hallelujah!
As we go marching on.

We are done with hoeing cotton, we are done with hoeing corn,
We are colored Yankee soldiers, as sure as you are born;
When massa hears us shouting, he will think 'tis Gabriel's horn,
As we go marching on.

[Chorus]

Father Abraham has spoken, and the message has been sent;
The prison doors have opened, and out the prisoners went,

To join the sable army of African descent,
As we go marching on.[56]

Just as African-American regiments had songs that grew out of their ethnic and cultural heritage, so did other American minorities. The song "Kelly's Irish Brigade" tells of immigrant Captain Joseph Kelly who in 1861 commanded a regiment in the sixth division of the Missouri State Guard:

Come all you that hold true communion with southern Confederates bold,
I will tell you of some men who for the Union in the northern ranks
    were enrolled;
Who came to Missouri in their glory, and thought by their power we'd be
    dismayed;
But we soon made them tell a different story when they met with Kelly's
    Irish Brigade.

[Chorus:]
Three cheers for the Irish Brigade
Three cheers for the Irish Brigade.
And all true-hearted Hibernians
In the ranks of Kelly's Irish Brigade!

You call us rebels and traitors, but yourselves have thrown off that name
    of late.
You were called it by the English invaders at home in seventeen and ninety-
    eight.
The name to us is not a new one, though 'tis one that never will degrade
Any true-hearted Hibernian in the ranks of Kelly's Irish Brigade

[Chorus]

You dare not call us invaders, 'tis but state rights and liberties we ask;
And Missouri, we ever will defend her, no matter how hard be the task.
Then let true Irishmen assemble; let the voice of Missouri be obeyed;
And northern fanatics may tremble when they meet with Kelly's Irish
    Brigade

Sometimes ethnic interests mixed in unusual ways. While the following is not a regimental song per se, "Sambo's Right to Be Kilt" addresses the specific values and political issues of Irish soldiers. The lyrics were set to the Irish tune "The Low-Backed Car" and sung on January 13, 1864, in New York's Irving Hall for a banquet in honor of General Thomas F. Meagher

and officers of his Irish Brigade. The song reflects the occasionally intense
debate among white Union soldiers as to whether blacks should be allowed
to fight. The words are attributed to a Private Miles O'Reilly, but in fact no
such character existed. Instead, the text—aimed at Irish soldiers, who tended
to be strongly opposed to fighting alongside black soldiers—was written by
Charles G. Halpine, who served for a time on the staff of Major General
David Hunter:

> Some tell us 'tis a burnin shame
> To make the naygers fight;
> An' that the thrade of bein' kilt
> Belongs but to the white;
> But as for me, upon my soul!
> So liberal are we here,
> I'll let Sambo be murthered instead of myself
> On every day in the year.
> On every day in the year, boys,
> And in every hour of the day;
> The right to be kilt I'll divide wid him,
> An' divil a word I'll say.[57]

The German language hymn Die Fahnenwacht (The Color Guard) of the 3rd
Missouri Regiment was written by Ritter Peter von Lindpaintner with lyrics
by Feodor Loewe:

> Der Sänger hält im Feld die Fahnenwacht,
> in seinem Arme ruht das Schwert, das scharfe,
> er grüsst mit hellem Lied die stille Nacht
> und schlägt dazu mit blut'ger Hand die Harfe:
>
> [Chorus:]
> Die Dame, die ich liebe, nenn' ich nicht;
> doch hab' ich ihre Farben mir erkoren.
> Ich streite gern für Freiheit und für Licht,
> getreu der Fahne, der ich zugeschworen,
> getreu der Fahne, der ich zugeschworen.
>
> The singer is color guard in the field,
> In his arms rests the sharp sword,
> He greets the silent night with a clear song
> And plays the harp with blood-stained hand:

[Chorus:]
I won't name the lady I love,
But I chose her colors.
I gladly fight for liberty and light,
True to the colors to which I've sworn,
True to the colors to which I've sworn.

E. E. Bryant of the 3rd Wisconsin Infantry composed "Hamilton's Badger Boys." The song was evidently first sung to Colonel Charles S. Hamilton and his staff shortly after 1st Bull Run. The original tune to which the words were set is no longer known:

> We are Hamilton Badger boys
> And within have come
> From woody Wisconsin
> Our dearly loved home
> To fight for the Union
> To conquer or die
> And to raise on the foe's land
> Our wild battle cry
>
> [Chorus:]
> Charge away boys, away, away, away
> All hearts bounding high
> For Hamilton's Badger boys
> Will conquer or die[58]

Sometimes additions to songs were improvised during a march itself. Union Captain Francis Adams Donaldson of the Army of the Potomac wrote that:

> Among the men of my company who always kept up was Corporal John Montieth, and a more thoroughgoing fellow I never saw. He was jolly and lively all the time, making light of fatigue, and when the men were nearly used up, would inspire the whole command by singing a rattling good soldier song, called "I Come From the Old Granite State," with a chorus of boom! boom! boom! in an imitation of the bass drum, which had a most curious effect and was at once taken up by the regiment and rendered with a will. Indeed, the brigade took up the air and long after we were through,

they could be heard shouting the boom! boom! boom! chorus. Montieth had a rich, melodius voice and sang with great feeling.[59]

Billings notes that soldiers readily changed lyrics to fit their own circumstances:

> There was a song composed during the war, entitled the "Raw Recruit," sung to the tune of "Abraham's Daughter," which I am wholly unable to recall, but a snatch of the first verse, or its parody, ran about as follows:—
>
> I'm a raw recruit, with a bran'-new suit,
> Nine hundred dollars bounty,
> And I've come down from Darbytown
> To fight for Oxford County.
>
> The name of the town and county varied with circumstances.[60]

Civilian Interactions

Soldiers seem to have always been ready to take advantage of a good musical opportunity. Major James A. Connolly recorded the following in his diary entry of November 17, 1864:

> We arrived at Conyers at noon, and as our Division had four miles of R. R. to destroy before moving any further, [————], who plays the piano finely, and myself started out to walk around through the town and find a piano, so that we could have some music while our soldiers were destroying the track. Meeting a little girl on the street who told us where there was a piano, we went to the house and on knocking at the door a grey headed, meek, ministerial looking old rebel opened the door and asked what we wanted. I had agreed to do the talking so I told him "we wanted" to destroy the R. R. first, and asked him what he thought of it. The old gent looked wise and said nothing; I then asked him if he had a piano in the house; the old man looked worried and replied that his daughter had one. All right, said I, that's just what we want, we want some music; the old man said he didn't think his daughter could play, and looked incredulous when we pushed by him into the room, and the Captain sat down at the piano; but

the Captain's fingers soon made the keys dance to the air of the
Star Spangled Banner, and the old man sat there astonished at the
thought that a rough, vulgar, brutal Yankee should be able to play
so skillfully. Then the Captain played "Dixie" in excellent style;
this made the old man talkative, brought in the daughter and some
other young ladies, and we soon had them playing for us, while
the Captain and I sat back and quietly enjoyed the discomfiture of
the old man, and laughed at the efforts of the rebel damsels to
appear composed. Finally, to cap the climax, we induced these
Southern ladies to sing us the "Confederate Toast," which they
told us was their favorite song, and one verse of it I remember,
viz:

"Here's to old Butler and his crew,
    Drink it down!
  Here's to old Butler and his crew,
    Drink it down!
  Here's to old Butler and his crew,
    May the devil get his due,
Drink it down! Drink it down! Drink it down!"

We left them, though, notwithstanding their elegant and patriotic songs—they, no doubt, hoping we might be shot before
night.[61]

He was probably correct. The civilities of music offered only brief, and often
uncomfortable, moments of truce. With the Union army camped in the fields
around her Virginia home, Lucy Rebecca Buck, who had two older brothers
in the Confederate army, wrote in her diary of June 18, 1862 that:

After supper Father begged us to play and sing, to which move I
strenuously objected until they called for Southern music—where-
upon I sat down and played "Johnson's March to Manassas," "Bonnie Blue Flag," and "Maryland," in this [Union] Captain S
accompanied me. He then proposed the "Red, White and Blue"
which I respectfully declined. [Younger sister] Nellie would not
even go into the parlor where we were.[62]

On this night, social duty trumped political differences. Still, for Lucy, playing Southern music must have seemed an act of defiance. She had surrendered to her father's wishes, but resisted the enemy. Angry as she was, the
event made a deep impression. Such encounters affected battle-hardened

veterans as well, as the following excerpt of remembrances from the battle of Franklin, Tennessee, suggests. One fellow wrote the following to G. F. Root:

> About four o'clock, after the General had left for the field, there lingered a Colonel, from Indianapolis, in my parlor, who asked my daughters to sing and play a piece of music. My daughters asked what they should play. He replied that he did not know one piece of music from another, except field music. I spoke and asked the young ladies to sing and play a piece which had recently come out, "Just before the battle, mother." At my request they sat down and sang, and when about half through, as I stepped to the door, a shell exploded within fifty yards. I immediately returned and said, "Colonel, if I am any judge, it is just about that time now!" He immediately sprang to his feet and ran in the direction of his regiment, but before he reached it, or about that time, he was shot, the bullet passing quite through him. He was taken to Nashville, and eighteen days after, I received a message from him through an officer, stating the fact of his being shot, and that the piece of music the young ladies were executing was still ringing in his ears, and had been ever since he left my parlor the evening of the battle. In April, four months later, after the war was over, he had sufficiently recovered to travel, when he came to Franklin, as he stated, expressly to get the young ladies to finish the song, and relieve his ears. His wife and more than a dozen officers accompanied him. He found the ladies, and they sang and played the piece through for him in the presence of all the officers, and they wept like children.
>
> If you have made any music that will ring for four months in the ears of a person that doesn't know one tune from another, I thought you ought to know it.[63]

Camp Religion

The nineteenth century was marked by massive religious revivals. One such event in August 1801 at Cane Ridge, Kentucky, for example, had attracted a crowd estimated as high as 20,000. Camp meetings, as they were also called, became popular from North to South and were frequented by

Presbyterians and Methodists, Shakers and Millerites. Penitents would pray, sing, and feel the Holy Spirit pulse through and cleanse their jerking bodies. People would swoon in their ecstasy.

Not surprisingly, since death was so close, religion was a powerful force in army camps. Services were often accompanied by the singing of time-worn hymns, many of which—such as "Amazing Grace," "Rock of Ages," or "I Am a Soldier of the Cross"—are still sung today.

Beginning in the early months of 1863, the first of a series of religious revivals swept through Confederate camps. While the movement died down somewhat with approach of the spring and summer military campaigns, there was a resurgence of religious activity in the winters of 1863–1864 and 1864–1865. Music was generally a part of the various services.

Hymns, like popular songs, were published in collections that generally included at least 100 songs. The following three were all published in Raleigh, North Carolina: *Hymns for the Camp* (1862), *A Collection of Sabbath School Hymns* (1863), and *The Southern Zion's Songster; Hymns Designed for Sabbath Schools, Prayer, and Social Meetings, and the Camp* (1864). Published elsewhere were *The Soldiers Hymn Book* (South Carolina Tract Society, 1862) and *The Army Hymn Book* (Richmond Presbyterian Committee of Publications), 1863.

While salvation may have been the ultimate goal, it is impossible to miss the political and military imagery found in so many of the lyrics. Set to the tune "God Save the Queen" ("America") was:

> Our loved Confederacy,
> May God remember thee
> And warfare stay;
> May he lift up his hand
> And smite the oppressor's hand
> While our true patriots stand
> With bravery.

Another example of religious militancy was "The Sunday School Army," which appears in at least two of the collections above:

> Oh, do not be discouraged,
> For Jesus is your friend;
> Oh, do not be discouraged,

For Jesus is your friend.
He will give you grace to conquer,
He will give you grace to conquer,
And keep you to the end.

[Chorus:]
I am glad I'm in this army,
Yes, I'm glad I'm in this army,
Yes, I'm glad I'm in this army,
And I'll battle for the school.

Fight on ye little soldiers,
The battle you shall win:
Fight on ye little soldiers,
The battle you shall win;
For the Saviour is your Captain,
For the Saviour is your Captain,
And he hath vanquished sin.

Mississippi private David Holt also mixed religious and military imagery in the following description of a service that took place sometime in 1864:

> [The chaplain] gave out the hymn:
>
> How firm a foundation ye saints of the Lord
> Is laid for your faith in his excellent word.
>
> Everybody sang with a will. We could feel the Spiritual presence of our Lord as a kind of heart manifestation of His love. The men all stood at "Attention" with shoulders back and heads up, as though they were receiving a command from the Superior Officer. I never heard such singing in my life. I looked around at the glowing faces of these seasoned warriors who seemed to be receiving some kind of inspiration, and a new hope, and the impulse of a sublime courage. The hymn ended the service, the men lit their pipes and, in small groups, went their different ways without words.[64]

Religious music could be found at the most desperate of times, such as the Confederate band playing "Nearer My God to Thee" during the retreat following Pickett's Charge. If in this case the hymn served to acknowledge a return of the living from the hell of combat, hymns were also there to smooth the transition to death. Remembered Fannie A. Beers who worked in the hospitals during the war:

> He was a Kentuckian, cut off from home and friends, and dying among strangers. An almost imperceptible glance indicated that he wished me to take up his Bible. The fast-stiffening lips whispered, "*Read.*" I read to him the Fourteenth Chapter of St. John, stopping frequently to note if the faint breathing yet continued. Each time he would move the cold fingers in a way that evidently meant "*go on.*" After I had finished the reading, he whispered, so faintly that I could just catch the words, "*Rock of Ages,*" and I softly sang the beautiful hymn.
>
> Two years before I could not have done this so calmly. At first every death among my patients seemed to me like a personal bereavement. Trying to read or to sing by the bedsides of the dying, uncontrollable tears and sobs would choke my voice. As I looked my last upon dead faces, I would turn away shuddering and sobbing, for a time unfit for duty. *Now,* my voice did not once fail or falter.[65]

Often there was singing to spell the grief and horror that accompanied the life of a soldier. But just as soldiers were ready on a moment's notice to move from the peaceful routine of camp life to deadly combat, so too their moods shifted from godliness to godlessness. In a diary entry from December 23, 1862, John Beatty recorded the words of men singing and then added his own wry comments:

> We are going home, we are going home,
> To die no more.
>
> Were they to devote as much time to praying as they do to singing, they would soon establish a reputation for piety; but, unfortunately for them, after the hymn they generally proceed to swear, instead of prayer, and one is left in doubt as to what home they propose to go to.[66]

Certainly the sounds of hymns and exhortations of camp preachers had a profound, if often only temporary, effect on many men of the North and

South. Yet, these activities were just a small part of the multifaceted musical life of soldiers and preachers in camp. Beatty had a keen eye and ear for the diversity of camp life. In the following diary entries from October 10 and 12, 1862, he describes the social life of Parson Strong as well as his friend, the African-American violinist Willis, whose musical knowledge was so broad that he could perform excerpts from Italian composer Vincenzo Bellini's 1831 opera *Norma*:

> [10 October] Mr. Strong, the chaplain, has a prayer meeting in the adjoining tent. His prayers—and exhortations fill me with an almost irresistible inclination to close my eyes and shut out the vanities, cares, and vexations of the world. Parson Strong is dull, but he is very industrious. . . .
>
> While Parson Strong and a devoted few are singing the songs of Zion, the boys are having cotillion parties in other parts of the camp. On the parade ground of one company Willis is officiating as musician, and the gentlemen go through "honors to partners" and "circle all" with apparently as much pleasure as if their partners had pink cheeks, white slippers, and dresses looped up with rosettes.
>
> There comes from the chaplain's tent a sweet and solemn refrain:
>
> Perhaps He will admit my plea,
>   Perhaps will hear my prayer;
> But if I perish I will pray,
>   And perish only there.
> I can but perish if I go,
>   I am resolved to try,
> For if I stay away I know
>   I must forever die.
>
> While these old hymns are sounding in our ears, we are almost tempted to go, even if we do perish. Surely nothing has such power to make us forget earth and its round of troubles as these sweet old church songs, familiar from earliest childhood and wrought into the most tender memories, until we come to regard them as a sort of sacred stream on which some day our souls will float away happily to the better country.[67]
>
> [12 October] The parson is in my tent doing his best to extract something solemn out of Willis' violin. Now he stumbles on a

strain of "Sweet Home," then a scratch of "Lang Syne"; but the latter soon breaks its neck over "Old Hundred," and all three tunes finally mix up and merge into "I Would Not Live Away, I Ask Not to Stay," which, for the purpose of steadying his hand, the parson sings aloud. I look at him and affect surprise that a reverend gentleman should take any pleasure in so vain and wicked an instrument, and express a hope that the business of tanning skins has not utterly demoralized him.

Willis pretends to a taste in music far superior to that of the common "nigger." He plays a very fine thing, and when I ask what it is, replies: " 'Norma,' an opera piece." Since the parson's exit he has been executing "Norma" with great spirit, and, so far as I am able to judge, with wonderful skill. I doubt not his thoughts are a thousand miles hence, among brown-skinned wenches, dressed in crimson robes and decorated with ponderous eardrops. In fact, "Norma" is good, and goes far to carry one out of the wilderness.[68]

The distance between sacred and secular song was often short. While men may have believed deeply in a Christian god and salvation in the Hereafter, they also applied a similar religious-like fervor to their relationship with state and country, comrade and family. North Carolinian Walter Clark wrote in early January of 1864, of being on the march as they:

were carried through Richmond and Petersburg, and thence to Baryburg, N.C. Our men began almost to believe the rumor that we were being carried to North Carolina to hunt up deserters. Unpleasant as such duty would have been, there was rejoicing at the thought of being nearer home, and with a pathos that cannot be described, the men sang Gaston's glorious hymn:

"Carolina, Carolina, Heaven's blessing attend her,
While we live we will cherish, protect and defend her,"[69]

In addition, sacred songs, or at least their melodies, could easily be transformed into secular songs by changing the lyrics. Writing from White Plains, Virginia, during the early days of the Fredericksburg campaign, Captain Francis Adams Donaldson tells of the pastiche that was so commonplace:

The men changed the words of a song which goes "Hard times! Come again no more," into the following, and sang it with much vigor and vim:

> 'Tis the voice of the hungry,
> Hard tack, hard tack,
> Come again once more!
> Many days I've wandered,
> From my little tent door
> Crying hard tack, hard tack
> Come again once more!"[70]

An excellent recorder of the scenes he observed, Donaldson also wrote about the way music was used in executions. In a letter to his brother Jacob dated August 29, 1863, he described the execution of five "bounty jumping" deserters. The scene, sketched by Alfred R. Waud, was depicted in the September 26, 1863, issue of *Harper's Weekly*:

> Every detail had been arranged for the special object of making a solemn impression. There was an oppressive silence, not a sound was heard save the mournful notes of the Army Headquarters band playing the dead march from Saul, slow, measured, sorrowful. Deliberate and regular was the step of the band, which came first, sad and mournful was their music. . . .
>
> Our regiment was posted close up to the graves, a little to the right of them, close enough to hear the earnest words and prayer of men of God who pleaded so fervently that God would have mercy on their souls. . . . After a few parting words the ministers of the gospel stood aside and the poor fellows were left alone on the brink of Eternity. They hadn't long to wait. "Attention guard," in clear ringing tones called Capt. Orne, "shoulder arms." "Forward march," and the solid steady tramp of the detail sounded appalling on the ear. When within 6 paces, "Halt," ordered the Captain. "Ready." "Aim." "Fire," and the sixty pieces flashed full in the breasts of the deserters, and military justice was satisfied.

After the executions, wrote Donaldson, "The lines were now put into motion and the troops returned to their Camps to the tune of 'The girl I left behind me.' "[71]

Prison Life

William Tecumseh Sherman famously noted that "war is hell."[72] But if combat was brutal, at least it was quick. A man could stand up for himself and put up a fight. And one way or another, the ordeal would soon be over. Not in the prison camps. There the suffering was slow, debilitating, and often deadly. Amid the sick and the slowly dying, men clung to hope.

They often had little else. Early on in the war, release could be achieved through prisoner exchanges. That was to change when Grant ended the system because the South refused to release African-American Union soldiers. Thus, all prisoners now had to wait until the war's conclusion. Survival depended to a great extent on a man's ability to extricate himself mentally from the setting's physical hardships and debasements. Music provided one means of escape.

Few songs dealt specifically with prison experience. Instead, prisoners defiantly sang songs of freedom. Friends and family waiting at home were generally buoyed by notions of glorious victories and honorable deaths, but capture, as Root's disturbing "Starved in Prison" (1865) suggests, resided in an uncomfortable no-man's-land. The lyrics of this maudlin song evoke a dreary limbo in which hapless prisoners slowly waste away while hard-hearted guards turn their backs. Helpless friends and family agonize from afar:

> Had they fallen in the battle,
> With the old flag waving high,
> We should mourn, but not in anguish,
> For the soldier thus would die;
> But the dear boys starv'd in prison,
> Helpless, friendless and alone,
> While the haughty rebel leaders
> Heard unmov'd each dying groan.

Far more compelling for prisoners themselves was Root's defiant "The Battle Cry of Freedom." Prisoner of war William H. Bentley of the 77th Illinois recalled singing the song while being marched off to a prisoner-of-war camp:

> A day or two after leaving Mansfield, a courier arrived with orders to change the line of march in the direction of Marshall, Texas, and they arrived at that place on the 13th. There was great curiosity among the people to see the captured "Yankees," and the whole population of the city and surrounding country, seemed to be present to see the circus. As our boys marched through the streets of

the city, they treated the citizens to the music of that stirring battle-song:

The Union forever, hurrah, boys, hurrah,
Down with the traitors, up with the stars,
While we rally round the flag, boys, rally once again,
Shouting the battle cry of freedom.

Some of the ladies protested loudly against what they considered a profanation of the atmosphere surrounding their sacred persons, and called upon the officer of the guard to stop the music. But that worthy paid no attention to their demands, and the show continued, much to the satisfaction of the guard and the prisoners, and the vexation and annoyance of the spectators.[73]

Music was a form of resistance and a fundamental part of prison life, wrote Robert Sneden, who was incarcerated in both Richmond, Virginia, and the notorious Andersonville Prison in Sumter County, Georgia. Sneden reports that prisoners sang to pass the time and raise their spirits. They also sang to annoy guards who complained of their "infernal howling."[74] Recalling New Year's Day 1864, during which time he was held in a converted tobacco house one block north of Richmond's Libby Prison, Sneden wrote:

Clear day and warmer. There was some unusual excitement last night over at Libby. Singing was heard by our prisoners over there, lanterns flashed on the upper stories, which showed that the Rebel officers and guards were "Stirring up the animals" in some man-ner. We kept up our singing last night until after 12 p.m. in spite of the Rebel guard who did not molest us. The scene was novel as 300 men sat on the floors in a bright moonlight singing in chorus to "Rally round the Flag," etc., in which the line "Down with the traitor, up with the Stars" were loudly emphasized for the benefit of the traitor guard on the front sidewalk. When Ross came in this morning to call the roll, he said that, "if any more howling was heard at night we would all be sent to Belle Island to cool off." We jeered and chaffed him in return, and by shifting our places in line, he was compelled to call the roll four times before he satisfied himself that none had escaped.[75]

Andersonville Prison was used for just fourteen months after it was opened in February 1864. Some 13,000 men died there. At its population height during the summer of 1864, the prison held approximately 33,000 Union soldiers. Thus, it was the fifth largest "city" in the Confederacy. Yet even in Andersonville, amidst terrible suffering, men sang. Sneden's reminiscences graphically convey both the prison's horrors and the resiliency of the incarcerated. In an entry marked July 11, he wrote:

> Down by the north and south gates are daily brought dead men, mostly entirely naked, who lay piled on top of each other, all swollen up, dirt stained and as black as Negroes from exposure to sun and rain, while millions of flies hover over the ghastly corpses! These are waiting for the ration wagon to carry to the graveyard! At night, the scene is solemn enough for the most hardened sinner. The ragged skeleton forms clustered around a small fire singing hymns or a comrade prays. The pile of naked corpses in the firelight, etc. The solemn looks of haggard men. A perfect stillness of all noises in the vicinity gives an impression never to be effaced from one's memory. All around were sick or dying men lying in their ragged shelters, or without any shelter; propped up by their comrades to hear and listen to the singing, some crying, others cursing in delirium, others joining in singing the old familiar hymns of long ago when they were then in their happy homes far away, little thinking that they would be in such a hell upon earth as this place! Sometimes four or five groups were having prayers and singing at one time among us.[76]

Most nights were subdued, like the one described above. Some were not. Sneden recorded a remarkable event in which the prisoners united through song. With prisoner agitation increasing, camp commander Captain Henry Wirz called for assistance from Howell Cobb, Confederate general and former Georgia governor. Cobb's address to the prisoners was met with defiance. "From 10,000 to 20,000 voices were now singing 'The Star Spangled Banner,' " and other songs, wrote Sneden. Cobb ordered the men to silence but his voice was soon "completely drowned out by the booming tornado of sound and melody." Sneden continued:

> The singing was very good considering that so many thousand voices without any leader [were] doing it. Good time was kept too throughout. Poor half starved prisoners, cripples and sick fellows caught at their comrades who helped them to stand, and waving

their bony hands united their hollow voices with enthusiasm in vocation. This was about noon time.

After this, when the Rebel troops were seen to go to their camps, every one quieted down. The sailors had managed to get some whiskey, and a fiddle from somewhere outside and they kept up a noisy jubilee as long as the whiskey lasted. Singing and dancing until rations came in after 6 p.m. when all were hungry enough to eat some of the mule or rotten meat.[77]

Music also expressed the inchoate thoughts of dispirited and broken men. One such fellow, recorded fellow prisoner John McElroy, sounded out his misery through long low tones on the flute:

> Near us an exasperating idiot, who played the flute, had estab-
> lished himself. Like all poor players, he affected the low, mournful
> notes, as plaintive as the distant cooing of the dove in lowering
> weather. He played or rather tooted away in his "blues"-inducing
> strain hour after hour, despite our energetic protests, and occa-
> sional fling of a club at him. There was no more stop to him than
> to a man with a hand-organ, and to this day the low, sad notes of
> a flute are the swiftest reminder to me of those sorrowful, death-
> laden days.[78]

Intense memories did not fade with time. Speaking in Hyde Park High School in Chicago on March 8, 1889 in a ceremony honoring G. F. Root, Dr. H. H. Belfield, who had served as an adjutant in the Iowa Cavalry Volunteers, remembered the following event from the summer of 1864, when he was a prisoner of war in Charleston:

> Late one afternoon in September our attention was directed to the
> entrance of men into the adjoining prison-yard. We rushed to the
> windows on that side of the prison-house, and anxiously inspected
> the new comers. With faces blacked by sun and stained with dirt,
> their clothing scant and torn, they wearily dragged themselves into
> the prison-pen. Before they came within speaking distance the
> faded army blue of their uniforms suggested the truth. "Who are
> you?" we asked. "Andersonville prisoners." May I never behold
> another such sight. Their piercing eyes, their emaciated features,
> their shrunken limbs, now concealed, now revealed by their ragged
> uniforms, their bloody bandages, told the awful story of slow star-

vation. We shared with them our scanty rations, and after a frugal
meal on each side of the wall, which neither party could cross, we
did all we could for them; we sang Doctor Root's songs, and
cheered their hearts with our sympathy. Never had poor performers so attentive an audience. Long into the night we sang, and in
the early morning we dismissed them, Doctor Root, with your
ringing chorus, in which their feeble voices were heard—

Tramp, tramp, tramp, the boys are marching,
Cheer up, comrades, they will come;
And beneath the starry flag we shall breathe the air again
Of the free-land in our own beloved home.[79]

African Americans in Civil War Music

AFRICAN-AMERICAN MUSIC

Genres and Styles

By the onset of the Civil War, African-American music had been undergoing nearly three centuries of development. The sounds were altogether new, neither African nor European. But they borrowed elements from each. Compared to European models, phrasing was looser and rhythms more syncopated. In-the-moment embellishments and improvisations were standard. The music's formal structure was simpler in design, but more open-ended. The music had also shed aspects of its African heritage. Bards no longer sang praises or detailed family histories. Drum languages had been lost, and with them, much of the music's rhythmic complexity.

In short, African-American music resided betwixt and between both African traditional music and either European folk or classical music. Curiously, while African-American musical and dance styles had been parodied by blackface minstrels since the 1820s, it was not until the Civil War actually broke out that a large percentage of Northern whites began to have direct contact with, and take serious notice of, the music of the slaves. They found a rich tradition.

African Americans sang in a fashion termed call and response (or some-

times known as leader and chorus style). One person sang, and often improvised, a line to which the rest of the group answered with a set phrase.
The following example is typical. This work song might have been performed
while shucking, husking, or grinding corn:

> Dis lub's er thing dat's sure to hab you, [solo]
> Roun' de corn, Sally! [group]
> He hole you tight, when once he grab you, [solo]
> Roun' de corn, Sally! [group]
> Un ole un ugly, young un pritty, [solo]
> Roun' de corn, Sally! [group]
> You needen try when once he git you. [solo]
> Roun' de corn, Sally! [group][1]

Music was often tied to work activities, as well as rituals involving birth,
puberty, marriage, and death. Where relatively non-acculturated forms of
African religious belief survived, as was the case with Vodun in New Orleans,
there were songs, rhythms, and dances for each of the many different spirits
that were worshipped.[2]

African-American spirituals were based on biblical verses. But often im-
bedded within those ancient images were new ones of contemporary freedom. The spiritual "Go Down Moses," for example, invited comparisons
between the fate of the ancient people of Israel and the modern oppression
of the African-American slaves:

> When Israel was in Egypt's Land,
> Let my people go.
> Oppressed so hard they could not stand.
> Let my people go.
> Go down, Moses, way down in Egypt's Land,
> Tell old Pharaoh, let my people go.

Egypt's Pharaoh stood for the slave master. Moses may have brought to mind
the dedicated and fearless former slave Harriet Tubman (ca. 1820–1913), one
of many conductors on the Underground Railroad who repeatedly went
"down in Egypt's Land" (the slave South). Tubman helped more than 300
slaves escape northward to freedom.

With its vivid imagery of oppressor and oppressed, "Go Down Moses" was
one of the first spirituals to become known by a white audience. In October

1861 the Reverend Lewis C. Lockwood published its first stanza in the New York–based *National Anti-Slavery Standard* newspaper.[3] Shortly afterwards, twenty additional verses were published in the New York *Tribune*. On December 14, 1861, the *National Anti-Slavery Standard* returned to "Go Down Moses" and published it with music notation so that Northern abolitionists might learn to sing it.[4]

Another song, "Follow the Drinking Gourd," is widely believed to have helped direct slaves escaping northward to freedom. Generally traveling alone, away from the roads, and under cover of darkness, slaves relied on the North Star, or in overcast weather the moss on the trees, to tell them the way:

When the sun comes back and the first quail calls,
Follow the drinking gourd.
For the old man is waiting for to carry you to freedom
If you follow the drinking gourd.

[Chorus:]
Follow the drinking gourd,
Follow the drinking gourd
For the old man is a-waitin'
To carry you to freedom
Follow the drinking gourd.

The river bed makes a mighty fine road,
Dead trees to show you the way
And it's left foot, peg foot, traveling on
Follow the drinking gourd.

[Chorus]

The river ends between two hills
Follow the drinking gourd
There's another river on the other side
Follow the drinking gourd.

[Chorus]

I thought I heard the angels say
Follow the drinking gourd
The stars in the heavens
Gonna show you the way
Follow the drinking gourd.

What does all this mean? The text seems to be a set of coded instructions telling the resolute traveler how to make his way north. The "drinking gourd" refers to either the constellation of the Little Dipper (Canus Minor), which holds the North Star at the end of its handle, or possibly, the "gourd" may be the Big Dipper (Canus Major), whose "pointer stars" at the end of the pot point almost straight to the North Star. The first stanza instructs the traveler to begin the journey around the winter solstice when "the sun comes back" to the northern hemisphere. The "old man" is perhaps Peg Leg Joe, an abolitionist who was said to have marked a trail, or any of the Underground Railroad conductors. The riverbank of verse two was evidently the Tombigbee River, which stretches from Tennessee to the Gulf of Mexico. From there, travelers follow the Tennessee River until it joins with the "great big" Ohio River. After completing that crossing, preferably in the winter when the river was frozen, people would be waiting on the other side to "carry you to freedom."

Frederick Douglass recalled music making in the days preceding his own escape from slavery:

> I am the more inclined to think that [the slave master] suspected us, because, prudent as we were, as I now look back, I can see that we did many silly things, very well calculated to awaken suspicion. We were, at times, remarkably buoyant, singing hymns and making joyous exclamations, almost as triumphant in their tone as if we had reached a land of freedom and safety. A keen observer might have detected in our repeated singing of
>
> "O Canaan, sweet Canaan,
> I am bound for the land of Canaan,"
>
> something more than a hope of reaching heaven. We meant to reach the *north*—and the north was our Canaan.
>
> "I thought I heard them say,
> there were lions in the way,
> I don't expect to stay
>   Much longer here.
> Run to Jesus—shun the danger—
> I don't expect to stay
>   Much longer here,"
>
> was a favorite air, and had a double meaning. In the lips of some, it meant the expectation of a speedy summons to a world of spirits;

but, in the lips of *our* company, it simply meant a speedy pilgrimage toward a free state, and deliverance from all the evils and dangers of slavery.[5]

Other songs with such double meanings included "Swing Low, Sweet Chariot," "Good News, de Chariot's Coming," and "Steal Away to Jesus."

Music was an important pastime for free urban African Americans as well. Middle-class families often included trained musicians who played on the piano or guitar what historian Eileen Southern has termed the "rather superficial music favored by white society."[6] Presenting more "elevated" fare was "the Black Swan," Elizabeth Taylor Greenfield (ca. 1824–1876) a former slave from Natchez, Mississippi, who in the 1850s sang in a number of American cities as well as in England, where she performed for the queen. Greenfield directed a black opera troupe during the 1860s.[7]

African Americans were active in a variety of genres. Dance and concert bands were popular in Philadelphia and New York as early as the 1820s. Francis "Frank" Johnson (ca. 1792–1844) toured the eastern United States as well as England. Other band composers and arrangers included Boston's Henry F. Williams (1813–1900) and St. Louis–based Joseph William Postlewaite (1827–1889). New Orleans saw the formation of the Negro Philharmonic Society in the 1830s. Some of these musicians also performed for the "free colored" at the Theatre de la Renaissance.[8] In New York City, the African Grove Theatre opened in the summer of 1821 at the corner of Bleecker and Mercer. The locale, which also became popular with whites, featured a wide range of dramatic productions as well as musical fare.

The Lucas Family Singers from Connecticut developed a successful career singing abolitionist music. On occasion they sang with the Hutchinson family. Interracial concerts were not always well received, as the following February 25, 1859, review from Freemont, Ohio, suggests:

> When we went to the concert, we anticipated a rare treat; but alas! how woefully were we disappointed! . . . We have, perhaps, a stronger feeling of prejudice than we should have felt under other circumstances, had their abolition proclivities been less startling; but to see respectable white persons (we presume they are such) traveling hand in hand with a party of negroes, and eating at the same table with them, is rather too strong a pill to be gulped down by a democratic community.[9]

The War Years

The Civil War emancipated both the slave and African-American music. One of the war's little-noticed consequences was that for the first time authentic African-American music making, rather than the various caricatures meted out through blackface minstrel shows, was heard by large numbers of white Northerners. For many, the experience was a revelation.

This happened for two reasons. First, emancipated slaves carried their music with them as they moved northward or attached themselves to the invading Union armies. Second, many Northerners traveled to the slave South for the first time. Most of these Northerner observers served in the military, although some worked as teachers, or were involved in relief efforts. A few took it upon themselves to document the music they heard. The following account appeared in *Dwight's Journal of Music* on September 7, 1861:

> It is one of the most striking incidents of this war to listen to the singing of the groups of colored people in Fortress Monroe, who gather at their resorts after nightfall. Last evening, having occasion to "visit" an officer of the garrison sick in his tent, I passed around by the fortress chapel and adjacent yard, where most of the "contraband" tents are spread. There were hundreds of men of all ages scattered around. In one tent they were singing in order, one man leading, as extemporaneous chorister, while some ten or twelve others joined in the chorus. The hymn was long and plaintive, as usual, and the air was one of the sweetest minors I have ever listened to. It would have touched many a heart if sung in the audiences who appreciate the simple melody of nature, fresh and warm from the heart. One verse ran thus:

"Shout along, children!
Shout along children!
Hear the dying Lamb:
Oh! Take your nets and follow me
For I died for you upon the tree!
Shout along, children!
Shout along, children!
Hear the dying Lamb."

> There was no confusion, no uproar, no discord—all was as tender and harmonious as the symphony of an organ.

There was also no Jim Crow, Zip Coon, or Brudder Bones. In fact, there was none of the shallow sensibility that decades of blackface minstrel show entertainment, with its dehumanizing subtext, had taught white audiences to expect. Experiences like the one above must have been sobering to all whites who witnessed them. It is instructive that Dwight, who generally devoted his journal to European classical music, was so struck by the report that he published it.

White and African-American Northerners worked with contrabands and newly enlisted Union soldiers near Beaufort, South Carolina, where, just seven months into the war, Union forces had invaded Port Royal Sound and freed some 10,000 slaves. Suddenly homeless, often starving, and perhaps "covered only with blanket, or bits of old carpeting," these former slaves enjoyed the security offered by Union military protection.[10] Civilian teachers and relief workers also came to their aid. From the latter conjunction came some of the war's most intriguing musical documents.

Beaufort served as a hub around which a coterie of fascinating personalities formed. One was Charlotte Forten, an African-American teacher from Salem, Massachusetts, who worked from 1862 to 1864 on Helena Island, South Carolina, as part of the North-based missionary group "Gideon's Band."[11] She and her colleagues were early members of what historian Willie Lee Rose has termed the "Port Royal Experiment," so named because its practices would help shape government policy when the war was over and reconstruction began.[12]

Forten's teaching agenda entailed more than imparting the three R's. She taught her charges about the world outside Port Royal. They learned "the 'John Brown' song" as well as about Haitian nationalist Toussaint L'Ouverture, "thinking it well they should know what one of their own color had done for his race."[13] Resisting the oppressor was sweet, she discovered:

> We thought how easy it would be for a band of guerillas, had they chanced that way, to seize and hang us; but we were in that excited, jubilant state of mind which makes fear impossible, and sang "John Brown" with a will, as we drove through the pines and palmettos. Oh, it was good to sing that song in the very heart of Rebeldom![14]

Forten also discovered a culture far from her own. Her description of an 1862 boat trip to Ladies Island, undertaken in the subtle half light of evening, suggests how deeply she was impacted by her various experiences:

> We glided along, the rich tomes of the Negro boatmen broke upon
> the evening stillness,—sweet, strange, and solemn:—
>
> Jesus make de blind to see,
> Jesus make de cripple walk,
> Jesus make de deaf to hear.
>   Walk in, kind Jesus!
>   No man can hender me.[15]

Forten's images suggest an otherworldly, even mystical atmosphere. As Forten listens, she becomes aware of the depth of culture to be found in the
people she has come to aid and educate. She understands that they will also
have much to teach her.

Yet even as bonds developed, Forten remained acutely aware of the distance between them and her. Forten's ways of making music and praising
God were more constrained, less physical. She found the differences both
fascinating and troubling:

> In the evenings, the children frequently came in to sing and shout
> for us. These 'shouts' are very strange,—in truth, almost inde-
> scribable. It is necessary to hear and see in order to have any clear
> idea of them. The children form a ring, and move around in a
> kind of shuffling dance, singing all the time. Four or five stand
> apart, and sing very energetically, clapping their hands, stamping
> their feet, and rocking their bodies to and fro. These are the mu-
> sicians, to whose performance the shouters keep perfect time. The
> grown people on this plantation did not shout, but they do on
> some of the other plantations. It is very comical to see little chil-
> dren, not more than three or four years old, entering into the
> performances with all their might. But the shouting of the grown
> people is rather solemn and impressive than otherwise. We cannot
> determine whether it has a religious character or not. Some of the
> people tell us that it has, others that it has not. But as the shouts
> of the grown people are always in connections with their religious
> meetings, it is probable that they are the barbarous expressions of
> religion, handed down to them from their African ancestors, and
> destined to pass away under the influence of Christian teachings.
> The people on this island have no songs. They sing only hymns,
> and most of these are sad.[16]

The muscular scene Forten describes—ring dancing and communal singing—has its roots in West Africa, where similar styles can still be found.

Moreover, the account foreshadows the path into an American future. So do others. Consider the description of a Christmas night religious service as recorded by Elizabeth Hyde Botume, who went to Beaufort in the fall of 1864 on an appointment by the New England Freedman's Aid Society:

> [One of the leaders] chose the "one t'ousand nine hundred and sebenty-eight hymn," and proceeded to "line off"
>
> "Why do we mourn departed friends,"
>
> which we thought very appropriate under the circumstances. Then the whole congregation sang with tremendous force, drawling the words. . . . I read the whole of Christ's Sermon on the Mount. . . . They gave breathless attention to all this, ejaculating from time to time, "My Lord! is dat so?"[17]

Similar scenes take place in African-American churches today.

Forten became friends with Colonel Thomas W. Higginson, who in November 1862 had taken command of the 1st South Carolina Volunteers, a regiment made up of emancipated slaves (with the exception of its officers, who were white).[18] Forten also met Colonel Robert Gould Shaw who commanded the 54th Massachusetts Volunteer Infantry, another African-American regiment.[19] Higginson wrote compellingly about wartime African-American music. So too would William Francis Allen, Charles Pickard Ware, and Lucy McKim Garrison, who worked in the same region and together published *Slave Songs of the United States* in 1867.

Despite the attention to detail and empathy for the people about whom they write, these early accounts are invariably idealized and naive. In a diary entry from November 27, 1862, Higginson relates listening to a soldier entertaining his comrades with a comic narrative of his escape from slavery. During the course of the tale, the soldier tells how he duped his thick-witted white oppressors by playing the fool himself.[20] Placing himself in the role of the insider, Higginson notes that such a story would not have been for the ears of Southern whites. Higginson does not, however, continue with this logic to note that perhaps much of this soldier's culture, the sea of meaning upon which the story floated, was also not open to him, or to whites in general, even abolitionists. New to the South, and despite his obvious empathy for the plight of the slave, Higginson could not possibly have understood the meanderings of the complex social world and system of codes in which these men had learned to survive under slavery.[21]

Higginson's understanding is never more than partial. He repeatedly writes of his soldiers' "childlike" emotions, such as in his camp diary entry of December 3, 1862:

> What a life is this I lead! It is a dark, mild, drizzling evening, and as the foggy air breeds sand-flies, so it calls out melodies and strange antics from this mysterious race of grown-up children with whom my lot is cast.[22]

Even as late as April 1864, he would describe his men as "dusky innocents."[23]

But if Higginson was naïve, he was also a keen observer and recorder of his soldiers and their world. A freethinking Transcendentalist who held radically progressive beliefs in the areas of social reform, abolition, women's suffrage, and labor, Higginson was fascinated by, and non-judgmental of, the culture he discovered at Beaufort. He continues his December 3, 1862, diary entry:

> All over the camp the lights glimmer in the tents, and as I sit at my desk in the open doorway, there come mingled sounds of stir and glee. Boys laugh and shout,—a feeble flute stirs somewhere in some tent, not an officer's—a drum throbs far away in another,—wild killdeer-plover flit and wail above us, like the haunting souls of dead slave-masters,—and from a neighboring cook-fire comes the monotonous sound of that strange festival, half pow-wow, half prayer-meeting, which they know only as a "shout." These fires are usually enclosed in a little booth, made neatly of palm-leaves and covered in at top, a regular native African hut, in short, such as is pictured in books, and such as I once got up from dried palm-leaves for a fair at home. This hut is now crammed with men, singing at the top of their voices, in one of their quaint, monotonous, endless, Negro-Methodist chants, with obscure syllables recurring constantly, and slight variations interwoven, all accompanied with a regular drumming of the feet and clapping of the hands, like castanets. Then the excitement spreads: inside and outside the enclosure men begin to quiver and dance, others join, a circle forms, winding monotonously round some one in the center; some "heel and toe" tumultuously, others merely tremble and stagger on, others stoop and rise, others whirl, others caper sideways, all keep steadily circling like dervishes; spectators

applaud special strokes of skill; my approach only enlivens the
scene; the circle enlarges, louder grows the singing, rousing
shouts of encouragement come in, half bacchanalian, half devout,
"Wake 'em brudder!" "Stan' up to 'em, brudder!"—and still the
ceaseless drumming and clapping, in perfect cadence, goes steadily on.[24]

Is this America or Africa? The distinctions blur. In the mystery of the firelit
night among the "African" huts the old slave masters have been reduced to
innocuous spirits who "flit and wail" harmlessly above. On the ground, a
vital "half bacchanalian, half devout" African life thrives in the New World.
Higginson is irresistibly drawn in.

Importantly, and despite a life spent in a culture that might easily have
led him to the opposite conclusion, Higginson did not see his soldiers as
racially inferior. He did, however, need time to gain his focus, to become
aware of his unconscious biases, and to put a lifetime of abolitionist theory
into practice. In the book's penultimate chapter he writes:

I cannot conceive what people at the North mean by speaking of
the negroes as a bestial or brutal race. Except in some insensibility
to animal pain, I never knew of an act in my regiment which I
should call brutal. In reading Kay's "Condition of the English Peas-
antry" I was constantly struck with the unlikeness of my men to
those therein described. This could not proceed from my prejudices as an abolitionist, for they would have led me the other way,
and indeed I had once written a little essay to show the brutalizing
influence of slavery. I learned to think that we abolitionists had
underrated the suffering produced by slavery among the negroes,
but had overrated the demoralization.[25]

Besides the many insights to African-American culture, these early writers
collected large amounts of song texts and melodies. Higginson, for example,
collected words to thirty-six spirituals, which he published in 1867 in *Army
Life in a Black Regiment*:[26]

The favorite song in camp was the following,—sung with no accompaniment but the measured clapping of hands and the clatter
of many feet. It was sung perhaps twice as often as any other. This
was partly due to the fact that it properly consisted of a chorus

alone, with which the verses of other songs might be combined at random.

I. HOLD YOUR LIGHT.

"Hold your light, Brudder Robert,—
  Hold your light,
Hold your light on Canaan's shore.

"What make ole Satan for follow me so?
Satan ain't got notin' for do wid me.
  Hold your light,
  Hold your light,
Hold your light on Canaan's shore."

This would be sung for half an hour at a time, perhaps, each person present being named in turn. It seemed the simplest primitive type of "spiritual."[27]

This was dance music as much as vocal music. The focus was tripartite: on physicality (ecstatic religious experience mediated through dance), social inclusion ("each person present being named in turn"), and freedom ("Hold your light on Canaan's shore").

Also significant was Higginson's observation that this chorus would be combined with other songs. These collectors invariably found different versions of the same songs. Higginson records the spiritual "Bound to Go" as:

"Jordan River, I'm bound to go,
  Bound to go, bound to go,—
Jordan River, I'm bound to go,
  And bid 'em fare ye well.
"My Brudder Robert, I'm bound to go,
  Bound to go, &c.

"My Sister Lucy, I'm bound to go,
  Bound to go," &c.[28]

This particular version is just one of a potentially endless variety. Higginson notes:

I had for many years heard of this class of songs under the name of "Negro Spirituals," and had even heard some of them sung by friends from South Carolina. I could now gather on their own soil these strange plants which I had before seen as in museums alone.

> True, the individual songs rarely coincided; there was a line here,
> a chorus there,—just enough to fix the class, but this was unmis-
> takable. It was not strange that they differed, for the range seemed
> almost endless, and South Carolina, Georgia, and Florida seemed
> to have nothing but the generic character in common, until all
> were mingled in the united stock of camp-melodies.[29]

Such fluidity is at the heart of an African-American oral tradition in which
music is remembered, rather than written, and adapted to fit ever changing
circumstances and tastes. Allen and his colleagues found the variations "endless, and very entertaining and instructive."[30] The spiritual "Bound to Go" is
transcribed twice in *Slave Songs of the United States*, once by Ware and, as
below, by Allen:

> I build my house upon de rock
> O yes, Lord!
> No wind, no storm can blow 'em down,
> O yes, Lord!
> March on, member,
> Bound to go;
> Been to de ferry,
> Bound to go;
> Left St. Helena,
> Bound to go;
> Brudder, fare you well.[31]

Of the three versions, Higginson's transcription is the most repetitious. It
also takes advantage of the technique used in "Hold Your Light" in which
each member of the choir is called by name. Perhaps Higginson's version,
with its shorter and more rhythmically active phrases, was a variation derived
from the song's chorus. Perhaps also, the lyrics were simplified because the
piece was danced and "shouted" in a manner that the surreptitious Higginson describes below:

> Often in the starlit evening I have returned from some lonely ride
> by the swift river, or on the plover-haunted barrens, and, entering
> the camp, have silently approached some glimmering fire, round
> which the dusky figures moved in the rhythmical barbaric dance
> the Negroes call a "shout," chanting, often harshly, but always in

the most perfect time, some monotonous refrain. Writing down
in the darkness, as best I could,—perhaps with my hand in the
safe covert of my pocket,—the words of the song, I have afterwards
carried it to my tent, like some captured bird or insect, and then
after examination, put it by.[32]

Each version of "Bound to Go" provides a snapshot of a particular time and
place in the song's trajectory. Higginson notes that since all songs were
learned "by ear, they often strayed into wholly new versions, which sometimes became popular, and entirely banished the others." But accounting for
variations was just one of many difficulties. Allen, Garrison, and Ware noted
that their transcriptions were invariably problematic:

The best that we can do, however, with paper and types, or even
with voices, will convey but a faint shadow off the original. The
voices of the colored people have a peculiar quality that nothing
can imitate; and the intonations and delicate variations of even
one singer cannot be reproduced on paper. And I despair of con-
veying any notion of the effect of a number singing together, especially in a complicated shout. . . . There is no singing in *parts*,
as we understand it, and yet no two appear to be singing the same
thing—the leading singer starts the words of each verse, often
improvising, and the others, who "base" him, as it is called, strike
in with the refrain, or even join in the solo, when the words are
familiar.[33]

Thus, these various musical transcriptions and performance descriptions
provide a picture that is tantalizing to behold, but incomplete.

While spirituals constituted just a portion of African-American music from
the Georgia Sea Islands, they accounted for the bulk collected by Allen and
his colleagues. Indeed, as the authors relate, obtaining secular songs was far
from simple:

Our intercourse with the colored people has been chiefly through
the work of the Freedman's commission, which deals with the
serious and earnest side of the Negro character. It is often, indeed,
no easy matter to persuade them to sing their old songs, even as
a curiosity, such is the sense of dignity which has come with freedom. It is earnestly to be desired that some person, who has the

opportunity, should make a collection of these now, before it is too late.[34]

Perhaps this was a matter of "dignity." Perhaps, however, these people were simply reluctant to share certain parts of their musical repertoire and social culture with whites. At any rate, spirituals clearly had a place in secular contexts, especially as work songs. Higginson notes that "The Coming Day" was "timed well with the tug of the oar":

> I want to go to Canaan,
> I want to go to Canaan,
> I want to go to Canaan,
> To meet 'em at de comin' day.[35]

Laborers adjusted the song for different tasks. The work song "Poor Rosy," for example, was "an even *andante*" when sung for rowing, but would "fly" when sung to work at the hominy mill.[36]

How could the same song be so different? Higginson searched for the source of African-American compositional techniques. He concluded that music was framed in and for the experiences at hand. An oarsman described how a song might come into being:

> "Once we boys," he said, "went for tote some rice and de nigger-driver he keep a-callin' on us; and I say, 'O, de ole nigger-driver!' Den anudder said, 'Fust ting my mammy tole me was, notin' so bad as nigger-driver,' Den I made a sing, just puttin' a word, and den anudder word."
>
> Then he began singing, and the men, after listening a moment, joined in the chorus, as if it were an old acquaintance, though they evidently had never heard it before. I saw how easily a new "sing" took root among them.

> "O, de ole nigger-driver!
>   O, gwine away!
> Fust ting my mammy tell me,
>   O, gwine away!
> Tell me 'bout de nigger-driver,
>   O, gwine away!
> Nigger-driver second devil,
>   O, gwine away!
> Best ting for do he driver,

O, gwine away!
Knock he down and spoil he labor,
    O, gwine away!"[37]

Higginson's notion of songs "taking root" gives shape to the fundamentally different approaches to music composition within white and African-American culture of that period. Generally speaking, individual white composers wrote for publication and profit. African Americans, individually and collectively, created their music within an oral community-based performance tradition. As Allen and his colleagues noted, "words of the verse are changed at the pleasure of the leader, or fugleman, who sings either well-known words, or, if he is gifted that way, invents verses as the song goes on."[38]

In Port Royal and across the South, freedom was a constant musical theme. Boston journalist and historian Charles Carlton Coffin, who traveled with Grant's army as it advanced along Virginia's North Anna River in May 1864, published the following observations of contrabands who were attaching themselves to the Union army:

> The negroes came from all the surrounding plantations. Old men with venerable beards, horny hands, crippled with hard work and harder usage; aged women, toothless, almost blind, steadying their steps with sticks; little negro boys, driving a team of skeleton steers,—mere bones and tendons covered with hide,—or wall-eyed horses, spavined, foundered, and lame, attached to rickety carts and wagons, piled with beds, tables, chairs, pots and kettles, hens, turkeys, ducks, women with infants in their arms, and a sable cloud of children trotting by their side.
>
> "Where are you going?" I said to a short, thickset, gray-bearded old man, shuffling along the road; his toes bulging from his old boots, and a tattered straw hat on his head,—his gray wool protruding from the crown.
>
> "I do'no, boss, where I'se going, but I reckon I'll go where the army goes."
>
> "And leave your old home, your old master, and the place where you have lived all your days?"
>
> "Yes, boss; master, he's gone. He went to Richmond. Reckon he went mighty sudden, boss, when he heard you was coming. Thought I'd like to go along with you." . . .
>
> It was the Sabbath-day,—bright, clear, calm, and delightful.

There was a crowd of several hundred colored people at a deserted farm-house.

"Will it disturb you if we have a little singing? You see we feel so happy to-day that we would like to praise the Lord."

It was the request of a middle-aged woman.

"Not in the least. I should like to hear you."

In a few moments a crowd had assembled in one of the rooms. A stout young man, black, bright-eyed, thick-wooled, took the centre of the room. The women and girls, dressed in their best clothes, which they had put on to make their exodus from bondage in the best possible manner, stood in circles round him. The young man began to dance. He jumped up, clapped his hands, slapped his thighs, whirled round, stamped upon the floor.

"Sisters, let us bless the Lord. Sisters, join in the chorus," he said, and led off with a kind of recitative, improvised as the excitement gave him utterance.

We are going to the other side of Jordan,
So glad! so glad!
Bless the Lord for freedom,
So glad! so glad!
We are going on our way,
So glad! so glad!
To the other side of Jordan,
So glad! so glad!
Sisters, won't you follow?
So glad! so glad!
Brothers, won't you follow?

And so it went on for a half-hour, without cessation, all dancing, clapping their hands, tossing their heads. It was the ecstasy of action. It was a joy not to be uttered, but demonstrated. The old house partook of their rejoicing. It rang with their jubilant shouts, and shook in all its joints.

It was late at night before the dancers ceased, and then they stopped, not because of a surfeit of joy, but because the time had come for silence in the camp. It was their first Sabbath of freedom, and like the great king of Israel, upon the recovery of the ark of God, they danced before the Lord with all their might.[39]

As the sinews of Southern authority weakened, similar scenes must have taken place virtually everywhere the advancing Union army went. The "crippled" and "almost blind," claimed their freedom. So too, perhaps unaware of the act's significance, did the children. It was long overdue, but the year of jubilee had finally arrived. The slaves were free and they would celebrate.

With the end of the war the government finally had the ability to enforce the 1863 Emancipation Proclamation and the South's "peculiar institution" came to an end. Former slaves could now sing anything they wished. "Sech rejoicing an' shoutin' you never he'rd in you' life," said former slave Mrs. Fannie Berry, who vividly recalled her day of emancipation during an interview some seventy-two years after the fact:

> Glory! Glory! yes, child the Negroes are free, an' when they knew
> dat dey were free Oh! Baby! [They] began to sing:

> Mamy don't yo' cook no mo',
> Yo' ar' free, yo' ar' free.
> Rooster don't yo' crow no, mo',
> Yo' ar' free, yo' ar' free.
> Ol' hen don't yo' lay no mo' eggs,
> Yo' free, yo' free.[40]

Berry spoke in Petersburg, Virginia, in 1937 as part of an initiative to collect slave narratives that was undertaken from 1936 to 1938 by employees of the Federal Writers' Project.[41] The collection has flaws, of course. Stories were sometimes confused; some may have been pure imagination. Berry, for example, claims to remember events from the Nat Turner Rebellion of 1831. Still, the words above ring with the spontaneity of truth.

Former slave "Parson" Rezin Williams was 116 years old and the oldest living African-American Civil War veteran when interviewed in 1937. Williams wrote a number of spirituals, including: "Roll de Stones Away," "You'll Rise in de Skies," and "Ezekiel, We'se Comin Home." He dictated the following verses. Both speak of freedom:

> When dat are ole chariot comes,
> I'm gwine to lebe you;
> I'm bound for de promised land
> I'm gwine to lebe you.

> I'm sorry I'm gwine to lebe you,
> Farewell, oh farewell
> But I'll meet you in de morning
> Farewell, oh farewell.

For Williams, and many who told their stories during these years, the images of the promised lands Jordan, Jerusalem, and Canaan continued to resonate with the ideals of personal freedom. If there is room for doubt as to the double nature of the "promised land" in the verses above, there is no such question with the following text. Williams claimed to have written these lines shortly before the Civil War:

> I'm now embarked for yonder shore
> There a man's a man by law;
> The iron horse will bear me O'er
> To shake de lion's paw.
> Oh, righteous Father, will thou not pity me
> And aid me on to Canada, where all the slaves are free.[42]

Some songs explicitly referred to freedom and the promise of liberty that would accompany Union occupation. Ninety-one-year-old James Calhart James narrated one example for the Federal Writers' Project. The son of a light-skinned slave and her master, James was raised on a plantation near Fort Sumter. He remembered the following song:

> Oh where shall we go when de great day comes
> An' de blowing of de trumpets and de bangins of de drums.
> When General Sherman comes.
> No more rice and cotton fields
> We will hear no more crying
> Old master will be sighing.[43]

On December 31, 1862, the day before Lincoln's Emancipation Proclamation was to take effect, thousands of freedmen and former slaves joined in singing "Go Down Moses" at a District of Columbia contraband camp. Following several renditions of that particular song, a woman came forward and sang a song that asked for action of a quite different nature:

> If de Debble do not ketch
> Jeff Davis, dat infernal retch,
> An roast and frigazee dat rebble,
> Wat is de use ob any Debble?[44]

Of course, it is a mistake to believe that all slaves longed for freedom. Upon Emancipation many found great difficulty in breaking from a crushing symbiotic relationship generations in the making.[45] James Lucas was over 100 when he recorded for the Federal Writers' Project in Natchez. Some of Lucas's memories are certainly invented—he claimed, for example, to have been owned by Jefferson Davis in the mid-1840s and been present at both the Battle of Vicksburg and Lee's surrender at Appomattox—but his insights suggest the depth of conflict that freedom brought:

> Folks dat ain' never been free don' rightly know the *feel* of bein' free. Dey don' know de' meanin' of it. Slaves like us, what was owned by quality-folks was sati'fied an' didn' sing none of dem freedom songs.[46]

Maria Sutton Clemments was in her late eighties at the time of her 1937 interview. Like Lucas, she too had no use for emancipation. Clemments remembered the following song:

> Jeff Davis is President
> Abe Lincoln is a fool
> Come here, see Jeff ride the gray horse
> And Abe Lincoln the mule.[47]

Remembrances of first encounters with Union soldiers also reveal the mixed emotions and experiences of these suddenly liberated slaves. Ninety-four-year-old Charley Williams of Tulsa, Oklahoma narrated the following story in 1937 for the Federal Writers' Project:

> De Yankees didn't seem to be mad wid old Master, but jest laughed and talked wid him, but he didn't take de jokes any too good.
>
> Den dey asked him could he dance and he said no, and dey told him to dance or make us dance. Dar he stood inside a big ring of dem mens in blue clothes, wid dey brass buttons shining in de light from de fire dey had in front of de tents, and he jest stood and said nothing, and it look lak he wasn't wanting to tell us to dance.
>
> So some of us young bucks jest stood up and say we was good

dancers, and we start shuffling while de rest of de niggers pat [slapped their thighs].

Some nigger women go back to de quarters and git de gourd fiddles and de clapping bones made out'n beef ribs, and bring dem back so we could have some music. We git all warmed up and dance lak we never did dance befo'! I speck we invent some new steps dat night!

We act lak we dancing for de Yankees, but we trying to place Master and old Mistress more than anything, and purty soon he begin to smile a little and we all feel a lot better.[48]

Yankee interest in black dance was common. Seventy-seven-year-old Margaret Thornton of Four Oaks, North Carolina, recalled the following incident during her 1937 Federal Writers' Project narrative:

I wus jist five years ole when de Yankees come, jist a few of dem to our settlement. I doan know de number of de slaves, but I does 'member dat day herded us tergether an' make us sing a heap of songs an' dance, den dey clap dere han's an' dey sez dat we is good. One black boy won't dance, he sez, so dey puts him barefooted on a hot piece of tin an' believe me he did dance.[49]

It's difficult to imagine soldiers going to the effort of heating a piece of metal just to make someone dance, but even if the story is part imagination, these were hardly the actions of enlightened liberators.

The first sight of Union soldiers made a strong impression on many slaves. Martha King must have been about fifteen years old when she got her first sights and sounds of the Yankees:

"They hung Jeff Davis to a sour apple tree!
They hung Jeff Davis to a sour apple tree!
They hung Jeff Davis to a sour apple tree!
While we go marching on!"

Dat was de song de Yankees sang when they marched by our house.[50]

Eighty-seven-year-old Lewis Bonner remembered his first sightings of Yankees as well: "I tell you it was some war. When it was all over, the Yankees come thoo' singing, 'You may die poor but you won't die a slave'."[51] The Yankee's words presaged a hard truth. The war would bring emancipation,

but for most Southern-based African Americans, social and economic hardships lay ahead. Change would be slow in coming but always music would
help to facilitate transformation. Just as the spirituals of antebellum America
had once swelled with a people's hopes and pulsed with their sufferings,
they would also ring forth 100 years later with equal fervor during the Civil
Rights Movement.

RACE-RELATED MUSIC

The Minstrel Show

The beginning of minstrelsy is often dated from February 6, 1843, when
the Virginia Minstrels, snappily dressed in calico-blue swallowtail coats, took
the stage of New York City's Bowery Amphitheatre and presented America's
first full-scale evening of "Ethiopian" entertainment.[52] With faces blackened
by the residue of burnt cork, the quartet delivered an evening of song, dance,
and repartee that, as their later publicity would claim, demonstrated the "odd-
ities, peculiarities, eccentricities, and comicalities of that Sable Genus of
Humanity."[53] Their songs were written in lively pseudo-African meters and
gapped scales. Lyrics and skits played on issues of race, class, and nationality.

Thousands of ensembles followed the Virginia Minstrels's model, and the
genre remained America's most popular entertainment style for the next
forty years. Throughout that time, black culture was at the butt end of most
of the jokes, but even from the beginning, humor was reaped from other
facets of American political and theatrical life. Parodies of Italian and English
culture were common. So too, were burlesques on opera, particularly those
in languages other than English.

Minstrel representations of African Americans tell us much about the
times. Characters reveal truths about race relations, of course, but as prod-
ucts of the white imagination, they also serve as a looking glass into the
white moral psyche. The "Ethiopians" were portrayed as children in grown-
up bodies who (at least when not dragging a hoe or under the lash) lived
the socially and sexually gregarious lives that stiff-lipped whites may have
both feared and envied. Curiously, these "Ethiopians" were "free" in ways
white audiences were not.

The burnt cork mask should not be interpreted as simply a racial marker.
The makeup, notes William Mahar, served at least three additional purposes.

First, it was a "disguise" through which performers could "satirize majority values while still reinforcing widely held and fairly conservative beliefs." Second, it was a "vehicle for the creation of an American [popular] style." Third, it was a "masking device" that allowed entertainers to "shield themselves from any direct personal and psychological identification with the material they were performing."[54] Such distancing can be seen in the sheet music cover of the 1844 Boston publication, "Songs of the Virginia Serenaders," in which the white artists are pictured twice, on the top half of the page in blackface and below in respectable "white" attire.

The instruments most closely associated with minstrelsy—fiddle, banjo, bones, and tambourine—reflect the sorts of mixing of cultural pedigrees that fascinated contemporary audiences. The fiddle, bones, and tambourine arrived in America via Europe; banjo prototypes (generally gourds covered by a membrane) arrived via West Africa. All four had long been incorporated into slave life, however.

Credit for the first detailed caricatures and imitations of black culture is generally given to Englishman Charles Matthews, who studied African-American traits during an 1822 trip to the United States. Quick to follow Matthews's innovations were soloists George Nichols, Bob Farrell, George Washington Dixon, Joe Sweeney, John N. Smith, and Thomas Dartmouth ("Daddy") Rice, who gave voice to the happy-go-lucky country-bumpkin character Jim Crow in the 1829 song by the same name:

> Come, listen all you gals and boys,
> Ise just from Tuckyhoe;
> I'm goin, to sing a little song,
> My name's Jim Crow.
>
> [Chorus:]
> Weel about and turn about and do jis so,
> Eb'ry time I weel about I jump Jim Crow.
>
> I went down to the river,
> I didn't mean to stay;
> But dere I see so many gals,
> I couldn't get away.

Jim Crow's counterpart, the urban dandy Zip Coon, was popularized by George Washington Dixon. The Zip Coon lyrics were set to an anonymously composed tune best known today as "Turkey in the Straw":

O ole Zip Coon he is a larned skoler,
O ole Zip Coon he is a larned skoler,
O ole Zip Coon he is a larned skoler,
Sings posum up a gum tree an conny in a holler.
Posum up a gum tree, coony on a stump,
Posum up a gum tree, coony on a stump,
Posum up a gum tree, coony on a stump,
Den over dubble trubble, Zip Coon will jump.

[Chorus:]
O Zip a duden duden duden zip a duden day.
O Zip a duden duden duden zip a duden day.
O Zip a duden duden duden zip a duden day.
Zip a duden duden duden zip a duden day.

In the course of the song's many verses this gibberish-speaking "larned sko-ler" dines on chicken foot and possum heel with his "blue skin" lover and prophesizes his ascendancy to the presidency (with no less a figure than the free-spirited frontiersman Davy Crockett as his vice president). Zip Coon has nothing, but imagines that he has it all.

Over the next decades this coarse view of the African-American experience would be central to the minstrel perspective. Some composers—most prom-inently Stephen Foster with songs like "Nelly Was a Lady" (1849) and "Old Folks at Home" (1851)—would attempt to break the tradition's most vulgar stereotypes by presenting African Americans as richly feeling. Invariably, however, song texts would be used to mitigate the incendiary issues of race and slavery. Songs generally portrayed life on the Southern plantations as being carefree, although some highlighted slavery's cruelty. Rarely however, and despite the growing sentiments towards abolition in the North, was slavery politicized in song or skit. Even as the Civil War unfolded, minstrelsy sought to preserve the status quo.

Consider, for example, the protagonist in Henry Wood and Gustavus Geary's "Isn't It a Wonder" (1862) who does not give much thought to his freedom, but just wants some peace and quiet. He nags that "Sister Norf and Sister Souff, / Cut a pooty figger, / Fightin' like two Thomascats; / All about the Nigger." All this is just plain silly, he says. Forget about the "Nig-ger":

De Nigger is a jolly bird,
You cannot do widout him;

> So quit de war and make it up,
> And say no more about him.

John G. Whittier and J. W. Dadman's "Song of the Negro Boatman" (1862)
is somewhat more proactive.[55] The sheet music's cover pictures three runaway slaves rowing a boat across a broad river. They smile as they point to
the Union army and freedom on the distant shore. They are not angry, do
not long for revenge. They praise God, not the army, for their upcoming
deliverance:

> We know de promise nebber fail,
> An' nebber lie de word;
> So, like de postles in de jail,
> We waited for de Lord;
> An now he open ebery door,
> An' trow away de key;
> He tink we lub him so before,
> We lub him better free.

Most of the minstrel publications were unremarkable in verse and melody.
The best, however, combined verbal wit with musical invention. Consider
Work's euphoric "Kingdom Coming (Year of Jubilo)" (1862). The lyrics present a world upside down—"bottom rail on top," as a contemporary African-
American expression had it. But more than that, Work gives these suddenly
liberated slaves a powerful voice that uses inference and exaggeration to
reveal philosophical truths. It's the "massa" who runs away, not the slave.
It's the "massa" who is contraband, not the slave.[56] The keys and whip are
lost, so, apparently, is "massa." The "han'cuffs" are broken, so is the South's
"peculiar institution" of slavery. Ultimately, the listener wonders just whose
"year ob Jubilo" this may be.[57] Abolition, after all, broke chains of mutual
dependency:

> Say darkies hab you seen de massa,
> Wid de muff-stash on his face,
> Go long de road some time dis morn-in'
> Like he gwine to leab de place?
> He seen a smoke way up de ribber,
> Whar de Linkum gum-boats lay;

He took his hat, an lef' berry sudden,
An' I spec' he's run away!

[Chorus:]
De massa run, ha, ha!
De darky stay, ho, ho!
It mus' be now de kingdom comin',
An' de year ob Jubilo!

He six foot one way, two foot tudder,
An' he weigh tree hundred pound,
His coat so big, he couldn't pay de tailor,
An' it won't go half way 'round.
He drill so much dey call him Cap'n,
An' he got so drefful tanned,
I spec' he try an' fool dem Yankees,
For to tink he's contraband.

[Chorus]

De darkeys feel so lonesome,
Libing in de loghouse on de lawn,
Dey move dar tings to massa's parlor,
For to keep it while he's gone.
Dar's wine an' cider in de kitchen,
An' de darkeys dey'll hab some;
I spose dey'll all be cornfiscated,
When de Linkum sojers come.

[Chorus]

De oberseer he make us trouble,
An' he dribe us 'round a spell;
We lock him up in de smokehouse cellar,
Wid de key trown in de well.
De whip is lost, de han'cuff broken,
But de mass'll hab his pay;
He's old enough, big enough, ought to known better
Dan to went an' run away.

Whatever the deeper implications, the song was light-spirited enough that it became popular both North and South. Troops of Lee's half-starved Army of

Northern Virginia, many who were disgusted by the easy lives lived by politicians and other privileged non-combatants, reportedly sang it during that army's desperate evacuation of Richmond on April 2, 1865.[58] Union African-American troops sang it the following day as they marched in to occupy the city. After the war, the song would be popular with African American minstrel troupes.

Just what did whites imagine slaves were up to when "massa" was away? Libidinous hijinks, it would seem. Typical was T. Ramsey and E. W. Mackney's voyeuristic "Sally Come Up" (1863). "Massa's gone to town the news to hear, / And he has left de overseer," the song begins. This recipe for carnal pleasure must have held considerable fascination for white audiences:

> [Chorus:]
> Sally, come up! Sally go down!
> Sally, come twist your heel around;
> De old man he's gone down to town
> Oh, Sally come down the middle!

> [Verse 5:]
> Sally can dance, Sally can sing,
> De cat chocker reel, and breakdown fling;
> To get de Niggers in a string,
> Dar's not a gal like Sally

Unsettling in a different way was "I Cant Help Dat. Taint My Fault" (1862, "Written by Somebody" and "Composed by Nobody"), in which the African-American protagonist sees the war going on around him, senses that he is the cause of all the trouble, but is powerless (and anyhow unwilling) to do anything about it. Notice the verb tense shift in the last four lines. White men suddenly would prefer their skin be black, it seems. Blacks once wished for white, but no longer, evidently:

> I duzzent hab to go to war
> To hear de cannon rattle;
> Dey draf de white folks in de Norf
> An' makes dem go to battle
> De white folks used to put on ars,
> An' cut tremengus figgers,

De Niggers wished dat dey wor white,
De whites wish dey wor Niggers.

Unusual for its militancy was Frank Howard's "Who Says the Darkies Wont Fight?" (1863):

Some white folks have been heard to say de niggers would not fight,
But I guess that they look at it now quite in another light;
Hush up you mouf, you "Copperheads" dont take dat for a plea
To keep us from de battlefield where all ob you should be.

George Cooper and Stephen Foster took up the theme of African-Americans soldiers in "A Soldier in the Colored Brigade" (1863). Such is the strength of this recruit's optimism that the two-line chorus needed to be continually modified to reflect his increasingly grandiose visions:

Old Uncle Abram wants us, and we're coming right along,
I tell you what it is, we're gwine to muster mighty strong;
Then fare you well my honey dear! Now don't you be afraid,
I's bound to be a soldier in de colored brigade.

A soldier! a soldier in de darkey brigade!
I's bound to be a soldier in de colored brigade.

O! when we meet de enemy I s'pect we make 'em stare,
I tink he'll catch a tartar when he meets de woolly hair.
We'll fight while we are able and in greenbacks we'll be paid,
And soon I'll be a Colonel in de Colored Brigade.

A Colonel! A Colonel in de darkey Brigade,
And soon I'll be a Colonel in de Colored Brigade!

The subsequent verses detail various African-American contributions to past wars. Yet, as the finale makes clear, optimism must be tempered by social reality:

Some say dey lub de darkey and dey want him to be free,
I s'pec dey only fooling and dey better let him be;
For him dey'd break dis Union which de're forefadders hab made,
Worth more dan twenty millions ob de Colored Brigade.

Other songs depicted slaves uncomfortable with their newfound freedom. Consider J. B. Murphy's "Young Eph's Lament: or Oh, Whar Will I Go If dis War Breaks de Country Up?" (1863). The protagonist, apparently overwhelmed at the prospect of being in charge of his own fate, longs to return to the uncomplicated life of the antebellum South:

> Oh where will I go if dis war breaks de country up,
> And de darkeys hab to scatter around,
> Dis dam bobolition, mancipation and sesession
> Am a gwine to run de nigger in de ground!
> De bobolition here, De secession dare,
> And neather one nor t'other of 'em's right,
> But one says dis, de oder says dat,
> And dey both got de country in a fight,
> But what can a poor nigger do.

Along the same lines was I. W. Lucas and Gomez's "Come Back Massa, Come Back" (1863). Here the faithful, but emasculated, slave speaks of the escalating troubles at home since Massa has gone to war:

> Since Massa went to war de deuce has been to pay,
> De cotton-pickin' darkies hab all run away;
> Some are up at Richmon', de good for noffin scamps,
> And some are digin' muck in de Union Army camps.
>
> [Chorus:]
> Den come back Massa, come back!
> O come back Massa, come back!
> Shake hands wid Uncle Sam, and be a Union man
> And sabe de ole Plantation!

As Grant's offensives of 1864 continued, as Atlanta fell to Sherman, and especially with Lincoln's reelection, it became clear that the Union would press the war to victory. With manumission inevitable, minstrel views shifted with the tide. Minstrels came to "favor emancipation because it removed a blot against American ideals, rewarded Negro war allies, and punished the South." Minstrels did not, however, accord "blacks a 'place' in the North or a position as the equals of whites."[59] Emmett's "Road to Richmond" (1864) is typical. As slaves, African Americans had been lazy: "When I was young and in my prime, / I used to work but took my time." As freedmen, they are lost, even willing slaves: "All hail! for we are underway. / Yah! we belong to the Union Army." The song "Nicodemus Johnson" (1865, attributed to J. B. Murphy) also takes this perspective:

> I wish dis war would only end,
> And peace come frew de nation,
> I'd go right back to Dixie's land an stay dar;
> For I isn't any contraband,
> I love the old plantation.

Stories of other minorities or star-crossed lovers were also frequent topics for minstrel lampoons. But because they lack the searing history of slavery, they receive relatively little notice in contemporary minstrel song discussions. Many, like Will Hays's love song "Will You Remember Me?" (1864) would seem to fit better with songs written for the parlor than the minstrel stage. There is no ethnic stereotyping, no mention of war. Yet, the many faces of love—pursued, gained, or lost—were also frequent minstrel topics. A. Jones and Frederick Buckley wrote of "Gentle Annie Ray" (1862) whose forlorn lover sighs that "I'm sitting by thy grave tonight, / I'm weeping weeping bitter tears." Tony Pastor and Nell Bryant wrote the upbeat Irish song "Lanigan's Ball" (1863):

> We "lather'd the flure" till the ceiling did fall,
> For I spent three weeks at Brooks' Academy,
> Leaning a step for Lanigan's Ball.

Eugene T. Johnston's "The Jersey Lovers (A Pathetic Ballad)" (1865) was purportedly used by Woods's, Campbell's, and Bryant's minstrels. It tells the story of a hapless lover who spies his sweetheart with another man:

> Then he ran down to the river side,
> But being out of breath,
> He fell down on a big clam shell,
> And scraped himself to death
>
> When Sari Jane she heard of this,
> She gave a piercing squall,

Then tied a grind-stone round her neck,
And jumped in the raging canawl.

Songs of Abolition

The slavery controversy, with its many varied rationales and inconsistencies, was as old as the nation. Thomas Jefferson, for example, held the seemingly impossible ground of Virginia slaveholder and abolitionist. Even Lincoln, early in his political career at least, was reluctant to take a stand on the issue.

The nineteenth-century anti-slavery movement is most closely tied to New England where one of its important leaders was Massachusetts-born William Lloyd Garrison (1805–1879), also an advocate of women's rights. The zealous and often inflexible Garrison found that song, with its sweeping paintbrush-like ability to cover complex matters under a layer of emotion, was an effective tool to rally public sentiment. He regularly published music in his weekly anti-slavery newspaper, the *Liberator*, which, from its initial issue of 1831 until its final edition at the end of the Civil War, served as one of the beacons of the abolition movement.

An early anthem was Jesse Hutchinson's pastiche "Get Off the Track!" (1844), which was published in the *Liberator* that same year and set to Emmett's popular 1843 minstrel tune "Old Dan Tucker."[60] The setting of new lyrics to existing melodies was effective for two primary reasons. First, since the melody was already familiar, providing music notation was unnecessary, and thus, songs could be inexpensively distributed and quickly learned with broadsides (lyric sheets). Second, the process of replacing the old text with the new text tended to conflate the original song's meanings and associations with those of the new one.

Consider the relationship between "Old Dan Tucker" and "Get Off the Track!" First, there is the character of Tucker himself. Larger than life, Tucker fought, drank, danced, and carried on to his heart's content. Because he lived outside the stricter codes of proper white society, Tucker was an object of fascination that white audiences could simultaneously mock, revile, and envy. Emmett's song recalls the broken chain of disconnected ideas and events along which Tucker lived his life. Printed below are the first, fourth, and seventh verses:

I come to town de udder night,
I hear de noise den saw de fight,
De watchman was a runnin roun,
Cryin Old Dan Tucker's come to town,

[Chorus:]
So get out de way! Get out de way!
Get out de way! Old Dan Tucker,
You're too late to come to supper.

Ole Dan Tucker an I got drunk,
He fell in de fire an kick up a chunk,
De charcoal got inside he shoe
Lor bless you honey how de ashes flew.

[Chorus]

Tucker was a hardened sinner,
He neber said his grace at dinner;
De ole sow squeel, de pigs did squall
He 'hole hog wid de tail and all

Compare these lyrics to Hutchinson's heightened speech in "Get Off the Track!" Dialect is gone; moral focus replaces mayhem. In a sense, "Get Off the Track!" liberates Dan Tucker, or at the very least, forces the listener to rethink him. Hutchinson's text moves from exaltation in the first verse (as if freedom were truly at hand) towards an increasingly militant and accusatory tone. The positive language of verse one—with words like "majestic" and "liberty"—is replaced with troubling images—"alarm" and "blunder" in verse four, "dangerous" and "false" in verse five. Although abolition will certainly come, Hutchinson forecasts a difficult future in which force may prove necessary to bring it about. The Hutchinson family singers led this, and similar songs, with great success at political rallies across the North. Printed below are the first, fourth, and fifth verses of the original eleven as they were published in the *Liberator*:

Ho! The car Emancipation
Rides majestic thro' our nation,
Bearing on its train the story,
LIBERTY! a nation's glory.
Roll it along, thro' the nation,
Freedom's car, Emancipation.

> Let the ministers and churches
> Leave behind sectarian lurches;
> Jump on board the Car of Freedom,
> Ere it be too late to need them.
> Sound the alarm! Pulpits thunder!
> Ere too late you see your blunder!
>
> Politicians gazed, astounded,
> When, at first, our bell resounded:
> Freight trains are coming, tell these foxes,
> With our votes and ballot boxes.
> Jump for your lives! Politicians,
> From your dangerous, false positions.

There was any number of variations on the pastiche technique. The song "My Country"—so enduringly popular that it was published in *The Free Soil Minstrel* (1848), *The Harp of Freedom* (1856), and the September 27, 1861, edition of the *Liberator*—was one of many songs set to the tune "America."[61] Here, the warm sentiments remembered from the original ("Sweet land of liberty" and "Land of the Pilgrim's pride") clash with the cold reality being lived in the slave states ("Dark land of slavery" and "Land where the slave has sighed"). "My Country" subverts the original song and casts the United States as a land of hypocrites in which a pretense of moral integrity shields a social reality built upon shame and injustice:

> My country,'tis for thee,
> Dark land of slavery,
> For thee I weep,
> Land where the slave has sighed,
> And where he toiled and died,
> To serve a tyrant's pride—
> For thee I weep.

Specific events also inspired musical responses. Pennsylvania Representative David Wilmot introduced the incendiary Wilmot Proviso in 1846. If passed, the bill would have banned slavery in territory taken during the Mexican War (1846–1848). The "Free Soil Chorus" of 1848 (sung to "Auld Lang Syne") talked of peace, but did so through the images of violence. Below are the song's second, fifth, and sixth verses:

We wage no bloody warfare here,
But gladly would we toil,
To show the South the matchless worth
For freedom and free soil.

[Chorus:]
For freedom and free soil, my boys,
For freedom and free soil,
Ring out and shout to all about,
For freedom and free soil.

Our southern neighbors feel our power,
And gladly would recoil;
But 'tis "too late," the cry's gone forth,
For freedom and free soil.

[Chorus]

Then let opponents do their best
Our spirits to embroil;
No feuds shall e'er divide our ranks
Till victory crowns free soil.

In fact, the spilling of blood seemed increasingly probable as Northerners and Southerners dug in their heels over which new states of the expanding nation would allow slavery. The Slave Act of 1850 strengthened slave owners' power to reclaim runaway slaves and thereby further animated Northern abolitionist sentiment. Now fugitive slaves, once relatively safe from pursuit once they had made across the Mason-Dixon Line, had to go to Canada if their liberty was to be guaranteed. Such was the topic of "The Bondsman's Home" sung to the tune "There Is a Happy Land":

We have a happy home,
Far, far away;
Where slavery is not known
    In Canada.
Here men have equal rights,
As the blacks, so are the whites,
There like a band of knights,
"All men are free."

Harriet Beecher Stowe's *Uncle Tom's Cabin* inspired both abolitionist and pro-slavery music. Representing the abolitionist perspective was "Little Eva;

Uncle Tom's Guardian Angel" (1852), written by poet and abolitionist John Greenleaf Whittier and composer Manuel Emilio:

> Dry the tears for holy Eva,
> With the blessed angels leave her,
> Of the form so sweet and fair
> Give to earth the tender care.
>
> For the golden locks of Eva
> Let the sunny southland give her
> Flowery pillow of repose
> Orange bloom and budding rose,
> Orange bloom and budding rose.

The lives of Little Eva and Uncle Tom were braided together by destiny. She, the innocent daughter of Tom's slave master, read Tom the Bible; Tom saved her life. Body and soul, the two were an essential part of Stowe's vision of how white and black might live together. Lyricist Charles L. Bennison and composer Isaac N. Bonney portrayed their reunion in the afterlife in "The Death of Little Eva and Uncle Tom" (1853). Below are the fifth and sixth verses. Tom lies dying from a brutal whipping:

> In mild resignation a dark form was lying,
> Awaiting the summons when he would be free,
> When Eva's bright cherub entered into the cabin,
> Whispering Uncle Tom, I linger for thee.
>
> A warm smile came over the face of the bondsman,
> As gently he folded his arms o'er his breast;
> The conflict is over, no mortal can harm thee,
> Their souls are united in the haven of rest.

Not surprisingly, Stowe was despised in the South where her book was banned and numerous pro-slavery novels quickly published. Southern lyricist Charles Soran and composer John Hill Hewitt used the 1853 blackface minstrel-styled song "Aunt Harriet Becha Stowe" to question Stowe's deeper commitment to the African American. In this song, the runaway slave, hoping to find shelter in the North, bemoans both his circumstances and Stowe's duplicity. As the narrative unfolds, not only is Stowe—who made a number of trips to England beginning in 1853—rebuked, but the song also takes aim at the capitalist wage labor system that makes "slaves" of its *white* workers:

> I went to New York city a month or two ago,
> A hunting for dat lady, Aunt Harriet Becha Stowe;
> I see'd de Abolitions dey said she'd gone away,
> Dey told me in de city it was no use to stay.
>
> She take away de dollars, and put 'em in her pocket,
> She laid her hand upon it, and dar she safely lock it,
> Dey said if Massa come for me, den dey would quickly meet,
> Dey'd make a lion of me, and gib me 'nuf to eat.
>
> Oh! Oh! Oh! Aunt Harriet Becha Stowe!
> How could you leave de Country and sarve poor nigga so.
>
> Dey treated dis here child, as doe I was a Turk,
> Den tole me for to leave dem and go away to work;
> I couldn't get no work, I couldn't get no dinner,
> And den I wish dis Fugitive was back to ole Virginny.
>
> Oh! when I was a picanin, Ole Uncle Tom would say,
> Be true unto your Massa, and neber run away,
> He tole me dis at home, he tole me dis at partin,
> Ned, don't you trust de white folks, For dey am quite unsartin.
>
> Oh! Oh! Oh! Aunt Harriet Becha Stowe!
> How could you leave de Country and sarve poor nigga so.
>
> Ole Massa's very kind ole Missus gentle too,
> And much I love my Dinah in old Virginny true,
> Now I'll go back and stay dar, and neber more will roam
> Lor bress de Southern Ladies, and my old southern home!
>
> But don't come back Aunt Harriet in England make a fuss,
> Go talk against your Country, put money in your puss
> And when us happy niggers you pity in your prayer,
> Oh! don't forget de WHITE SLAVES dat starvin ober dare![62]

Theatrical productions of *Uncle Tom's Cabin*—ranging from blackface minstrel skits to longer burlesques to full-length plays—were popular across the United States and Europe, where slavery was also an important social issue. Such fare would be produced throughout the nineteenth century. Edwin S.

Porter for the Edison Company made the first of many film versions of the story in 1903.

Slavery was a tinderbox ready to ignite and wrench apart the nation. A national crisis developed when Illinois Senator Stephen A. Douglas introduced the Kansas-Nebraska Act of 1854, which repealed the long-standing ban on slavery north of 36°30' north latitude. The legislation came just two months after Harvard Divinity School–trained theologian and Unitarian minister Thomas Wentworth Higginson and colleagues had stormed a Boston federal courthouse but failed to rescue escaped slave Anthony Burns, who was being held awaiting the arrival of his Virginia master. In this heated climate, Kansas-Nebraska struck hard at already heightened emotions, dealt a deathblow for the Whig Party, and opened a path for the new anti-slavery Republican Party.[63]

Once again, songs were created in response to unfolding events. James G. Clark's "Ho! For the Kansas Plains" (1856) called for a slave-free state. "Huzza," the song's opening cheer, would be used by Union soldiers in the coming war:

> Huzza for the prairies wide and free;
> Ho! For the Kansas plains;
> Where men shall live in liberty,
> Free from a tyrant's chains
> We ask no page in story,
> Prouder than the spotless glory,
> Of a land that gives her might
> To the battle of the right.

Another compelling abolitionist song was "Strike for Freedom and for Right" (1856). The song focused on white crimes by conflating the violence in Kansas with South Carolina Congressman Preston Brooks's vicious cane whipping of Massachusetts Senator Charles Sumner, an act committed in retribution for the latter's anti-Southern diatribe on the Senate floor. The text was sung to the "Old Dan Tucker" melody and published in *The Harp of Freedom*:

> From the bloody plains of Kansas
> From the Senate's guilty floor,
> From the smoking wreck of Lawrence,

From our Sumner's wounds and gore,
Comes our country's dying call—
Rise for Freedom, or we fall![64]

The slate of candidates in the presidential election of 1860 mirrored the widening fissures in the national psyche. The contest featured longtime Illinois rivals Democrat Stephen A. Douglas against Republican Abraham Lincoln. Dividing the generally pro-slavery Democrats was a second ticket headed by Kentuckian, Vice President, and future Confederate Secretary of War, John C. Breckinridge. Running for the newly formed Constitutional Union Party was John Bell of Tennessee, former secretary of war under William Henry Harrison.

Each candidacy was supported by music. Charles Grobe, with an eye for niche marketing, published piano works dedicated to each: the "Breckinridge Schottisch," the "Douglas Schottisch," "The Union Bell Polka," and the "Lincoln Quickstep," all in 1860. Songsters (books of song collections), included the pro-Lincoln *The Wide-Awake Vocalist; or, Rail Splitters' Song Book*, and *Hutchinson's Republican Songster for the Campaign of 1860*. Songsters offered a wide variety of music. Some songs highlighted a candidate's virtues; others attacked an opponent's weaknesses. Sensing that a victory for Lincoln would mean a resolution of the slavery issue once and for all, Hutchinson's songster ranged in tone, as the two following examples suggest, from that of homespun cloth (by referencing the 1840 presidential campaign of William Henry Harrison) to the iron fist of militant abolitionism:

"Honest Old Abe of the West"

Then bring out the music and banners,
The "fence rails" and orators too,
And we'll teach Loco-focos good manners,
As we did with "Old Tippecanoe."[65]

"Have You Heard the Loud Alarm?"

Steeped in infamous corruption,
Sold to sugar cane and cotton,
Lo! A nation's heart is rotten,
And the vampires suck her blood;
O'er our broad and free dominions
Rules the cotton king whose minions

> Clip our fearless eagle's pinions,
> And invite Oppression's reign.[66]

Another 1860 election song, this one would remain popular throughout Lincoln's presidency, was "Old Abe Lincoln Came Out of the Wilderness," which was set to the tune "Down in Alabam" (best known today as "The Old Gray Mare").

> Old Abe Lincoln came out of the wilderness,
> Out of the wilderness, out of the wilderness,
> Old Abe Lincoln came out of the wilderness,
> Many years ago.

Later verses would be added to reflect the evolving political situation:

> Old Jeff Davis tore down the government,
> Tore down the government, tore down the government,
> Old Jeff Davis tore down the government,
> Many years ago.
>
> But old Abe Lincoln built up a better one,
> Built up a better one, built up a better one,
> Old Abe Lincoln built up a better one,
> Many years ago.

4

Urban and Concert Music

NEW YORK CITY

As pianist Louis Moreau Gottschalk observed at the beginning of 1862, New York was "at least as brilliant as when [he had] left it for the South in 1857."[1] Opportunities abounded. By his own account, Gottschalk would play some ninety-five concerts in the city over the next two years. New York, or so it seemed to him, was immune from the deprivations the Civil War was inflicting elsewhere.

Gottschalk was only half right. The first half of the 1861–1862 season had been a tenuous one for classical music. Entrepreneurs were desperate to find any sort of entertainment that might sell tickets. The Austro-Hungarian impresario Bernard Ullman, who had previously brought in such virtuosos as Belgian violinist Henri Vieuxtemps (1820–1881) and Swiss-born pianist Sigismond Thalberg, opened the New York Academy season with entertainment of a decidedly more populist ilk, the German magician Carl Herrmann. Ullman rationalized his choice by noting Herrmann's unique talents, boasting that Hermann's "appearance has been a new revelation in the art of prestidigitation, as that of Jenny Lind has been in singing."[2] Well, perhaps. At any rate, the show proved plenty entertaining. To spice it up, Theodore Thomas (1835–1905) conducted works of Ferdinand Hérold, Mendelssohn, Wagner, as well as "the celebrated Strauss of Vienna['s] 'Herrmann Polka.' "[3] The magician's wife, Rosalie, in addition to claiming clairvoyance, was an accomplished vocalist and pianist. She performed in all three capacities.

Herrmann and company proved so popular with critics and public alike that the fall season was a financial success and Ullman's confidence was restored. Thus braced, he moved on to finding support for a spring opera season. Pleas went out to benefactors so that the "rebellion shall not interfere with opera," that the Academy stay open, and that:

> despite a Civil War that calls half a million men to the field, despite the treasure promptly found to supply their necessities and war's expensive requisites—we are not compelled to close our institutions of art and intellectual amusement, or debar citizens their usual pleasure of a season's opera.[4]

There were, it seems, endless entertainment niches to fill. Mid-March saw mechanical instrument performances in Dodworth's Hall. Most notable was the "Automoton," a clarinet-playing robot created in 1838 by Cornelis Jacobus van Oeckelen. The instrument had thirty-two notes and could play four different classical works. Also featured were the keyboard-manipulated "Clavier Oboe" and the "Clavier Contrabasso." Austrian pianist Gustav Satter and others performed recitals and chamber music, but they proved less of a draw than the machines. Chamber concerts were common throughout the city and were often given by members of the New York Philharmonic, as well as local or touring ensembles.

Choral societies were active as well. The New York Liederkranz, founded in 1847 and with 547 members by 1860, was probably the first of at least twenty German Männerchöre (male choruses) active in New York City in the years preceding the Civil War.[5] These groups, which invariably had a strong social component, were seen as a way to preserve German heritage within Manhattan's Lower East Side. The New York Liederkranz sang with the New York Philharmonic, the Brooklyn Philharmonic, and Theodore Thomas's orchestra. Personalities such as piano builder William Steinway sang with the group. Wartime performances included Mendelssohn's *Die erste Walpurgisnacht* (*The First Witches' Sabbath* 1861), Félicien David's *Le Désert* (1862), and Niels Gade's *Comala* (1863). Schubert's 1823 operetta *Die Verschworenen* (*The Conspirators*) was performed after two years' delay in 1866.[6]

In May 1861, lawyer and future New York Philharmonic president George Templeton Strong (1820–1875) found himself appointed to a committee formed to present an open competition for a national hymn. With a reward of $250, the committee put out advertisements and hoped to find musical gold, even though, as Strong acknowledged, the odds were "one chance in ten million that it may bring out something good."[7]

It did not. Writing in his diary a month later, a disappointed Strong noted that, "We got through possibly a third of our job between eight and twelve-thirty. There are 1,156 'hymns,' many of them with music. The great majority are consigned to the rubbish bin (or clothes basket) after reading the first three lines. A few were put aside as meritorious and worth looking at, and a few others as brilliantly absurd and therefore worth saving."[8] In the end, the entire enterprise turned out to be not only a waste of time, but also a major embarrassment for the judges and organizers.

Many of the city's musical events were linked to the unfolding war. "The pavement in Broadway is battered with the steady trap of pedestrians keeping step to the martial strains of military bands leading new-fledged warriors to the field of glory; and the possible widows of these same warriors begin to excite attention," wrote a perceptive, if irreverent, reporter for the *Albion* on June 1.[9] In the preceding two weeks, Colonel Louis Blenker's 1st German Rifle Regiment had held a Grand Military Festival intended to benefit the regiment's families. It featured vocal soloists, choirs of the Arion and Teutonia societies, an orchestra, and the regimental band. A few days later George Frederick Bristow had led a massive musical festival at the Academy of Music. As the summer unfolded, bandmasters Claudio S. Grafulla (1810–1880) and Harvey Dodworth (1822–1891) led military bands to great effect. Dodworth's outdoor concerts in Central Park regularly attracted audiences of 20,000 or more. Similar events would continue into the fall. Patriotism drove these events. In parks and theaters alike, the singing of nationalistic songs became surefire winners with audiences. The *Albion* noted cynically that, "when the word 'patriotic' is omitted from the bills there is a fearful exhibition of empty benches. And so it happens that no program is complete now without at least one National song among the pieces."[10]

While the war was good business for military bands, it was not so clear how symphonic music (especially the New York Philharmonic) would fare. Founded in 1842 as the country crawled out of the depression that followed the financial Panic of 1837, the New York Philharmonic Society was the nation's first permanent orchestral ensemble (preceding the Boston Symphony, the next city to come on line, by thirty-nine years). The orchestra was run cooperatively. Control was in the hands of the musicians, with revenues divided among the players. The 1842 debut concert featured mostly German works and was performed on December 7 in the Apollo Rooms, where musicians stood as they performed before an audience of some 600 to 650. In a review published three days after the concert, the *Albion* called the event "the commencement of a New Musical Era."[11] And it was. Opera was already well established; now there was an instrumental institution to match. Throughout most of the nineteenth century, the orchestra's membership would be filled largely by German immigrants or their immediate descendants. Just three years after its founding, the Philharmonic reached a milestone when it presented the American premiere of Beethoven's Symphony No. 9.

The ensemble's focus on the German repertory came at a public relations cost when, in 1854, music critic William Henry Fry took aim at the organization that he regarded as "an incubus on Art, never having asked for or performed a single American instrumental composition during the eleven years of its existence."[12] The assertion was almost true, but not quite. In 1847, the orchestra had played Concert Overture in E-flat by the Brooklyn native Bristow, one of the ensemble's members. Despite that single success, Bristow added his own fury to Fry's when he spoke out against his colleagues. Bristow complained that "the Philharmonic Society has been as anti-American as if it had been located in London during the revolutionary war, and composed of native born English Tories."

Fry and Bristow's anti-German tirades had little effect on the Philharmonic Society's popularity or musical direction. By 1856, the ensemble had moved to the spacious Academy of Music, which it easily filled with subscribers. Still, there were always new challenges. One of these was the Financial Panic of 1857, precipitated by the failure of the New York branch of the Ohio Life Insurance and Trust Company and exacerbated when a ship carrying one million dollars in commercial gold sank off South Carolina. There was a subsequent run on the banks which brought on a financial depression that lasted until the eve of the Civil War. The Philharmonic Society felt musical pressures as well, including increased competition with the arrival of a new wave of Italian opera performers and the founding of the Brooklyn Philharmonic.

In light of these developments, it is not surprising that the Philharmonic Society decided to retrench with the outbreak of war. Concerts were moved from the Academy of Music to the smaller and far less expensive Irving Hall for the 1861–1862 and 1862–1863 seasons. The move proved unwar-

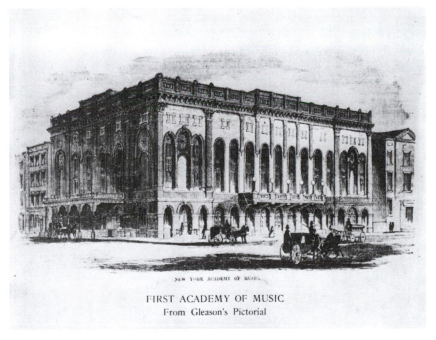

FIRST ACADEMY OF MUSIC
From Gleason's Pictorial

Interior and exterior of New York City's Academy of Music. Image courtesy of the New York Philharmonic.

Philharmonic Society
OF NEW YORK.

1861   **1862**

FIRST CONCERT, TWENTIETH SEASON.
IRVING HALL,
Saturday Evening, November 9th, 1861.

EIGHTIETH CONCERT.

PROGRAMME.
PART I.

GRAND SYMPHONY, No. 5, in C minor, Op. 67,...L. von BEETHOVEN.

   1. Allegro con brio.   3. Allegro.

   2. Andante con moto.   4. Allegro—Presto.

RECITATIVO e CAVATINA, from "La Sonnambula," "Care Compagne,"
MISS ABBY FAY.   BELLINI.

SECOND CONCERT, *for Piano and Orchestra*, in F. minor, Op 21,....
                                               CHOPIN

   1. Maestoso.   2. Larghetto.   3. Allegro vivace.

              (First time.)

        MR. S. B. MILLS.

PART II.

OVERTURE, le Carnival Romain,..................HECTOR BERLIOZ.

CAVATINA, from "La Niobe,—"I tuoi frequenti palpiti,".....PACINI.
        MISS ABBY FAY.

VARIATIONS DE CONCERT, sur "le Philtre" de Donizetti, *pour Piano*
solo, Op. 1,......................... ....A. HENSELT,

        MR. S. B. MILLS.

INTERMISSION OF A FEW MINUTES.

OVERTURE, "Rienzi,"........................R. WAGNER.

Mr. H. C. TIMM will preside at the Piano.

Conductor, MR. CARL BERGMANN.

TO COMMENCE AT 8 O'CLOCK P. M.

The Grand Piano used on this occasion is from the Factory of Messrs. STEINWAY & SONS,
No. 84 Walker Street, near Broadway.

Program of New York Philharmonic of November 9, 1861. Image courtesy of the New York Philharmonic.

Staff of the *New York Tribune*. Seated, left to right: George M. Snow, financial editor; Bayard
Taylor; Horace Greeley; George Ripley, literary editor; Standing, left to right: William Henry
Fry, music editor; Charles A. Dana; Henry J. Raymond. Library of Congress, Prints & Photo-
graphs Division.

ranted. After both seasons sold out, the orchestra returned to the spacious
Academy in the fall of 1863 and had no difficulty filling the seats with subscribers.

Opera also thrived. On September 22, 1862, as the fall season was just
getting under way, Fry noted that:

> The old Wallack's Theater is now alive with German opera. It is
> a striking elucidation of the cosmopolitan character of New York
> over that even of Paris or London, to find dramatic entertainments
> given steadily in English, Italian, French and German. What other
> city in the world can say as much of its many-sidedness in the
> tongues? The ever beautiful and glorious *Der Freischütz* was per-
> formed on Friday night. The best impersonation was by Madame
> Johannsen. The execution of her grand *scena* gave ample satisfac-
> tion to the German audience present—as much German almost
> as if assembled in Vienna, Berlin or Dresden.[13]

The following night Fry reviewed a performance of Vincenzo Bellini's opera *La Sonnambula*. "The opening last night, notwithstanding the troublous time, promised well. The house was full, brilliant, and in good temper with the opera," he wrote. Fry noted that the evening's success, quick on the heels of a German production the night before, suggested that not only would the war not cause the collapse of the musical season, but offered proof of opera's ability to undertake "the work of sweet solace in the face of great difficulties."[14] The evening saw the New York operatic debut of Carlotta Patti (1835–1889), the elder sister of the famed Adelina Patti (1843–1919), whose New York debut Fry had reviewed in 1859 and who was now singing in Europe.

Over a period of five days in mid-November, Fry reviewed productions of Giuseppe Verdi's *La traviata* and *Il trovatore*, as well as Bellini's *Norma*. The spring saw performances of Neapolitan composer Errigo Petrella's grand opera *Jone, o L'ultimo giorno di Pompei* (*Jone, or The Last Days of Pompeii*) as well as Christoph Willibald Gluck's *Orfeo ed Euridice*. In between these reviews, Fry found time to dismiss Hector Berlioz's massive *Benvenuto Cellini* on the shaky grounds that Berlioz was "not a melodist."

Fry was nothing if not opinionated. In January 1863 he began a series of articles in which he complained about America's slow development in the areas of composition, concert programming, and perhaps most importantly, artistry. He wrote that:

> If singers are scarce, composers are more so. By composers we do not mean the writers of "sheet music" any more than we would call poets the fillers-up of the corners of a village newspaper. . . . So rare are composers of any sort that even in our large cities the men who can detail with the pen, on paper, the abstract sonorousness and expression of musical effects—may be set down at one or two—or none—and out of the great cities there is nobody at all.[15]

The problem, Fry argued, was not that the bar set by European art music was too high, but rather that Americans were not confident or interested enough to attempt the leap. He continued:

> Nothing is so dreary, mean and stupid, art-wise, as an exclusive reference to Europe for musical high art. . . . Europe is not so fecund in operatic music that we need wait her motions. Italy, the

land of song, during twenty years has given the world one composer. Since the death of Von Weber, more than thirty years ago,
no master spirit in Germany has risen to take his place.[16]

The following March, Fry looked at the New York Philharmonic and, as he
had in 1954, found it wanting. He argued that it was not enough for the
orchestra to function as a living museum in which the works of the old
European masters were performed and preserved. Instead, the orchestra
needed to serve as a vehicle through which American composers and audiences could create and enjoy art music unique to their own society. This
was a revolutionary notion. Internationally, the United States was becoming
an economic and industrial powerhouse. Few, however, had thought to challenge Europe's artistic legacy. Fry was one of them. Despite his lukewarm
critique of the Philharmonic's premiere of Robert Goldbeck's (1839–1908)
Victory; Peace, Struggle, and Triumph, he wrote on March 23, 1863, that:

> We do not know what the Philharmonic Society is instituted for
> unless its office be equally to offer original American with original
> European music; and to labor might and main, heart and soul, to
> put America abreast with Europe in the adequate, constant and
> liberal productions of musical works suited to the concert room
> and especially to large orchestras. To see as we do, seventy or
> eighty musical gentlemen composing the orchestra, apparently
> content to advertise year in and year out, pieces of foreign pro-
> duction, when equally good pieces can be and are written in this
> country, is a sorry sight. . . . We apprehend that no other country
> is so wanting in artistic pride; and that the art in none can live at
> all unless as sedulously nursed as the mother nurses the child she
> loves. We say it with due respect and reverence for every man in
> Europe who seeks "to advance on chaos and the dark" by aiming
> to strike out new forms in musical art, that we have heard nothing
> of orchestral music of the most recent production in Europe that
> should induce its performance here in preference to an equally
> ready and liberal performance of works written in this country.[17]

These last sentences were an exaggeration. There was no American orches-
tral composer writing on a par with the European masters of the period.
Still, a handful of Americans were trying. Bristow, who had helped form the
American Music Association in 1856, was one of them. His eclectic career

as composer, violinist, conductor, teacher, and church organist reflected the many varied possibilities open to a talented musician in this vibrant city. Bristow's professional life had begun with comic opera and musical burlesques when he joined the pit orchestra of New York's Olympic Theater at the age of thirteen. He joined the Philharmonic in 1843 and stayed with the ensemble for thirty-six years. In addition, he served as the orchestra concertmaster when impresario P. T. Barnum sponsored soprano Jenny Lind's 1850–1851 American tour; he held the same position two years later in the orchestra of Frenchman Louis Jullien (1812–1860). Bristow conducted the New York Harmonic Society from 1851 to 1863 and the Mendelssohn Union from 1867 to 1871. He composed in a variety of genres ranging from chamber music to opera. Large-scale works included the operas *Rip Van Winkle* (1855) and *Columbus* (unfinished, although the Philharmonic performed the overture in 1866), as well as the Symphony in F-sharp Minor (premiered by the Philharmonic in 1859) and the oratorios *Praise to God* (1860) and *Daniel* (1866).[18]

Fry also composed. Curiously, however, little of his fiery oratory found a parallel on the music staff. Instead, he drew conservatively from European models. Drafts of his opera *Notre Dame of Paris* (adapted from Victor Hugo's *The Hunchback of Notre Dame* with a libretto by Fry's brother Joseph) suggest it was originally planned to be sung not in English, or even French, but Italian.[19] The music too was derivative of European models. *Hunchback* was premiered in Philadelphia on May 4, 1864, by the American Opera Company and ran for just a handful of performances, despite mostly positive reviews. On the podium was Theodore Thomas making his operatic conducting debut.[20]

With the qualification that getting American music onto a concert program remained as difficult as ever, the 1863–1864 New York season was even brighter than the previous one. Over twenty-five different operas were scheduled at the Academy of Music alone: seven by Donizetti, six by Verdi, three by Bellini, two by Meyerbeer, and works by Gounod, Wagner, and others. Outside of the Academy, however, finding appropriate venues was a problem. "The new singing birds are here, but where is the cage for them?" Fry asked in a November 12 column.[21]

In fact, there were plenty of "cages." They were just being used for other things, most notably, minstrel shows. Whatever opera's successes, it was minstrel shows and "the alcohol-dispensing concert saloons, with their superabundance of entertainment, that attracted the greatest crowds," reported

historian Vera Brodsky Lawrence. And why not? Such establishments suddenly had more quality entertainers than they knew what to do with, for "the
general shutdown of theatres throughout the Union had forced hordes of
entertainers of all descriptions to flock to New York, where—merely to survive—many accepted underpaid employment in places formerly beneath
their notice."[22]

Minstrel shows were most popular of all. Bryant's Minstrels, with Emmett
in the group from 1858 through much of the war, drew large crowds to
Mechanics' Hall. (In 1867, the ensemble would open its own venue, Bryant's
Minstrel Hall.) Among the many other groups active in the city were Hooley
and Campbell's Minstrels, Lloyd's Minstrels, and Sharpley's Minstrels. *New
York Tribune* editor and abolitionist Horace Greeley was a frequent target of
minstrel wrath. So were operas. Giacomo Meyerbeer's 1859 French opera
Dinorah, ou Le Pardon de Ploërmel was recast in blackface as *Dinah—The
Pardon Pell-Mell*. Gaetano Donizetti's 1833 opera *Lucrezia Borgia*, the story of
the infamously promiscuous daughter of Pope Alexander VI, was recast in
blackface by Buckley's Serenaders for, amazingly enough, an 1862 Christmas
holiday show at the Palace of Music Hall.[23]

WASHINGTON

The war transformed Washington. What at the beginning of 1861 had
been a slow-paced backwater of a town of 60,000 with geese and hogs
wandering the streets was by 1865 a modern bustling city with a population
of 120,000. Construction had been continuous, including some fifty hospitals to serve as many as 20,000 wounded at a time. Catering to soldiers, the
city's rousing nightlife included upwards of 450 bordellos, some of which
had government ratings as to their quality.[24]

The city's musical life was transformed as well. While its scope was perhaps less varied than was New York's, wartime Washington, with its seemingly endless supply of soldiers and their bands, may have had, notes to
population, more music than anywhere in the land. Throughout the war, the
Lincolns would host musicians in the executive mansion. Military bands
would serenade the president from the lawn or streets below. Opera companies would increasingly attract the public at large.

With seven states seceded and more to follow, President Lincoln's inauguration on March 4, 1861, was conducted under a pale of political uncer-

tainty. Civil war seemed inevitable. Even so, the inauguration was a grand enough affair. A 45-piece band led by L. F. Weber was the centerpiece of the evening's postinauguration party. The ensemble played six hours worth of dance music, with polkas, waltzes, and quadrilles by Strauss, Lanner, and other popular composers. Patriotic selections included the "Inauguration March," written by United States Marine Band director Francis Scala (ca. 1819–1903), as well as such popular tunes as "The Star-Spangled Banner," "Yankee Doodle," and "Hail to the Chief."

For that night, at least, Washington was a Yankee town.

That fact was not always so clear. Music of both the North and South resonated throughout Washington in the months leading to war. Early 1861 witnessed "a perpetual tinkle of . . . favorite secession airs" throughout the city, as a White House clerk noted.[25] Consider Emmett's "Dixie," which was already hugely popular with Confederate sympathizers. The song resounded in the restaurants, in the streets on mechanical hurdy-gurdies, and, as John Hutchinson complained, was sung in the rail stations. Washingtonians also received a steady diet of Union songs. "Yankee Doodle" and "The Star-Spangled Banner" were common. So were Joseph Hopkinson's 1789 song "Hail, Columbia" (written for George Washington's inauguration) and a host of other tunes, including one of Lincoln's favorites, the French Republican song "Marseillaise."

Band music was common in outdoor Washington throughout the war. In the weeks and months following the attack on Fort Sumter, arriving regiments from states ranging from Massachusetts to Minnesota paraded down Pennsylvania Avenue with bands blaring. Scala led the Marine Band at all important official events and the ensemble gave regular summer concerts on the south lawn of the White House. The Marine Band was the hometown darling. A reporter with the Washington *Evening Star* on May 9, 1861, testified that, "We in Washington flatter ourselves that this favorite band is an institution not to be beat anywhere."[26]

Still, the Marine Band had plenty of competition. At any time of the day or night, regimental bands passing through the city, or bivouacked nearby, might stop to serenade outside the White House. The repertoire at these occasions ranged from patriotic favorites to blackface minstrel tunes to popular sheet music to operatic arrangements. A spring 1861 concert attended by Lincoln at the Navy Yard offered a typical program. There Harvey Dodworth led his famed 71st New York Regimental Band in music that ranged from the grimly titled "Yes! Let Me Like a Soldier Fall" to a variety of excerpts from Verdi operas. And as if all that music were not enough for the president in one day, the Marine Band serenaded him that same evening.[27]

Of course, Lincoln heard far more than military bands. Although he had no musical training, Lincoln was a great aficionado who found in music an important relief from the pressures of office. He attended the opera nineteen times during his presidency. Programs at the White House were frequent. Song recitals were given by the Native American, but thoroughly acculturated, Larooqua, who was billed as the "aboriginal Jenny Lind," known for her recitations of Longfellow, and said to have had "a richness of melody in her notes which flow out in perfect control and an ease and grace that would do credit to our best singers."[28] Also performing was the Washington-born and European-trained opera singer Meda Blanchard, whose appearance marked the first time any opera singer had performed in that space. Child pianist Teresa Carreño did much to turn the White House upside down during her brief appearance. The most unusual entertainer may have been the diminutive Commodore Nutt who, at just twenty-nine inches tall, was a star for P. T. Barnum. An all-around performer, Nutt told jokes for the Lincolns and sang, among other things, "Hail, Columbia."[29]

The Hutchinson family singers, who had campaigned vigorously for Lincoln, gave an impromptu recital for the family on January 7, 1862. The evening included war-related songs as well as Macky and Russell's "Ship on Fire" (1840). A few days later the singers commenced what was intended to be a series of concerts for the Army of the Potomac. Events turned out differently, however. Midway through the first program, which was given at the Fairfax Seminary for the 1st New Jersey Infantry Regiment, the group sang an arrangement of John G. Whittier's abolitionist poem "We Wait Beneath the Furnace Blast," which had been set to the tune of the Lutheran hymn "A Mighty Fortress Is Our God." The third verse proved overly provocative:

> What gives the wheat-field blades of steel?
> What points the rebel cannon?
> What sets the roaring rabble's heel
> On the old star-spangled pennon?
> What breaks the oath
> Of the men of the South?
> What whets the knife
> For the Union's life?—
> Hark to the answer: *Slavery.*

WITH THE ORIGINAL

HUTCHINSON FAMILY,

"TRIBES of JOHN and JESSE."

With the original Hutchinson family. "Tribes of John and Jesse." Library of Congress, Prints & Photographs Division.

The Hutchinson family tribes of John and Jesse. Library of Congress, Prints & Photographs Division.

The verse nearly caused a riot. General Franklin, apparently acting on orders from General McClellan himself, subsequently revoked the Hutchinsons' singing permit. That was not the end of the matter, however. Upon his return to Washington, John Hutchinson complained to Secretary of the Treasury Salmon P. Chase. He, in turn, took the matter to a cabinet meeting.

In the end, the Hutchinson's singing permit was reinstated, with Lincoln's approval. Such was the concert's notoriety that "Furnace Blast" became an abolitionist rallying song.[30]

The city's musical life was infused with opera as well as recitals. Italian opera heard in 1862 and 1863 included works by Verdi, Rossini, and Donizetti. In April and June 1864 a German company performed works of Gounod, Weber, Flotow, and Beethoven. Lincoln, who had heard his first opera during a stopover in New York on February 20, 1861, attended performances in all three years, plus a March 24, 1864, recital at Willard's Hall featuring Gottschalk along with soprano Charlotte Varian, tenor Theodore Habelmann, and violinist Carlo Patti in a program of music by Beethoven, Rossini, Verdi, Gottschalk, and others. After the concert, Gottschalk candidly reminisced that:

> Lincoln is remarkably ugly, but has an intelligent air, and his eyes have a remarkable expression of goodness and mildness. After an encore I played my fantasia, *The Union*, in the midst of great enthusiasm. Lincoln does not wear gloves. I played very badly and was furious with myself, which, however, did not prevent many of my friends from coming to congratulate me on my success. One of them who was present at the [March 22] concert (at which, by the way, I played very well) said to me, "Well and good, you are in the vein tonight, for at the first concert one saw that you were badly prepared."[31]

Two days later Gottschalk again played in Washington. This time the famously tin-eared General Grant—whom Gottschalk characterizes as "a small man, of ordinary appearance, slender, modest"—and his staff were in the audience. The evening's patriotic spirit was such that each stanza of the "The Star-Spangled Banner" "was applauded to the skies and encored."[32]

NEW ORLEANS

Nineteenth-century America was ethnically diverse, but no city matched New Orleans with its mingling of French and Spanish, African and Native American peoples. Much of the city's population carried on lifestyles of near mythic excess. By day, entertainments included animal fights (ranging from

cocks to bulls), horse racing at the Metairie Course, bare-knuckled fist fighting, and lacrosse games played virtually rule free. Nights ushered in more
private passions. During the 1850s, prostitution was the city's second largest
industry, collecting sums second only to those of the city's port.

Latin-Catholic in the majority, the populace was not shackled by conservative Northern ideologies that often connected dance with lasciviousness.
Dance was central to social life. So, apparently, was lasciviousness. Balls
accompanied nearly every important concert prior to 1830.[33] A single venue
might hold four such events in a single week, many of which were open to
anyone who could afford the price of admission. Dancers, often masked and
with skin completely covered to hide race, freely mingled one and all.

If blacks perhaps crashed white balls, so too there were events designed
to allow the mixing of races. These were the famous quadroon balls for free
women of one-quarter African ancestry. The idea behind these affairs was
supposedly to find these young ladies white providers; socially speaking,
marriage was impossible. The reality, however, was quite different. White
men (much to the displeasure of white women) were certainly attracted to
the balls, but they came for the short-term thrill, not the long-term commitment. Prostitution was rife. By the 1850s interracial mixing was becoming taboo and society as a whole was becoming more hierarchical. Free
blacks increasingly opposed allowing slaves into their balls.[34]

Perhaps it is not surprising that such a city would be attracted to the often
steamy and lavish spectacle that was nineteenth-century opera. The city's
first documented opera performance was Grétry's Sylvain, which made its
city debut in 1796.[35] Soon New Orleans would be opera crazy. During a
nine-year run beginning in December 1810, the St. Philip Street Theatre
alone presented some 500 performances of over 100 different productions.
The St. Charles Theatre, which opened in 1835 when the city's population
was only 60,000, seated more than 4,000. Everyone—whites, free blacks,
and slaves—attended. The French Opera House opened in 1859; Meyerbeer's Dinorah was performed there in 1861. The city's fall and subsequent
Union army occupation put an end to opera, which was not produced again
until after the war.

Masquerading in the balls had its parallels in the pre-Lenten celebrations
of Mardi Gras, which began in 1837 amidst a reign of bad news ranging
from crop failures and widespread financial panic to an outbreak of yellow
fever. The first parade traveled through town and ended at the Théâtre
d'Orléâns, so that the masquers could pile onto the stage for the finale of

Auber's opera *Gustave III, ou Le Bal Masqué*. A far greater level of festivities was achieved on February 24, 1857, when the Mistick Krewe of Comus, a group founded by Mobile Anglo-Saxons rather than New Orleans Creoles, took up their torchlight parade. The war interrupted these celebrations, but the Mistick Krewe returned in 1866.

MUSIC IN THE MILITARY

Bands and Field Musicians

"I don't believe we can have an army without music," observed General Robert E. Lee after enjoying a brass serenade in 1864. Lee spoke for the majority of soldiers. For reasons both practical and emotional, instrumental musicians were an essential part of the Civil War military experience. Regiments awakened to the rattling beat of the drum and retired to the soft tones of the bugle. Band music energized soldiers on the march and broke the monotony of camp life. In combat, drums and bugles sounded commands; bands shored up men with patriotic airs like "Dixie" or "Rally Round the Flag." After a battle, in camp and at the hospitals, bands would play songs of home and country, love and family. If not performing during combat, musicians generally served as stretcher bearers or assisted the surgeons.

Army music was divided into two categories: field music and band music. Both were essential. Theoretically, their functions were different. In practice, however, duties often overlapped. Field musicians sounded calls to initiate basic camp duties; they were also used during military operations. These were the fifers, buglers, and drummers. Bands were full-scale concert ensembles made up of brass and percussion; woodwinds were uncommon.

From the soldiers' standpoint, both types of music were welcome. Like knives and forks, each served its special purpose. Francis H. Buffum of the 14th Regiment of the New Hampshire Volunteers prized the merits of each, writing that:

> It was never determined whether a crack drum-corps or a fine band appeared to best advantage [during a corps review, but] for marital music, purely, a drum-corps stands "par excellence," unrivalled; while a band possesses obvious advantages, and constantly tends to promote morale, strengthening the discipline and elevating the sentiment of the organization.[36]

Drum Corps of 10th Veteran Reserve Corps at leisure, Washington, D.C. Library of Congress, Prints & Photographs Division.

Band of 10th Veteran Reserve Corps, Washington, D.C. Library of Congress, Prints & Photographs Division.

Band of 107th U.S. Colored Infantry at Fort Corcoran, Arlington, Virginia. Library of Congress, Prints & Photographs Division.

The military's assignment of musicians followed clear guidelines. General Order 48 of July 31, 1861, allowed two principal musicians, up to twenty field musicians, and up to twenty-four band musicians per regular army infantry or artillery regiment, with sixteen band musicians in cavalry regiments. In practice, however, these numbers were rarely adhered to. Volunteer units sometimes had bands as large as fifty, some had bands under a dozen. Due to poor record keeping, we know next to nothing about most regimental bands. Estimates swing wildly as to how many musicians were even in uniform. Historians Lord and Wise state that by the end of 1861 the Union army had nearly 28,000 musicians enlisted of which about 14,000 were performing in 618 bands averaging about twenty-three members each.[37] In contrast, a December 9, 1861, report issued by the Sanitary Commission puts the total number of musicians at under 8,000. Estimates for the entire war reach as high as 53,600 musicians in service.[38]

Enlisting and outfitting these many musicians constituted an enormous expense. At the beginning of the war, a musician third-class earned $17 a month (more than a private), while a bandleader earned $105.50 (equivalent to a second lieutenant). The War Department spent $4,000,000 on bands in 1861.[39] Instrument costs added up as well. By the fall of 1863, Union armies had purchased some 13,000 drums and nearly 15,000 fifes. By war's end, numbers totaled over 32,000 drums, 21,000 bugles, and nearly 15,000 trumpets.[40]

Instruments

The mid-nineteenth century saw the rise and high point of the brass band. This phenomenon was made possible through advancements in instrument technology and metalworking skills. Historians generally date the modern era in brass instruments from 1810 Dublin where Irishman Joseph Haliday invented the five-keyed bugle. Haliday's idea was to imitate the system of keys used on woodwind instruments. His innovation gave musicians the ability to play a broader array of pitches than did the old natural horn with its fixed tube length. The idea took off. Additional keys were quickly added (up to twelve) and various instrument models were soon in use across Europe. By 1815, keyed bugles appeared in the United States where they were played by virtuosos such as Frank Willis (director of the West Point Military Academy Band), the African-American Philadelphian Francis "Frank" Johnson and Boston's Edward "Ned" Kendall (1808–1861). An important advancement followed in Paris in 1821 when instrument maker Jean Hilaire Asté patented an entire family of keyed brass instruments ranging in pitch range from soprano to bass. These also proved popular. By the mid-1830s, New York City's Dodworth Band, and in Massachusetts the Salem and Boston brigade bands, had put aside their woodwinds and converted to all brass instrumentations.[41]

Yet, while keyed mechanisms ushered in the brass band era, these instruments would ultimately prove little more than a bridge between natural horns and those using an airtight valve mechanism, the 1818 invention of German instrument makers Heinrich Stoelzel and Freiderich Bluhmel. Valved brass, with its relatively complex technology, was adopted more slowly than keyed brass, but the shift was inexorable as improvements were steadily adopted. Twin-piston valves were patented in 1830 by Viennese inventor Leopold Uhlmann; rotary-action valves were patented in the same city in 1832 by Joseph Riedl.[42]

Band before quarters at Camp Stoneman, District of Columbia. Library of Congress, Prints & Photographs Division.

Despite the mechanical superiority of valves over keys, both systems had ardent supporters. Celebrated in its time was the 1856 contest in Salem, Massachusetts, between keyed–bugle virtuoso Kendall and the valve-using cornet player Patrick Gilmore. There was no clear winner that day; the men's individual skills triumphed over their respective equipment. Yet, while key and valve systems existed side-by-side throughout the Civil War, keyed brass instruments gradually became obsolete.

The great variety of mechanical systems and instrumental shapes in use during the Civil War is not surprising if one considers the speed with which brass design was developing. Some instruments had bells pointing forward, some pointed skyward. In the 1840s and 1850s Paris-based Adolphe Sax (1814–1894) designed for military use a complete family of valve instruments with similar bores, pitch characteristics, and tone color. Saxhorns, as they were known, became popular across America by the mid-1850s and were used throughout the war. Also popular was bandmaster Allen Dodworth's (1817–1896) 1838 design of instruments that had their bells pointing backwards over the shoulder. This allowed soldiers marching behind the band to better hear the music. These instruments, reported Dodworth in his influential method book, *Dodworth's Brass Band School* (1853), were "for military purposes only . . . [and] for any other purpose are not so good."[43]

Before the war, the American instrument-making business was centered in New England. Graves & Company was based in Winchester, New Hamp-

Band of 10th Veteran Reserve Corps, Washington, D.C. Close-up of drums. Library of Congress, Prints & Photographs Division.

shire. Boston was often home base for Thomas D. Paine, who was the first to produce rotary valves with string linkage; J. Lathrop Allen, who invented the Allen rotary valve; and Elbridge G. Wright, who was the premier maker of the keyed bugle. Worcester, Massachusetts-based Isaac Fiske not only made improvements on the valve mechanism but also sponsored his own band.[44] Despite the growing popularity of brass instruments, because they were handcrafted, the total output before 1860 was slight, only a few thousand annually.

This would change with the introduction of interchangeable parts, an innovation soon known worldwide as the American system of manufacturing, and which revolutionized production of everything from rifles to watches to bugles. The Union army's orders for large quantities of brass instruments spurred manufacturers to implement new production techniques. John F.

Stratton's New York–based factory was soon turning out as many as 100 instruments daily, each with interchangeable parts. Because mass production brought with it greater financial rewards, new companies were attracted to the market. Philadelphia saw the establishment of the firms of William Seefeldt, Ernst Seltmann, Klemm & Brother, and Henry G. Lehnert; New York had the firms of Charles A. Zoebisch & Sons, Slater & Martin, John Howard Foote, Louis Schreiber, Christian R. Stark, and Wm. Hall & Sons. Kummer & Schetelich set up shop in Baltimore.[45]

In contrast to brass instruments, there were no significant developments in fife and drum technology in the years leading up to the Civil War. The fife (a small transverse flute with six to eight holes and no keys) was generally made of rosewood or some other hardwood. It was tuned to the key of C or B-flat major, though B-flat was evidently preferred because it was "louder in all the tones of the lower octave [and could] be heard at a greater distance than an instrument of any other pitch."[46] Because of the instrument's small size, playing in tune was invariably difficult, especially if notes were outside its home key.

Drums came in a variety of sizes and styles, and were built by dozens of manufacturers located from New England to Wisconsin. Field drums (also known as side or snare drums) ranged in size from 15 to 16 inches in diameter and from 10 to 12 inches in depth; bass drums were approximately 24 by 24 inches. Field drums were tuned by a rope tension system and used four to six animal-gut snares. Shells were generally made of maple, ash, or holly and were single, double, or triple ply. Specialty instruments were sometimes built from brass or German silver. The more elaborate wooden drums featured inlaid patterns. Union army guidelines, which were only loosely followed, stated that military drums were to be painted with the arms of the United States on a field that was blue for the infantry and red for the artillery. Company and regiment letters and numbers were placed beneath the arms or in a scroll.[47]

To outfit the shell for performance, the calfskin (or occasionally sheepskin) drumheads were soaked in water until pliable and then placed over and tucked in around a hoop that was just larger than the shell itself. When dry, the skins were placed over the shell and a heavier counter hoop (or rim) was seated on top to hold it secure. Drums were tuned by adjusting the tension of the heads with a rope strung back and forth WW-like along the outside of the shell from the batter (or struck) head to the thinner snare head. The pattern continued all the way around the drum. In order to further tighten the rope, leather tags, sometimes called "ears," were wrapped around adjoining turns in the ropes near the batter head. By pushing these tags down towards the snare head one could increase the tension exerted by the rope, thus pulling the counter rims together and raising the pitch. Near war's end, greater tension was achieved through the introduction of metal tension rods that worked on a screw system.

Field Musicians

Field musicians—fifers, buglers, and drummers—were at the nerve center of the military. Their duty was to transmit the various orders essential for the army's day-to-day functioning, whether in camp or on the battlefield. Some musical sequences were expansive. Others were precise, "just so many words of command."[48] Field musicians, often mere boys, studied to memorize these commands. Fighting soldiers were generally trained to follow them.

The music was bracing. Francis H. Buffum wrote that there is "no finer inspiration thrilling the entire nervous system of a vigorous man, than the first burst, crash, and roll of reveille when a crack drum-corps . . . rouses an entire regiment as by an electrical shock."[49] Indeed, reveille seems to have burst forth upon army camps with the inevitability of a force of nature. Edwin B. Houghton of the 17th Maine Regiment recalled how musical orders spread and multiplied across the vast army camps:

> As the first beams of the rising sun begin to tinge the eastern skies, the clear notes of the bugle, sounding reveille from headquarters are heard—repeated in turn by the regimental buglers. The drums of one regiment commence their noisy rataplan, which is taken up by the "Ear piercing fife and spirit stirring drum" of another, which is in turn echoed by another, till every drum corps of the brigade, with accompanying bugles and fifes, join in the din, and the morning air is resonant with the rattle of drums, the shrill notes of the fife, or the clarion tones of the bugle, sounding reveille. At the last tap of the drum every man is supposed to be "up and dressed" the companies are formed, the roll called by the first sergeants, and woe to the absentees! "Extra duty" is the customary punishment of tardiness, and is the horror of a soldier.[50]

Army regulations allowed for the enlistment of field musicians as young as twelve. Soldiers bearing arms were required to be eighteen. For players and fighters alike, however, those numbers were often ignored. Boys of nine and ten found their way into the musical ranks. At enlistment, few could read music; some could not even play an instrument. To survive, they learned fast. They also grew up fast. Boys shy upon enlistment soon learned to "stare the Devil out of countenance and [could not] be beat at cursing, swearing and gambling."[51] On fields of combat these courageous drummer boys of the "sheep-skin batteries" steadfastly beat out their rhythms amidst the rush of war.

There was much music to be learned for these boys who, with the tap of a drum or pipe of a fife, could roust men from sleep or send them to their deaths. Often musical training took place in camp where boys memorized not just the proper calls, but sometimes even learned how to play their instruments. Field musicians learned by rote, few ever learned to read notes.

Some boys received more formal training amidst the spartan conditions of either the School of Practice on Governor's Island in New York Harbor or Newport Barracks in Kentucky. Life there was hardly any easier than that in an army camp, maybe tougher. At Governor's Island, for example, the boys slept two to a bed on hay-filled sack mattresses. The building was without heat or warm water. Standard fare was salted pork or beef and potatoes. When adult supervision lagged there were often hazings, occasionally fist-fights. Every day included hours of lessons and practice on fife or drum. Students followed the rigorous schedule of the military day from reveille to taps.[52]

In the years leading up to the Civil War, army musicians studied from various texts, including Charles Stewart Ashworth's *A New, Useful and Complete System of Drumbeating* (1812) and Elias Howe's *School for the Fife* (1851).[53] In 1862, the army adopted George B. Bruce and Daniel Decatur Emmett's *The Drummers and Fifers Guide*. Bruce, a percussionist, had served as drum major in the band of the 7th New York Militia and taught at the School of Practice. Emmett had been a fifer in the 6th Infantry Regiment of the Regular Army, though he was best known as minstrel performer and composer of "Dixie." Their method book contained 148 pieces, all which were expected to be memorized. This was the standard text until 1869 when Gardiner A. Strube's *Drum and Fife Instructor* appeared. Of the three books, Bruce and Emmett's is the most complex in terms of the amount of material and difficulty.

Once in camp, field musicians sounded out the duties of the day with clocklike precision. Their duties were organized into three categories: regulatory calls, tactical signals, and various other obligations neither regulatory nor tactical. Regulatory calls organized the day, starting with the "Drummers' Call" at dawn and ending with "Taps." Tactical signals relayed field commands, such as instructions to march slower or faster, wheel a column left or right, rally to the flag, load and fire, or charge, halt, and retreat. These calls were shared between regiments, but were not fully standardized. Literally hundreds co-existed side by side.[54] The sundry duties of category three included providing music for dress parades or entertainment, funerals, cheers, discharges, and the meting out of corporal and capital punishments.[55]

There was an extensive amount of music to memorize. "Reveille" alone was made up of a sequence of six tunes and rhythms. Some are still familiar today. The series began with "Three Camps, or Points of War," and followed with "Slow Scotch," "Austrian," "Hessian," "Prussian," and "Quick Scotch." Sometimes additional tunes were inserted. Melodies were lively, replete with angular and snappy dotted rhythms. The accompanying drum parts were thick with driving rolls and ornamented notes. Tunes were attached one to the next by drum rolls and the whole cycle took nearly ten minutes to perform.[56] Through the course of a camp day, soldiers responded to at least eighteen different standard regulatory calls, including: "Assembly," "Guard Mounting," calls to meals or the infirmary, and, as the day came to a close, "Retreat" followed by "Tattoo," the return to quarters.

Early on, at least, much of the music was poorly played. Stories of incompetence are legion and frustrated commanders were sometimes driven to extremes. Colonel Ames of the 20th Maine Infantry, for example, was so incensed by the bumbling field musicians during his regiment's first dress parade that he "charged the drums corps with his sword" in order to shut them up.[57]

Pity the raw musicians, whose sense for music lagged well behind their spirit for adventure. Many must have been like young Charles W. Bardeen, who by July 1862 (and at the tender age of fourteen) was a member of the 1st Massachusetts Infantry drum corps. Bardeen wanted to enlist sooner but his age deterred him—until he thought of becoming a musician, that is. "I don't know why I did not happen to think of getting in as a drummer boy; perhaps because I didn't know how to drum or have any means of learning, though as I afterward discovered, that was no obstacle," he wrote.[58] Once in the army, Bardeen found his drum a lousy companion, too heavy to carry and too difficult to play. Daunted, but plucky, he switched to fife, "glad

Drum corps of 61st New York Infantry, Falmouth, Virginia. Library of Congress, Prints & Photographs Division.

enough to turn in an instrument that I played so poorly."[59] Unskilled though he was, Bardeen was probably no worse than many. Corporal Dan Owen Mason of the 6th Vermont Infantry was already in the army when he managed to get himself assigned duties as bugler. He found the job description attractive: no guard duty or drills, the possibility of better pay, and the chance to stay back near the Colonel during combat. He knew little about music.[60]

Whatever their instruments, these boys soon learned how to please their audiences. And with so much time to practice, they also became more than proficient. The best of these musicians may have been downright fabulous. F. H. Buffum remembered a drummer boy whose "arms [were] playing all about him like forked lightning, his drumsticks rattling down upon the doomed head like half a dozen magnificent hailstorms, each combination of sounds welling up and flying off like distinct peals of thunder with no room for reverberation between the claps."[61] Drummer boy Delavan S. Miller, was barely thirteen when he followed his father and joined the 2nd New York Artillery. When he and his mates played, the soldiers listened. He remem-

Drum corps, 93d New York Infantry, Bealeton, Virginia. Library of Congress, Prints & Photographs Division.

bered that "When a dozen or more of the lads, with their caps set saucily on the sides of their heads, led a regiment in a review with their get-out-of-the-way-Old-Dan-Tuckerish style of music, it made the men in the ranks step off as though they were bound for a Donnybrook fair or some other pleasure excursion."[62]

These boys could lighten the darkest event. Miller remembered the funeral of a fellow drummer boy who died in the fall of 1862:

> The next Sabbath afternoon with muffled drums and slow, measured tread, we escorted his remains to a little knoll 'neath a clump of pines near Arlington. The chaplain said "Earth to earth, ashes to ashes, dust to dust." A volley was fired over the grave, our drums unmuffled and back to camp we went, beat[ing] a lively quickstep.
>
> "Fold him in his country's stars,
> Roll the drums and fire the volley!

> What to him are all our wars,
> What but death be mocking folly!"[63]

The boys saw their share of death. When not on the front lines they could often be found working as stretcher bearers or in the field hospitals. George T. Ulmer of the 8th Maine Infantry remembered the horror of Civil War medicine as he experienced it at age sixteen:

> My duty was to hold a sponge or "cone" of ether to the face of the soldier who was to be operated on, and to stand there and see the surgeons cut and saw legs and arms as if they were cutting up swine or sheep, it was an ordeal I never wish to go through again. At intervals, when the pile became large, I was obliged to take a load of legs or arms and place them in a trench nearby for burial.[64]

Field musicians were sometimes also called upon to administer corporal punishments. Augustus Meyers, who once received thirty days in the guard-house for refusing to whip a man, wrote that:

> It had always been the custom in the army for flogging to be administered by one of the musicians. Why they were selected to do it, I never learned. When all was ready the officer of the day called one of the older boys from the ranks. He was handed the rawhide and told . . . to strike the prisoner hard blows from the shoulders to the loins.[65]

At least three boys received the Congressional Medal of Honor for their bravery under fire. Eleven-year-old drummer Willie Johnston of the 3rd Vermont Infantry became the country's youngest Medal of Honor recipient for his gallantry during the Seven Days Battles of the Peninsula Campaign. Fifteen-year-old fifer Julian Scott, also of the 3rd Vermont, won the Medal of Honor for bravery during the same engagement. Fourteen-year-old drummer Orion P. Howe of the 55th Illinois Infantry earned his a year later at Vicksburg where, although severely wounded and under continuing enemy fire, he refused to leave the field until he had informed General Sherman of his regiment's need for ammunition. Another famous drummer was Johnny Clem, the "drummer boy of Chickamagua," who ran away from home at age nine and tagged along as a drummer boy with the 22nd Michigan Infantry. Clem was formally enlisted as a drummer after a shell smashed his drum at Shiloh, an act that earned him the sobriquet "Johnny Shiloh." Clem soon exchanged his drum for a musket because he "did not like to stand and be shot at without shooting back." He earned the "drummer boy of Chickamagua" title after shooting a Confederate colonel off his horse in that battle. Clem went on to make the army his career. He retired in 1916 as a major general.[66]

Some regiments trained to take combat commands from drum cadences and bugle melodies. The idea was that these instruments might be heard more easily than a voice above the din of battle. Union General Daniel Butterfield took this idea a step further by creating an easily recognizable preliminary bugle call that imitated the cadence of his name. Under combat situations, the call preceded a tactical order so that Butterfield's soldiers knew the order was intended specifically for them. The call's rhythm fit with the following words, which the men would sometimes sing: "Dan, Dan, Dan, Butterfield, Butterfield." In the more trying of circumstances, "if the going promised to be rough," they sometimes sang "Damn, Damn, Damn, Butterfield, Butterfield."[67]

"Dan" or "Damn," conducting combat maneuvers by musical call took practice. Butterfield evidently pushed his men hard. Wrote Major Fredrick C. Winkler of the 26th Wisconsin Infantry from Lookout Valley in a letter from April 29, 1864:

> We had a grand division drill yesterday under the direction of General Butterfield. We went through the manoeuvres of a battle on one side; our infantry fired about thirty rounds of blank cartridges, and the artillery was not at all sparing of ammunition. It was a very interesting and instructive drill. This afternoon we had brigade drill again, thus you see we keep at it pretty rigidly. To-morrow we have division drill by bugle sound. These are things that we never practiced in our old brigade and division; we are, therefore, much behind and have to work and study to keep up.[68]

Few regiments met Butterfield's standards. Some gave it a half-hearted try, however. Cornet player Julius Leinbach of the 26th North Carolina recorded one such affair that took place in 1863 under the command of General William W. Kirkland, who also wanted bugle calls for his brigade drill. To his dismay, Leinbach was selected. He wrote of the event that:

[Kirkland] had sent a copy of tactics in which the various calls were given, and I was to memorize a few but there were so many and I could not know what commands he would give, that I was much in the condition of a small boy going to school without knowing his lessons. I had this consolation however, that if I did not know the different calls, neither did the General, nor the men and so if I gave the wrong one, no one would be the wiser, so I put on a bold front as I walked up to headquarters at the appointed hour. I was put on a "fiery" steed and followed the General as he rode to the parade ground. I could well imagine that the under officers and men were wondering what sort of circus performance was to come off.

The general gave his command as for instance, "By Batallion, Right Wheel," which was repeated by the regimental and company officers. Then instead of saying, "March," I was to give the pre-scribed call for that maneuver. Sometimes I remembered the cor-rect call, mostly I knew no more than the veriest dunce in the ranks as to what tomes I should play, but I blasted out something all the same and it answered the purpose. For two hours, this farce was kept up and then we rode back to camp, wiser men. I was never asked to repeat the performance.[69]

Butterfield is also associated with the field call "Taps," which was introduced into military tradition in July 1862 at Harrison's Landing, Virginia. Elements of the melody were derived from a tattoo long in use within the American military. Butterfield, with the assistance of brigade bugler Oliver Wilcox Nor-ton of the 83rd Pennsylvania Volunteers, is credited with molding those notes into their present form.[70]

Bands in the Field

Bands added to the spectacle and improved the quality of military life. In concert settings, regimental bands provided entertainment. On the battle-field, their patriotic airs helped shore up frightened men. When staffed by competent musicians, bands were a source of considerable pride. On parade, regiments showed off their bands with the élan of an officer carrying a fancy dress sword. Music's brassy flamboyance encouraged men to stand taller and added snap to a marching column.

Early in the war, entire bands, sometimes made up of already functioning civilian ensembles, enlisted with the regiments of their choice. This was often done concurrently with the regiment's recruitment or mustering into service because high-quality music making could help spur on new enlistments. This was especially true in the war's first year when naïve visions of war's glory, an idea so easily portrayed through military music, still overshadowed the bloody reality.

Fighting soldiers and bandsmen alike rushed to the enlistment offices in the spring and summer of 1861. The conflict, they were told, would soon be over and they did not want to miss their chance to "see the elephant." Many enlisted for three-month terms. That would be plenty of time to win the war, people thought.

Even in this short period, bandsmen could have many memorable experiences. The acclaimed Providence-based American Brass Band, for example, enlisted with the 1st Regiment Rhode Island Militia in April 1861 and was discharged the following July. During that time, the band performed for President Lincoln, served with the medical corps at 1st Bull Run, and performed for any number of dress parades.

Not all tours of duty were so rich, however. Consider the July to October 1861 enlistment of the 13th Illinois Infantry band. Morale was so low and ennui so high that a system of twenty-five-cent fines (soon raised to fifty cents) had to be assessed to players who skipped out on rehearsals. Even that failed to deter some of the more wayward members.[71] The band of the 5th Connecticut Infantry could not have played even if they wanted to. Their instruments were lost or destroyed during the 1862 Union defeats in the Shenandoah Valley.[72] Such fiascos were common. The band of the 48th Ohio Infantry lost their instruments at Shiloh.[73] Both bands were mustered out of service shortly thereafter.

Weighing the various successes and failures of the army's many bands, Congress decided relatively early on that music's expenses generally eclipsed the benefits. A bill was passed (and approved by President Lincoln) on July 17, 1862, that slashed music expenditures. The War Department's subsequent General Order 91 of July 29, 1862, reduced band leaders' pay from $105.50 to $45 monthly. Bands were eliminated at the regimental level and reassigned at the brigade level (every four regiments). Records are murky, but in all, General Order 91 may have eliminated some 300 bands from service.[74] This may not have been a bad thing. The cutbacks purged any number of incompetent instrumentalists from the military.

Even with roster reductions, there would be plenty of music in the army, including as many as 100 brigade bands by war's end. In addition, some fifty regiments, perhaps more, found a way around the order and retained, sometimes even funded, their own bands. They did this partly as a matter of regional pride (brigades were less homogeneous and tended to combine regiments from broader geographic areas) and partly because they wanted guaranteed access to music. After Antietam, the 24th Michigan Volunteer Infantry, for example, mustered out the field musicians and kept their band.[75] The musicians were finally eliminated two years later after the bloody fight at Spotsylvania when, "its members [were] distributed among the woefully thin companies . . . [because] a band was a luxury the unit could no longer afford."[76] Musicians in the 2nd Minnesota performed as a band but were listed, and doubled, as field musicians. Buglers in the 1st New York Volunteer Dragoons apparently also doubled as a band.[77] The 7th New York Infantry remained so closely attached to its band that for each of its three separate three-month enlistment periods in 1861, 1862, and 1863, the regiment was automatically accompanied by its famous band, led by Claudio Grafulla. Men of the peripatetic Repasz Band (founded in 1831) of Williamsport, Pennsylvania, were so determined to serve that they took assignments with three different regiments: the 11th Pennsylvania Infantry in 1861, the 29th Pennsylvania Infantry in 1862, and finally (though not listed as a band in the regiment roster), with the 8th Pennsylvania Cavalry. They stayed with that unit until the end of the war.[78]

Soldiers sometimes paid their musicians directly. Writing to his brother from Antietam Creek on October 1, 1862, Edward King Wightman of the 9th New York Volunteer Infantry noted that his regiment's band, "one of the finest in the service," was "supported by a contribution of 25¢ per month from each member (and from $400 to $500 from officers)" and this despite the fact that the band "had been left behind as useless during the fighting season."[79] The 13th Connecticut Infantry, stationed in New Orleans for two years beginning in April 1862, raised funds to hire a seventeen-member band under the direction of Southerner Charles Brother. Just weeks earlier, the same ensemble had been at the battle of Shiloh, where they were attached to the Confederacy. With the Yankees, Brother's band was on hand at the battles of Labadieville, Irish Bend, Franklin, and others.[80]

The repertoire of a good military band was widely varied. Band books contained marches and patriotic melodies, popular songs, and traditional dances (polkas, waltzes, schottisches, and reels), hymns, and even operatic

transcriptions. An October 5, 1861, Boston concert given by the Gilmore
Band (attached to the 24th Massachusetts Infantry) opened with the overture
to Rossini's *The Barber of Seville*. The program continued with polkas,
marches, a clarinet solo, and additional operatic fare. Frank Rauscher, leader
of the fourteen-piece 114th Pennsylvania band recorded an 1863 concert for
General Meade and other officers at army headquarters in Culpepper, Virginia. That program opened with "Hell on the Rappahannock" and continued
with operatic selections. Rauscher was proud of his band's skill with this
orchestral repertoire. It was, he wrote, "Such a selection as . . . had probably
never been given at the Headquarters in the field by any of the army
bands."[81] Confederate band books were equally eclectic. The books of the
26th North Carolina Infantry band contained dances, Irish traditional songs,
selections composed in honor of Confederate regiments and officers ("21st
Regiment Quickstep" and "Col. Kirkland's March"), and transcriptions from
Italian, French, and German operas ("Trovatore Quickstep," " 'The Prophete'
March," and "Quartet from the Opera 'Sharp Shooter' " [*Der Freischütz*]).
North and South, concerts might also have included vocal soloists and sing-
a-longs, banjo or fiddle performances, and perhaps even a display of rudi-
mental drumming.

Bands got their music from a variety of sources. The more skilled groups
wrote their own arrangements. Bands also often exchanged music with another. There was also a small-scale band music publishing industry (though
output was modest in comparison to song sheet music). *Dodworth's Brass
Band School* included eleven straightforward and mostly homophonic band
arrangements in transposed score format. Among the included titles were
"Yankee Doodle," "Star-Spangled Banner," "Hail to the Chief," "Home,
Sweet Home," and "Marseillaise Hymn." The *Brass Band Journal* of 1854
offered twenty-four arrangements. Many of these selections were duplicates
of Dodworth's book, but the arrangements were more difficult to perform.
Also used during the war were *The Companion* (1854), Patrick Gilmore's
Brass Band Music (1859), and the *Journal for Brass Bands*, which was published in serial form and included selections from *Il trovatore, Lucrezia Borgia*, and other operas. In all of these publications, melodies were generally
given to the E-flat soprano cornet, sometimes doubled in unison or at the
octave by an E-flat or B-flat cornet.

Many of the tunes above, and even the specific arrangements, made it into
hand-copied band books. Although surviving band books are rare, Union
examples can be examined in the collections of the Wisconsin State

Historical Society (3rd Wisconsin Volunteers) and the Manchester [New Hampshire] Historical Society (perhaps from the 4th New Hampshire).[82] Sets of books from the "Port Royal Band" under the direction of Gustavus Ingalls are held at the Library of Congress, as well as the New Hampshire Historical Society and New Hampshire Antiquarian Society, in Concord and Hopkinton respectively. The Moravian Music Foundation in Winston-Salem holds six sets of books that once belonged to the 26th North Carolina band.

Esteemed Bands

There were many important bands and renowned band leaders. Irish-born bandleader, composer, and cornetist Patrick Gilmore was one of the best. In his early thirties at the time the war broke out, Gilmore had taken over the Boston Brigade Band in 1859 and changed its name to the Gilmore Band. Shortly thereafter, he presented a successful summer series on the Boston Common as well as winter programs in Boston Music Hall. In October 1861 Gilmore and the entire band enlisted in the 24th Massachusetts Volunteers. They traveled with the regiment as it fought with General Burnside's corps in Virginia and North Carolina. As recorded in *Dwight's Journal*:

> Gilmore's celebrated band has been engaged to accompany Col. Stephenson's Regiment to the war. The band will consist of *sixty-eight pieces*, including twenty drummers and twelve buglers. Such a band was never enjoyed by a regiment before, and it will probably incite the men to heroic deeds if loyal men can need any new stimulus in such a time as this. The band will appear three times more before the Boston public at the Promenade Concerts.[83]

The band, with its combination of woodwinds and brass, was evidently equally impressive during its tour in North Carolina. Wrote John to his girlfriend Fannie L. Partridge in April 1862:

> I don't know what we should have done without our band. It is acknowledged by everyone to be the best in the division. Every night about sundown Gilmore gives us a splendid concert, playing selections from the operas and some very pretty marches, quicksteps, waltzes and the like, most of which are composed by himself or by Zohler, a member of his band. . . . Thus you see we get a great deal of *new* music, notwithstanding we are off here in the

Bandmaster Patrick S. Gilmore. Library of Congress, Prints & Photographs Division.

woods. Gilmore used to give some of the most fashionable we had
at home and we lack nothing but the stringed instruments now.
In place however we have five reed instruments, of which no other
band can boast.[84]

The Gilmore Band was mustered out of service in accordance with the War
Department's General Order 91 and Gilmore returned to Boston in September 1862. There he reinstituted his Boston Music Hall series at reduced rates
from his prewar price. As was typical of the time, repertoire for the concerts
was decidedly eclectic. It ranged in style and emotional affect from minstrel
tunes like Stephen Foster's "Oh! Susanna," to "The Star-Spangled Banner,"
to French composer Charles Gounod's "Ave Maria."

Gilmore was rarely far from the war. In 1863, at the request of Massachusetts Governor Andrew, he helped organize the bands of the state militia.
His own band was busy as well. The Gilmore Band played at both the 1863
Boston send-off and 1865 homecoming of the 54th Massachusetts Volunteer
Infantry.[85]

These were important services but Gilmore is better remembered for his
concert of March 4, 1864 when he organized a band of 510 musicians and
a chorus of 5,000 American flag-waving children to perform in New Orleans
as part of the festivities surrounding the inauguration of Michael Hahn as
governor of Louisiana. The event was the first in a series of ever more gargantuan concerts that would culminate in 1872 with the Boston-based World
Peace Jubilee.

What Gilmore was to Boston, so was the Dodworth family to New York
City. Trombonist Thomas Dodworth (1790–1876) and his eldest son Allen
had arrived in New York from England in 1828. Shortly afterwards, both
joined the Independent Band of New York, a group formed in 1825 by William Peterschen and Thomas Dilks. After an 1834 instrumentation change
to all brass, the band went through a number of personnel and name
changes. It eventually emerged in 1836 as the Dodworth Band. Thus began
a New York institution.

It was Allen's younger brother Harvey (1822–1891), the conductor of the
13th New York Regiment Band since 1839, who was to direct the Dodworth
Band during the war. Harvey took over the group from Allen in 1860 while
also keeping control of the 13th Regiment Band. At the beginning of the
war, Harvey, his younger brother Thomas (1830–1896), and the rest of the
Dodworth Band took on a three-month Union enlistment.[86] During their

term of service, and in addition to performing, band members helped attend to the wounded at the Battle of 1st Bull Run. When their enlistment expired, the musicians returned to New York City where the brothers continued to teach music and perform with the band.

Stationed in Washington was the Civil War's most visible ensemble, the United States Marine Band, formed in 1798 under the direction of Drum Major William Farr. From 1855 to 1871 the band was under the leadership of Francis Scala, who oversaw its expansion and rise in importance. Neapolitan by birth and a virtuoso E-flat clarinetist, Scala had immigrated to the United States after entering the U.S. Navy in 1841. He joined the Marine Band in 1842, when the ensemble consisted of only ten or twelve field musicians. Under Scala's leadership the band would gradually grow until it reached a membership of thirty-two in 1862. That same year Congress raised the organization's status from an ensemble of field musicians to that of concert band. Throughout the war, the Marine Band frequently performed concerts at the White House, the Capital, and Lafayette Park, offering a varied repertoire ranging from patriotic favorites to the latest operatic literature. The group also functioned as a dance band at balls and other social functions. The band played at Lincoln's inauguration festivities as well as at Gettysburg for the November 19, 1863, dedication of the national cemetery at that site.

Other important early military bands included the one at West Point, which began to play concerts around 1816; the 4th Artillery Band, which was placed at Fortress Monroe in 1825 and stayed through the Civil War (even though its regiment had long been transferred elsewhere); and the Navy Academy Band, which was formed in 1853 by John Phillip Pfeiffer and stationed in Newport, Rhode Island, during the war.

Contributing to the rising esteem of military band music in the years immediately preceding the war was Elmer Ephraim Ellsworth, who in 1859 took command of the hapless Chicago-based National Guard Cadets and turned them into the nation's finest drill team. A lawyer by profession, Ellsworth modeled his ensemble on the steely brilliance with which the French marched and deployed their armies to the signals of bugle and drum. He outfitted his men in the style of the French colonial army in Algeria (baggy pants and short jackets, fezzes and gaiters), renamed the ensemble the United States Zouave Cadets, and taught them to follow complex rifle and marching drills. In the summer of 1860, the Cadets toured eastern cities where they defeated in competition every drill team that dared challenge

Band of the 114th Pennsylvania Infantry. Library of Congress, Prints & Photographs Division.

them. Thousands attended the performances. The Cadets became the paradigm that other drill units would emulate.[87]

One such regiment was the 114th Pennsylvania Volunteers (known as the Collis Zouaves) of the Army of the Potomac. Organized in 1861 by Charles H. T. Collis, this well-disciplined regiment imitated exactly the dress of the French Zouaves: red pants and white leggings, Zouave jacket, blue sash, and white turbans. The regiment's cornet band had been formed before the war and was directed by Frank Rauscher, who left important memoirs of his time in the service. The band was a favorite of General Meade.[88]

There were fewer Confederate bands than Union bands. This was partly because there were fewer available musicians, but brass instruments were also less available (though guitars and violins occasionally filled out a band's instrumentation). Perhaps most important, however, was the fact that the increasingly undermanned Confederates needed their men to fight more than they needed them to play. Section 75, Article XII of the 1863 Regulations stated that musicians could be called upon to serve in the ranks if needed. They often were.

The most famous Confederate ensemble was the Stonewall Brigade Band, which was formed in 1855 as the Mountain Saxhorn Band of Staunton, Virginia. The band quickly established a reputation for itself. It performed for President Pierce, as well as 1860 presidential candidates Stephen A. Douglas and John C. Breckinridge. With the outbreak of the Civil War, the Mountain Saxhorn Band joined General Jackson's 1st Brigade, Army of the Shenandoah. The band was given the name "Stonewall Brigade Band" after Jackson earned the "Stonewall" moniker for his fortitude at 1st Manassas (known in the Union as 1st Bull Run). In late 1862, below Fredericksburg and along the Rappahannock River, the band alternated concert pieces with Federal bands on the opposite shore. The band remained active after the war, including a performance at Grant's funeral in 1885. As late as 1900, six members of the Civil War–era configuration continued to play in the band. The band still performs today. Current members claim to have in their possession the only complete, unbroken set of Confederate band instruments in existence.[89]

Another highly acclaimed Confederate band was that of the 26th North Carolina Regiment under the direction of cornet player Samuel T. Mickey and made up of Moravians, a German Methodist sect well respected for their musical abilities. Sporting elegant brass-buttoned non-regulation uniforms, the Salem-based band enlisted in March 1862 with eight brass players and no drummer. (At various points during the war it would reach a full compliment of twelve.) In addition to military duties, the band performed at church functions and fund-raising events. Despite bouts of yellow fever, malaria, typhoid, dysentery, and other illnesses that killed at least one member, the band stayed on until their capture outside Richmond on April 5, 1865.

Instrumentation and Sound

For most ensembles, instrumentation varied according to available personnel. Musicians themselves made due with whatever instruments were available. Yet, these accommodations do not mean there was no sense of what an ideal instrumental arrangement might consist. Generally accepted was the format outlined in *Dodworth's Brass Band School*. Dodworth asserted that bandsmen should strive for balance across an instrumental range that he divided into six categories: soprano, alto, tenor, baritone, bass, and contrabass. A minimum ensemble of four brass players should include E-flat soprano, B-flat alto, tenor, and bass, for example. Then, as the ensemble's

The 26th North Carolina Band. Courtesy of The Moravian Music Foundation, Inc.

size increased, instrumentation additions would solidify important timbres, expand pitch range, and fill in gaps. A six-member ensemble would double the soprano and tenor. Should a seventh instrument be added, it should be a contrabass.[90]

Despite instrumentation differences between ensembles, period bands had a distinctive sound. This was due to the use of conical-bored tubing and mouthpieces that produced a mellower tone than today's more common cylindrical-bored tubing. Instruments had a variety of shapes, with bells facing back, front, or up. Backward-facing bells were most popular on the march so that troops in the rear could hear. The cavalry preferred either backward or upward facing bells so that the sound would be directed away from the horse's ears. Of course, because over-the-shoulder instruments sounded best when musicians turned away from the audience, they were inferior concert instruments. And as Bufkin notes, it is unlikely that musicians would have felt comfortable turning their backs on ranking officers, even if this might have improved the sound.[91] Some instruments had a swiveling mouthpiece that would allow the bell to be directed either over the shoulder or upwards.

Melodies were generally played by the first E-flat soprano cornet and often doubled at the octave with a B-flat cornet. Bass lines tended to stay with the roots of the chords and were often doubled by E-flat and B-flat horns, in unison or at the octave. Chord progressions were simple, rarely venturing past tonic, subdominant, and dominant relationships. Bands generally played in the flat keys of B-flat, E-flat, and A-flat. Meters were generally confined to 2/4, 3/4, and 6/8 time. Instruments were often cheaply made, the metal soft and thin. Tuning deviated considerably between manufacturers. Intonation and timbre problems were compounded because many bands played with instruments of mixed design and manufacture. Thus, sounds were not homogeneous.

Musical Quality

These various instrumental discrepancies, when combined with substandard musicianship, made for some dreadful music making. Wrote James J. Kirkpatrick of the 16th Mississippi Volunteers in his diary on October 30, 1863:

> Camp, 2 miles South of the Rappahannock. Drilling as usual. Went over to the Band in the evening to hear some vocal and instrumental music. Our band is a great institution. It always keeps its numbers undiminished, and labors with the greatest assiduity at "tooting." Their music, however, is never the sweetest nor most harmonious.[92]

Timothy H. Pendergast of the 2nd Minnesota Infantry wrote that his band was so incompetent that the camp mules mistook the ensemble's braying for the sounds of an incoming wagon train.[93] Events surrounding performances of the band of the 13th New Hampshire Volunteer Infantry surpassed dreadful and entered the absurd. S. Millet Thompson wrote in his diary that:

> While the Band is playing at guard-mounting this morning, the valves in the instruments keep freezing, and the music is very bad indeed—a compound of squeaks, yelps and blares. After a little, a small dog—a homely small dog—appears and coolly takes a seat on the ground, a little way to the front of the Band, looks the players full in the face, screws his own face into the most comical,

droll and pitiful expression, and begins to whine and howl. He proceeds with his accompaniment all the time while the Band is playing. The scene is a severe strain upon military discipline, nearly causing both Band and guard to break up in laughter. Inasmuch, however, as no one has been specially detailed to kick that particular dog, Army Regulations cannot permit any interference. Later, by special order, this dog is excluded from parades.[94]

Incompetence was often amplified by alcohol. Spirits of all qualities were readily available and caused problems at all levels within the armies. Occasionally, drink led to musical bedlam. William Wiley of the 77th Illinois Infantry wrote in his diary that, "All was excitement after the colonel fell [in combat]. Lem Wiley had got pretty full and went taring around and falling down over roots and brush until he mashed his bugle as flat as a pancake."[95] Liquor was such a problem in the 7th Ohio Infantry band that a ten-dollar fine was instituted for each incidence of drunkenness. In at least one instance, bad playing was actually rewarded with drink. Wrote Robert Sneden of the 40th New York Volunteers on July 23, 1862:

> Regimental bands were serenading at each general's headquarters after dark. That which serenaded General Kearny must have been the worst one in the army. It was a regular "sheet iron band," I did not learn of which regiment. General Kearny gave this band a gallon of whiskey "to go *away!*" It was [a] "regular circus."[96]

Soldiers' letters and diaries suggest that morale was also difficult to maintain. Missouri bandmaster Charles Monroe Chase had a laundry list of complaints about his musical comrades. He wrote in his diary on August 2, 1861, that:

> It is a tedious thing for me to drill the band when interest and ambition flags. I want to see every member in his place at the proper time, ready and anxious for the word "play . . ." I have anticipated that laziness would sometime seize the band, that band practice would seem like work, like above, that members would want to beg off, that they would conclude their health was endangered by a little work—and in fact that anything and everything would "turn up" to prevent work in the band. But I have firmly concluded that when that time arrives I want a discharge from the

service. I won't be connected with a lazy loafing Brass Band, the
desire to hear and to make *good music* is stimulating enough to
me to induce labor for nothing, but labor will get up good music.
And he who thinks he plays well enough is no musician . . . But
members seem unwilling to get their parts by themselves, they
prefer lying around the tent to studying like *earnest musicians.*[97]

Yet while the dearth of "earnest" musicians may have infuriated Chase, his
band could hardy have been busier. Writing in his diary less than two weeks
earlier on July 22, 1861, Chase described a day of band duty:

At eight this morning we performed duty mounting guard. It is
this, we play one quickstep for the guard to march onto the
ground, then a waltz or whatever we please for inspection of arms,
then a slow march and march to the head of the ground, then
turn, cheer and march back to place on a quickstep, then a short
quickstep to march the guard off. The boys want to get off this
duty as it consists of the same thing as dress parade. Our regular
duty at mounting guard and dress parade requires nine times per
day. After mounting guard we proceeded to the court house and
drilled an hour and a half.[98]

Bands stationed in the east could have similarly draining schedules:

A brigade band in the 9th Army Corps received orders December
14, 1864, that after guard mount in the morning each man should
practice by himself for one hour, that at 2 p.m. the full band
should play at headquarters for one and a half hours, and at 4
p.m. the band should play for dress parade. Moreover, after the
parade, "a few pieces" had to be played in front of the brigade
commander's quarters, and that evening rehearsal should last
from 6 to 8 p.m. making a total of 7 $1/2$ hours per day for each
man.[99]

Hardworking as many of these bands appear to have been, sometimes winter
weather made playing brass instruments impossible. When this was the case,
the musicians turned to other entertainments. Wrote "Wisconsin's Singing
Soldier" Edwin Kimberley to his parents in Brodhead on January 14, 1862,
from Frederick, Maryland:

We are getting the coldest weather; our instruments freeze almost every time we go out to play. We are now enjoying ourselves for the first time since we left home; we do have bully times; only have to play twice a day or once, the remainder of the time we sing, dance, play fiddles. And we have a dance every night, one of our boys being the best fiddler in the regt.[100]

Even when well played, music was not for everybody. Nor was it for all occasions. Wrote Walter Lord, who edited the diary of British Colonel Arthur James Fremantle:

The Confederates loved to have bands around, and they were kept playing whenever possible. General Dick Taylor describes how his Louisiana Creoles pulled up after a long march to support Stonewall Jackson, and immediately started their band going with a waltz. They were newcomers or they probably wouldn't have tried such levity directly in front of Jackson, who was perched on a fence watching them and, as usual, sucking a lemon. "Thoughtless fellows for serious work," was his only remark.[101]

While Jackson sometimes found music frivolous, the Union's General Grant seems not to have appreciated it at all. For Grant, "the appreciation of music was a lacking sense and the musician's score a sealed book," wrote his aide General Horace Porter. As for Porter himself, he had a keen eye and a cutting wit, if not a sensitive ear. Porter described an encounter with a band that was interrupting Grant's dinner conversation:

[I] offered to go . . . see whether [the band] would obey an order to "cease firing," and my services were promptly accepted. The men were gorgeously uniformed, and the band seemed to embrace every sort of brass instrument ever invented, from a diminutive cornet-à-pistons to a gigantic double-bass horn. . . . The broad-belted band-master was puffing with all the vigor of a quack-medicine advertisement, his eyes were riveted upon the music, and it was not an easy task to attract his attention. Like a sperm-whale, he had come up to blow, and was not going to be put down till he had finished. . . . On my return the general said: "I fear that band-master's feelings have been hurt, but I didn't want him

to be wasting his time upon a person who has no ear for
music."[102]

Historian Bruce Catton describes a review Grant made of the Army of the
Potomac on March 10, 1864:

> [Grant and General Meade] made an occasion of it, and when
> Grant reached headquarters they turned out the guard. The guard
> included a Zouave outfit, 114th Pennsylvania, which had seen
> much hard fighting before the luck of the draw pulled it out of
> combat ranks and assigned it to headquarters, and it was natty
> with baggy red pants, white leggings, short blue jackets, and
> oriental-looking turbans. With the guard came the headquarters
> band, also of the 114th Pennsylvania; a melodious group, distin-
> guished from most of the other army bands by the fact that all of
> the players were always sober when time came to make music. It
> had learned to play the kind of music Meade liked—something
> soft and sweet, usually—and it tootled away vigorously today, quite
> unaware that the lieutenant general [Grant] was completely tone-
> deaf, disliked all music rather intensely, and could not for the life
> of him tell one tune from another.[103]

Bands and Morale

For the average soldier and the military as a whole, however, brass bands
were a boon. Bands rallied spirits on the march and in battle; they conferred
grandeur upon military spectacles in general. A November 20, 1861, Union
review at Bailey's Cross Roads outside of Washington included up to
100,000 soldiers and fifty bands, including General Butterfield's impressive
brigade band of 120 instrumentalists. President Lincoln, members of his
cabinet and their families, and General McClellan all attended.[104]

Stories of music's efficacy pepper diaries and regimental histories. At the
end of a dreary march to camp following the burial of General Joseph Plum-
mer, for example, Francis Buffum of the 14th New Hampshire wrote that
the band:

> wheeled into the head of the column and struck up the most pop-
> ular piece in their *répertoire*. . . . First [came] a cheer, loud and long,
> then a feeling of marvelous refreshment and renewed strength.

The spirits of the men were wonderfully revived; stragglers found
their places in the ranks; the files aligned and closed up. The step
was caught, and the regiment marched into camp easily and with
enthusiasm.[105]

On September 22, 1862, and following the battle at Antietam, a portion of
McClellan's Army of the Potomac was sent fourteen miles southwest to Harper's Ferry. Upon reaching the Potomac on this unseasonably hot day, the
tired and dirty soldiers found the bridges had been destroyed. Misery soon
changed to elation, however, when as the first soldiers plunged into the
swiftly moving waist-deep river, the band struck up "Jordan Is a Hard Road
to Travel." This melody was soon followed with "Dixie," "Yankee Doodle,"
and other songs. Colonel Frederick L. Hitchcock of the 132nd Pennsylvania
remembered the entire division singing along to the band's rendition of
"John Brown's Body."[106]

Perhaps most importantly, bands reinforced the spirit and pride of an
army. James I. Robertson, Jr., with Stonewall Jackson's brigade in Winchester, Virginia, wrote that:

> By 3 p.m. the whole army was in motion, down the dusty streets
> and eastward toward the browning-green hills that rose majesti-
> cally in the afternoon sun. Residents of Winchester lined the
> streets, cheering, singing, and shouting words of encouragement
> to loved ones and relatives. Regimental Bands began to blare out
> lively choruses of "Dixie" and "The Bonnie Blue Flag."[107]

Even in combat men often felt they needed music to do their best. Sneden
attested to this in his diary entry of July 4, 1862 (written at Harrison's Landing, Virginia), in which he recounted his experiences of the previous spring
with General George McClellan and the Army of the Potomac during the
poorly led Peninsula Campaign. The Union army was turned back outside
the Confederate capital of Richmond:

> During the evening the regimental bands played at all the head-
> quarters of generals, lasting until midnight. This is the first music
> we have been treated to since leaving Williamsburg, and was fully
> appreciated by all. All the time we lay in front of Richmond, music
> by the bands was prohibited by General McClellan, so that the
> enemy would not know our position in the woods and swamps of

the Chickahominy. There was no "reveille" or "tattoo" by the drum corps even. No bugles were heard, except during the hours of battle, which then transmitted orders. Consequently the army was continually in low spirits, and fought with less enthusiasm than if the music had been allowed. The only thing that held Hooker's decimated lines . . . at the battle of Williamsburg was the music from a band playing "the Flag of the Free," by General Heintzelman's personal orders. Hooker's men thought reinforcements were close at hand in the woods behind them, when in fact Kearny was struggling through muddy and overcrowded roads two miles in the rear to get to the front. Hooker held on though until Kearny did come up, and dashed at the enemy with victorious results.[108]

The ever aggressive Union General Phil Sheridan was also convinced of the inspirational effect that music could have during combat. He sent bands onto the field at the November 24, 1863, battle of Lookout Mountain. In the March 31, 1865, fight at Dinwiddie Court House (during the Appomattox campaign), Catton writes that Sheridan, "rounded up all of the regimental bands and ordered them to play the gayest tunes they knew—play them loud and keep on playing them, and never mind if a bullet goes through a trombone, or even a trombonist, now and then."[109]

At Chancellorsville, the band of the 14th Connecticut Infantry was ordered to the front to help slow the Union rout. Colonel Frederick L. Hitchcock called this "charge of a band of music" a "most heroic" deed, writing that for twenty minutes, "with shot and shell crashing all about them," the band played national favorites to "magical" effect. "Imagine the strains of our grand national hymn . . . bursting upon your ears out of that horrible pandemonium of panic-born yells, mingled with the roaring of musketry and the crashing of artillery."[110]

Such feats depended on the bravery of the bandsmen. Sometimes they fell short. Following similar orders in the same battle, the band of the 12th New Jersey had "stopped right in the middle of the tune, played 'Yankee' but missed the 'Doodle,' " when the shells came too close.[111]

Music gave spirit and solace to the soldiers at Gettysburg. Wrote James P. Sullivan, a sergeant in company K of the 6th Wisconsin Volunteers of the famed Iron Brigade:

It may seem odd for men to be marching toward their death, singing, shouting and joking as if it were a street parade or a

holiday show. . . . Before we were done cheering [on the news that
Meade had replaced Hooker at the head of the Army of the Po-
tomac], Gettysburg came in sight and our lads straightened up to
pass through in good style, and the brigade band struck up the
"Red, White and Blue," when all at once hell broke loose in front.
The cavalry had found the Johnnies [Confederates] and they were
driving them back on us. The band swung out to one side and
began "Yankee Doodle" in double quick time and "Forward, double quick," sang out the colonel.[112]

In the fight that followed, 160 of the 6th Wisconsin's 360 men were killed,
wounded, or missing in action after they and the rest of the Iron Brigade
attacked and subsequently trapped hundreds of men from the 2nd Mississippi Infantry in an unfinished railroad cut. As a whole, the Iron Brigade
suffered casualties of some 61 percent at Gettysburg. Other units on both
sides fared even worse during those first three days of July 1863.

Even so, the music continued. Confederate musicians at Gettysburg also
found themselves in the thick of battle. Fremantle, who was often shocked
at the "braying" sounds Confederate bands were wont to make, wrote in his
diary that, "When the cannonade was at its height, a Confederate band of
music, between the cemetery and ourselves, began to play polkas and
waltzes, which sounded very curious, accompanied by the hissing and bursting of shells."[113]

The band of the 26th North Carolina was plenty busy those three days in
July. Remembered Julius A. Leinbach:

> It was therefore with heavy hearts that we went about our duties
> caring for the wounded. We worked until 11 o'clock that night. . . .
> At 3 o'clock [the next morning] I was up again and at work. The
> second day our regiment was not engaged [because casualties were
> so high], but we were busily occupied all day in our sad tasks [of
> caring for the wounded]. While thus engaged, in the afternoon we
> were sent . . . to play for the men, and thus, perhaps, [to] cheer
> them somewhat. . . . We accordingly went to the regiment and
> found the men much more cheerful than we were ourselves. We
> played for some time, the 11th N.C. Band playing with us, and the
> men cheered us lustily. Heavy cannonading was going on at the
> time, though not in our immediate front. We learned afterwards,
> from Northern papers, that our playing had been heard across the

lines and caused wonder that we should play while fighting was going on around us. Some little while after we left, a bomb struck and exploded very close to the place where we had been standing, no doubt having been intended for us.

We got back to camp after dark and found many men in need of our attention. Some of those whom we had tried to care for during the day had died during our absence.[114]

Captain D. S. Redding of the 45th Georgia Regiment recorded bands playing such wide-ranging fare as "Listen to the Mocking Bird," "Marseilles," and favorites of the British Isles.[115] The 2nd New Hampshire's band performed as General Longstreet's forces attacked the Union left at the Peach Orchard on July 2; the Union's General Winfield Scott Hancock ordered the Philadelphia Brigade's band to play during the July 3 Confederate artillery barrage on the Union center. Terrible to imagine, but also infinitely moving, is the performance by the Confederate band playing Lowell Mason's hymn "Nearer My God, To Thee" as the grim survivors of Pickett's Charge fell back into their lines following the failed attack. On the morning of July 4, the fighting now over and Lee's army in retreat, Union bands played "The Star-Spangled Banner," "Hail, Columbia," and other national melodies. During the three days of fighting at least two bands put down their music and picked up rifles, the 20th Maine and 12th New Jersey.

Bands were also used to deflate and even confuse the enemy. L. D. Young of the Confederate "Orphan Brigade" wrote that the "softly and sweetly" played "national airs" coming from the Union camps outside Dalton, Georgia, "haunted me for days."[116] In June 1863, and as the Gettysburg Campaign was just getting underway, the undermanned Confederate General Thomas Rosser had his band perform in one location, then quickly move to another, in order to make the enemy think there were multiple bands in the area and thus his force was larger than it really was. During the Atlanta Campaign, Sherman's army used frontline bands to disguise the rumble of moving artillery. Near war's end, music of Confederate bands helped cover the Army of Northern Virginia's nighttime evacuation of Richmond. Unaware of the ruse, "Federal musicians responded . . . with national airs until the night was filled with melody."[117] The Confederate music continued until the musicians were also evacuated and only a picket line remained in place.

Sometimes, bands simply entertained the enemy. Confederate soldiers gathered on a bridge on the Rappahannock River to listen to a Union band before the Battle of Fredericksburg. Colonel James C. Nisbet of the 66th Georgia wrote in his memoirs of a Confederate cornet player along the Kennesaw Mountain line who was much appreciated by the Yankees:

> [He] was the best I have ever heard. In the evening after supper he would come to our salient and play solos. Sometimes when the firing was brisk he wouldn't come. Then the Yanks would call out: "Oh, Johnnie, we want to hear that cornet player."
>
> We would answer: "He would play, but *he's afraid you will spoil his horn!*"
>
> The Yanks would call out: "We will stop shooting."
>
> "All right, Yanks," we would reply. The cornet player would mount our works and play solos from the operas and sing "Come Where My Love Lies Dreaming," or "I Dreamt that I Dwelt in Marble Halls," and other familiar airs. He had an exquisite tenor voice. How the Yanks would applaud! They had a good cornet player who would alternate with our man.[118]

Catton writes of Union bands performing along the Rappahannock River in the winter of 1862–1863 when, after a concert that included both "The Star-Spangled Banner" and "Dixie," 150,000 men from both sides of the river choked back tears as they sang together "Home, Sweet Home."[119] Rufkin cites various (mostly) friendly musical rivalries across the lines. Asbury L. Kerwood of the 57th Indiana Volunteers wrote of a night in which a Union band played "national airs" from the parapets of Fort Wood outside Chattanooga. Soon afterwards, a Confederate band:

> struck up "Dixie," continuing for some time, and when they ceased a cheer went up from their lines. Instantly our own musicians took up the same tune, and when it was finished, a yell went up from our lines, followed by a "bah" from the rebels.[120]

Displeasure with the opposing side's music making sometimes escalated beyond hoots and hollers. Two examples, perhaps remembering the same event, come from Spotsylvania, Virginia. S. Millet Thompson described the affair thus:

> This evening the Band of the Thirteenth goes into the trenches at the front, and indulges in a "competition concert" with a band that

is playing over across in the enemy's trenches. The enemy's Band renders Dixie, Bonnie Blue Flag, My Maryland, and other airs dear to the Southerner's heart. Our Band replies with America, Star Spangled Banner, Old John Brown, etc. After a little time, the enemy's band introduces another class of music; only to be joined almost instantly by our Band with the same tune. All at once the band over there stops, and a rebel battery opens with grape. Very few of our men are exposed, so the enemy wastes his ammunition; while our Band continues its playing, all the more earnestly until all their shelling is over.[121]

Colonel George A. Bruce of the 20th Massachusetts Volunteers remembered soldiers from each side cheering the dueling bands as they played their various "national airs":

When our bands struck up the "Star-Spangled Banner," theirs would break out with "Bonnie Blue Flag," and "America" was matched with "My Maryland." Once when "Old John Brown" was given with much vigor and snap, the rival concert ceased and twenty cannon thundered an answer to the insolent song.[122]

A more gentle across-the-lines musical rivalry was undertaken between the band of the 13th New Hampshire Regiment and the citizens of Hampton, Virginia, during the Peninsula Campaign when:

At one aristocratic mansion . . . a number of young ladies had shut themselves in, and refused to be seen. After a little, our Band is drawn up on their lawn; and a grand vocal and instrumental concert, or serenade, is immediately in full chorus, with many fine male voices rendering popular airs, in rich measure. This proves to be more than the pretty girls can resist, and soon the mansion doors are wide open. Later the Band moves up on the piazza, and with their instruments very near the open windows plays our National airs, responded to by the young ladies at the piano with "Stonewall Jackson," "My Maryland," "Bonnie Blue Flag," and other Southern airs.[123]

While rarely documented, such encounters must have been frequent. Nineteen-year-old Virginian Lucy Rebecca Buck of Front Royal, Virginia, in the Shenandoah Valley was alternately infuriated and moved to tears by the music of the Union bands camped around her home. She wrote in her diary on May 15, 1862, that:

> The band, a very fine brass one[, had] struck up an inspiring air . . . and had the performers been any other than they were, I should have enjoyed it unspeakably. . . . As it was, I liked it until they struck up "Yankee Doodle" and "Dixie"—*that* would not do *any way* [so we] gave them to understand by turning our backs to the window and dropping the curtains. . . . We were a good deal provoked and I had just gone to Grandma's room to try and regain my temper by reading when another band more magnificent than the first commenced discoursing sweet music under the windows. Dear absent brothers! when they played the "Mocking Bird," "Annie Laurie," "The Dearest Spot on Earth" and "Be Kind to the Loved Ones at Home," songs so often sung together in our home in so many happier hours—I could not restrain my tears.

After this, however, the new band also played "Yankee Doodle." Buck fell into a fit of rage. Suffering from a headache, she:

> begged Father and Ma to let me go into the parlor and play "Johnston's March to Manassas" as a restorative. They consented provided I would not announce the name, as they thought it unnecessary to aggravate the Yankees.

Hardly aggravated, the bandsmen seem to have appreciated the music. They returned two days later with their own arrangement of the piece. That was too much for Ms. Buck, who fumed that:

> A company of Yankees came in about four o'clock the band playing "Johnston's March to Manassas." Thieves! they come to steal our liberty, steal our property, our slaves, and, not satisfied with this robbery, actually steal our *National music*, which I should think would be the very last thing they would desire to do.[124]

There were also challenges thrown down between bands within their own armies. Kimberley described one such event in a letter from Etoway, Georgia, in September of 1864 where he was serving as leader of the regimental band for the 3rd Wisconsin Infantry under Sherman. The following incident developed after his band had been making the rounds through the various army encampments serenading officers and doctors:

> Another band struck up about 50 rods from us, which proved to be a band of the regiment we had just left. They were a very fine Band, they would play a piece and then we would. After playing 3 or 4 pieces we then played a new piece we had just learned, a fine thing; after finishing it, they struck up with the *same thing*, which of course was considered an insult. Our boys then swore they would run them out, determined to play the last piece, and then their band also made the same determination that they would play the last piece and run the D——d Badgers out. Of course, on such occasions both bands had been drinking freely and were excited and [illegible] to no small pitch. . . . as soon as they would finish a piece we were ready to start in playing every piece they did if we had it. They sent a man over so to see what we had to say and we done the same. Their colonel was with them and swore he would hang the first man that gave out. The whole affair was just like a hard contested battle. At one o'clock we were still going in. As quick as they would stop we would start right in. We were determined to play till 8 o'clock in the morning if necessary. The Doctor said he would get us some breakfast. Liquor was set out on a table for the boys to drink just when they had a mind to. Both bands kept on till 3 o'clock; it was their turn to play but they failed to come out. We waited patiently. Our spy came back and informed us they had given up. We played Yankee Doodle *double quick* the boys shouting *Victory!* We had whipped them and forced a retreat. It was the most interesting affair I have experienced for a long while.[125]

Bands were also needed for dishonorable discharges, executions, and other unpleasant events. In one of the stranger "discharges" of the war, Rauscher described the fate of a journalist during the Wilderness Campaign who had criticized the army brass, thereby invoking their wrath. The fellow was summarily arrested and "drummed out" of camp for suggesting that had Meade been in charge instead of Grant, the Union army would already be in full retreat. The hapless fellow was arrested and had a card pinned on his back proclaiming him a "Libeler of the Press." After this:

[The] bugler loudly [called] attention to his humiliation and the drum corps [played] the "Rogue's March." In this way the offender was paraded along the whole line, causing a great deal of merriment and odious remarks among the soldiers. After passing through this ordeal, he was sent off and forbidden ever to come within the lines of the army again.[126]

Rauscher also recalled an execution that took place in Petersburg, Virginia, in 1864:

All the troops in the vicinity were called out and formed a square. Our band again took the head of the line, followed by an army wagon, in which the condemned men sat. The band had often played at military funerals, but there was something singularly sad in this proceeding—men listening to their own funeral march— to the roll of drums that had their death-knell in it. On arriving at the place of execution General Patrick read the sentence of death pronounced upon them by the Court, the Chaplain made a short prayer, and at the tap of a drum the platform on which they stood was suddenly pulled from their feet and in an instant all was over. The Provost Marshal General then made an address to the soldiers assembled, warning all against the commission of like deeds, asking them to remember their mothers, sisters, and daughters. He said that both Grant and Meade were determined that the sanctity of home should be respected. This closed a sad ceremony and an unwelcome duty, when the band struck up a sprightly air, as was always the custom, and the troops marched back to their camp.[127]

Bands often participated in religious services. After Antietam, services in an oak grove were accompanied by the band of the 14th Connecticut Volunteers. "Flag-draped drums [served as] a pulpit and the inspiring music of the band [served] as church bell and orchestra."[128] During the winter of 1864, band members of the 114th Pennsylvania provided outdoor music to call the congregation to church and a vocal quartet to perform during services.[129]

In the end—whether mustering men into the army or honoring them in death, whether competing amongst themselves or across enemy lines— bands, and the music they played, were about pride and honor, family and country. Wrote a member of the 114th Pennsylvania Volunteer Regiment to Rauscher shortly before the latter published his book, *Music on the March*:

Don't forget to put in the book how we boys used to yell at the band for music to cheer us up when we were tramping along so tired that we could hardly drag one foot after the other. Since the war I have often thought how cruel we were to do so; for, if we were tired, wasn't the band members equally so? and yet we wanted them to use up what little breath they had left to put spirit in us. But then, you know, that good old tune we called "Hell on the Rappahannock" had enough music in it to make a man who was just about dead brace up, throw his chest out, and take the step as if he had received a new lease of life. Those were hard days, but even after a long march, if we were only rested a little we could be as happy as the day was long, knowing that we were doing our duty to our country and the flag, and that was reward enough for tired limbs and blistered feet.[130]

Conclusion

Musicians were present at the war's beginning and end. The Union's 1st Regiment of Artillery Band (also known as Chandler's Band of Portland, Maine) served at Fort Sumter on April 12, 1861, when the Civil War's initial battle commenced. These musicians did not play during the Confederate bombardment. Instead, they were busy "filling cartridge bags with powder and carrying ammunition."[131] After the thirty-four-hour fight had finished, Union honor maintained, and the surrender successfully negotiated, the bandsmen took out their instruments. They played "Yankee Doodle" and "Hail to the Chief" as the regiment marched out of the fort to board the Union ship *Baltic* for the long trip northward. These soldiers would eventually receive a hero's welcome in New York Harbor. At war's end, marching bands lent splendor to massive army reviews through the streets of Washington, D.C. The review of April 23, 1865, featured a daylong parade by General Meade's 80,000-man Army of the Potomac. General Sherman's 65,000-man western armies marched the following day.

The sounds of camp and combat were never to be forgotten by those who lived with them. The following story occurred twenty-five years after the battle of Gettysburg and during a reunion of the 20th Maine. These were the men who fought the decisive July 2, 1863 battle for Little Round Top:

A bugler went up on Little Round Top and sounded the old Dan Butterfield call. Veterans who had been scattered all over, exam-

ining half-remembered positions, came hurrying to the hill in answer to the call, many with tears in their eyes. Echoing sharp and
clear among the rocks and trees where they had fought, it had
awakened the memories they were seeking with a sudden and
breath-taking sense of reality.[132]

The War's End, and Forward

As the cannons fell silent, the armies dissolved with breathtaking speed. On April 10, 1865, the day after Lee's surrender, Union presses began printing over 28,000 Confederate paroles. Five days later, the task completed, the Army of Northern Virginia no longer existed. An era in American life had ended, noted despondent cornetist Julius Leinbach:

> Farewell home and friends, farewell Southern Confederacy, farewell 26th North Carolina regiment, farewell 26th North Carolina Regimental Band. No more would we play for guard mount and dress parade. Never again shall your familiar airs cheer and be cheered by the men, who for three years were wont to call you, "our band."
> There is no more any 26th North Carolina regiment. It has passed into history, and such a history as any organization might well be proud.[1]

More than military music was passing into history, of course. So was a way of life. The South was exhausted, its heritage and families torn apart. An astounding one in five white Southern males had died in the war. Richmond, Columbia, and Atlanta, and the Southern economy as a whole, were in ruins.

The emancipated slaves would be hard pressed as well. The thirteenth, fourteenth, and fifteenth amendments (of 1865, 1868, and 1870 respectively) ended slavery, granted African-American citizenship, and guaranteed the right to vote regardless of race, but bringing those rights into practice would be another matter. Southern states passed "black codes" that restricted African-American rights. The Ku Klux Klan, established in 1866, added terror to repression. Southern blacks remained economically disenfranchised.

The old made way for the new. Territorial growth continued as eyes recently cast northward and southward turned once again to the Great Plains and beyond. There were numerous social initiatives. The year 1867 brought the Alaskan Purchase, the founding of Howard University, the Reconstruction Act, and renewed activism for women's suffrage. The year 1869 saw the completion of the transcontinental railroad. In Cincinnati, the Redstockings became the nation's first paid baseball team.

Music marked many of these events. Lyrics promoting women's suffrage and temperance were grafted onto melodies recently used to promote abolition. Minstrel and parlor songs turned away from topics of war and death to explore unfolding race relations and cultural activities. Classical music was rejuvenated with an influx of European virtuoso performers, such as Norwegian violinist Ole Bull, who had toured the country extensively in the 1840s and 1850s.

FOLK MUSIC

Antebellum American folk music had been dominated by ballads from the British Isles. After the war, African-American songs would gain an ever increasing hold on the broader public consciousness. As African Americans took to the rails, river docks and levees, western plains and Northern cities, they responded to changing conditions by creating new genres of work songs and ballads. Adventurers sang of women they left behind; prisoners sang of Black Betty, the driver's whip. Slowly, and irrepressibly, these songs seeped into white culture. Still sung today is "John Henry," the ballad of the 220-pound "steel driving" former slave railroad laborer who pitted his own strength against the newly invented steam drill. John Henry served as a poignant model for the African-American experience as a whole; he battled against all odds and won, but he worked himself to death in the process. The lyrics come in many variations, few give evidence to the song's African-

American heritage. The following verse was collected by John and Alan Lomax:

> John Henry was a li'l baby, uh-huh
> Sittin' on his mama's knee, oh, yeah,
> Said: "De Big Bend Tunnel on de C. & O. road
> Gonna cause de death of me,
> Lawd, Lawd, gonna cause de death of me."[2]

POLITICAL MUSIC

Abolition achieved, the activist Hutchinson singers directed their music toward other causes. In August 1867, John Hutchinson and members of his troupe headed out from their western home in Hutchinson, Minnesota, to Kansas to sing for women's suffrage. Concerts began in Atchison on September 2, where the Hutchinsons shared the stage with Susan B. Anthony, Senator S. C. Pomeroy, and others. Throughout their tour, the singing, if not always the politics, was applauded. In his autobiography, Hutchinson recorded the following story from the *Ottawa Home Journal*:

> [The Hutchinsons] are traveling under an engagement with the advocates of female suffrage, and are striving to sing the people of Kansas into an acceptance of the "pernicious proposition." Futile as their efforts will evidently be in this direction, they furnish a delightful evening's entertainment. They must be sacrificing many profitable engagements in large eastern towns in their zeal for this heresy, and much as we regret to see such talent so misdirected, we are thankful that such sweet singers can be heard upon these prairies.
>
> They were apparently hard driven to find poetry the sentiment of which could be made to sustain a proposition so hostile to poetic feeling as is female suffrage, and so their songs upon this subject were original.[3]

For the time being, at least, the *Ottawa Home Journal* had the people's pulse. Women's suffrage was soundly defeated in the nation's first popular referendum on the topic. Undaunted, the Hutchinsons switched their message from suffrage to temperance, singing their way out of Kansas with the same zeal with which they had sung themselves in.

POPULAR SONG

The Confederate army was defeated and the economy in shambles, but still, the Southern dream survived, in some quarters, at least. Confederate songs continued to be refashioned, such as in T. Von La Hache's "Improvisation on the Bonny Blue Flag" (1866), which was published in New York, St. Louis, and New Orleans. Southern animosities survived as well. As lyrics to the anonymously written "O I'm a Good Old Rebel" (no date) suggest, it would take years, even generations, for lingering emnities to heal:

> O I'm a good old rebel,
> Now that's just what I am,
> For this "fair Land of Freedom"
> I do not care AT ALL;
> I'm glad I fit against it—
> I only wish we'd won
> And I don't want no pardon
> For anything I done.

> Three hundred thousand Yankees
> Is stiff in Southern dust;
> We GOT three hundred thousand
> Before they conquered us;
> They died of Southern fever
> And Southern steel and shot,
> I wish they was three million
> Instead of what we got.

The sheet music's illustrated cover pictures a sour-faced bearded woodsman slouching against a fallen tree into which his ax, presumably in spite or anger, has been driven. The song is contemptuously "dedicated to the Hon. Thad Stevens," the Pennsylvania Congressman who had been an ardent abolitionist long before the war and who, after its conclusion, favored both African-American suffrage and the confiscation of Southern land and its redistribution to the former slaves.

In the North, Mrs. P. A. Hanaford and Reverend J. W. Dadmun's "The Empty Sleeve" (1866) reminded listeners that sacrifice and honor continued to be bound together:

> The strife for freedom is gone by;
> The war-cry sounds no more.
> But the heroes come with empty sleeves
> From out the battle's roar.
>
> [Chorus:]
> The empty sleeve, it is a badge
> Of bravery and of honor;
> It whispers of the dear old flag,
> And tells who sav'd our banner.
> Three hearty cheers for those who lost
> An arm in Freedom's fray
> And bear about an empty sleeve,
> But a patriot's heart today.

In fact, North and South, war-related songs quickly fell from favor as interests shifted to lighter issues. The ever popular Will Hays published songs on a variety of themes in the war's aftermath, including: "We Parted by the River Side" ("Tell me that you love me yet / For, oh! the parting gives me pain;") in 1866 and the homey ode to technology, "Song of the Sewing Machine" (1869). The "husband is away in the army" theme, played out with so much pathos during the war, became a topic for fun in the war's aftermath, as is seen in Hays's "Mistress Jinks of Madison Square" (1868):

> I am Mistress Jinks of Madison Square,
> I wear fine clothes and I puff my hair,
> And how the gentlemen at me stare,
> While my husband's in the army.
> Where e'er I go I'm talked about,
> I'm talked about, I'm talked about,
> I wear the latest fashions out,
> While the Captain's in the army.

Having more fun still with gender issues was British-born occasional female impersonator William Horace Lingard, whose "Walking Down Broadway" was published in 1868:

> The sweetest thing in life
> And no one dares say nay,
> On a Saturday afternoon,
> Is walking down Broadway.
> My sister thro' the Park
> And at Long Branch wish to stay,
> But I prefer to walk down the festive gay Broadway.

The American oil era had begun in 1859 when Edwin L. Drake drilled the world's first well in Titusville, Pennsylvania. Initially, the war had drawn attention elsewhere. Now the boom was on. The pervading optimism and excitement was captured in comic songs like Joseph B. Quimby's "Have You Struck Ile?" (arranged by A. Speculator) and Frank Wilder's "I've Struck Ile," both from 1865. Prospecting for oil, said Wilder, was a sure path to riches:

> "Pick up traps and come along,"
> We will "pump it" long and strong,
> And fill our barrels to the top,
> Hurry Up! don't stop!
> They say all round where you may go,
> Just give a "tap" and oil will flow.
> Abundance of it may be found
> Under, under ground!

People may have been looking to the ground for wealth, but they were looking up for love. British music hall star George Leybourne's (1842–1884) hit song "The Flying Trapeze" was published in England in 1867, in the United States the following year:

> Once I was happy, but now I'm forlorn,
> Like an old coat, that is tatter'd and torn,
> Left on this wide world to fret and to mourn,
> Betray'd by a maid in her teens.
> The girl that I lov'd, she was handsome,
> I tried all I knew, her to please,
> But I could not please her one quarter so well,
> Like that man upon the Trapeze.

[Chorus:]
He'd fly thro' the air with the greatest of ease,
A daring young man on the flying Trapeze;
His movements were graceful, all girls he could please,
And my love he purloin'd away.

America's long fascination with transportation continued after the war. Train songs remained popular, so was the pedal bicycle, or velocipede, as it was then known. The invention inspired dozens of piano pieces, such as William O. Fiske's "Velocipede" (1868), Henry Von Gudera's "Les Velocipedes Galop" (1869), and E. H. Sherwood's "The New Velocipede Song of the Last Sensation" (1869). Frank Howard's song "Velocipedia" (1868) highlighted the practical uses of the new invention:

Oh soon horses, mules or steam,
On our travels we'll not need,
But our journeys make with a two wheel'd team,
Call'd the French velocipede.

MINSTRELS AND THEATER

Minstrel shows continued to be popular well into the 1880s. Along the way the troupes grew from quartets to as many as 100 performers while ethnic content diversified with lampoons of Irish, German, Chinese, and other minorities. Female impersonators, of which Francis Leon was considered the greatest, were popular as well.

Minstrels continued to update their relationships with African-American culture. Eph, the simple character of the 1863 song "Young Eph's Lament," was revisited with Tom Russell's "That's what the niggers then will do: answer to 'Young Eph's lament' " (1865) and with J. B. Murphy's "Young Eph's Jubilee (Answer to Young Eph's Lament)" (1866). The 1863 Eph had wondered "what am a nigger to do," but by 1865 he had "help'd to save the flag [and] pull down the traitor rag." The Eph of 1866 had grown more still. He is strong but cautious. He asks for equality, but assures his listeners that he represents no threat:

Oh! dars room enough for all . . . white and black and great and small,
In dis great and happy land ob Liberty:
I can work as well as fight: and I'll do whate'er is right:
If you'll only try and do the same by me.
We soon will understand Our places in de land:
And could'nt hurt de country if we would.
And its plain enough to see: Dat now we all are free
We would'nt hurt de country if we could,
Dats what we neber wanted for to do.

The various sheet music covers also tell a story. The 1863 Eph stands in tattered suit, belongings tied to a stick over his shoulder. He looks out, hand extended, as if lost. Not so the Eph of 1866. He is dressed in red, white, and blue and walks down a path called Liberty. Above, plump black cherubs, their hoop earrings dangling, serenade on drum, bugle, and banjo. To the sides are depicted scenes from Eph's life as boy, contraband, soldier, and banjoist.

Not all songs showed such social movement forward. Even with emancipation, some slaves never left the plantation. With the song "The Little Old Cabin in the Lane" (1871), Will Hays paints the picture of a faithful servant staying on long after his master (and a way of life) has died:

I'm getting old and feeble now, I cannot work no more,
I've laid the rusty bladed hoe to rest,
Ole massas an' ole miss's am dead, dey're sleepin' side by side.
Deir spirits now are roaming wid de blest;
De scene am changed about de place, de darkies am all gone.
I'll nebber hear dem singing in de cane,
And I'se de only one dat's left wid dis ole dog ob mine,
In de little old log cabin in de lane.

Blackface minstrelsy provided the first extensive opportunities for African Americans to work within the music industry. These troupes formed immediately after the war. Curiously, African-American actors continued the tradition of lampooning African-American culture. Now, however, the formula was more complex. On the one hand, African-American ensembles succeeded because they offered "authenticity"; this was *their* music, after all. Yet, these groups also offered an uncomfortable new layer of meaning as

African-Americans occasionally reinterpreted, but often merely reinforced, stereotypes held within the white community.

Of the early troupes, the most important was Indianapolis native Charles ("Barney") Hicks's Georgia Minstrels, which toured extensively across North America and Europe. Other successful leaders included Charles Callender, Lew Johnson, and Ernest Hogan. James Bland was just eleven years old when the Civil War ended. He would go on to become one of the period's most famous minstrel songwriters. His songs include "Carry Me Back to Old Virginny" (1878), "Oh, Dem Golden Slippers" (1879), and "De Golden Wedding" (1880). The first of these, with its remarkable lyrics, was made Virginia's state song in 1940. It was given the status "emeritus" in 1997.

> Carry me back to old Virginny,
> There's where the cotton and the corn and tatoes grow,
> There's where the birds warble sweet in the springtime,
> There's where the old darke'ys heart am long'd to go,
> There's where I labor'd so hard for old massa,
> Day after day in the field of yellow corn,
> No place on earth do I love more sincerely
> Than old Virginny, the state where I was born.

Theaters thrived in the postwar years. In New York City, Tony Pastor, who had worked as a circus clown and ringmaster before the war, opened in 1865 the Bowery district–based Tony Pastor's Opera House. The name was decidedly more upscale than the entertainment within, but Pastor was looking to create a new style of popular entertainment that would appeal to women as well as men. To achieve that, he introduced a broad selection of minstrel and variety entertainment ranging from skits to musical numbers to animal acts. Thus was born vaudeville.

The year 1866 saw the opening of *The Black Crook*, a reportedly poorly crafted but wildly popular extravaganza that spiced a mundane melodrama concerning a man who has sold his soul to the devil with the talents of a 100-women pink-tight-clad French ballet troupe. In the tradition of English ballad opera, most of the music consisted of old songs fitted with new words. The show was a guaranteed hit the moment the clergy denounced its bawdy character. It ran for sixteen months. Romantic love was reduced to a series of flirtations. Typical was Kennick and Bickwell's "You Naughty, Naughty Men":

> I will never more deceive you, or of happiness bereave you,
> But I'll die a maid to grieve you, oh! you naughty, naughty men;
> You may talk of love and sighing, say for us you're nearly dying;
> All the while you know you're trying to deceive, you naughty men.

The song received a quick reply with Laurat and Cull's "You Naughty, Naughty Girls" (1867). The show spawned an imitator as well: *Humpty-Dumpty* (1868), starring pantomime great George L. Fox. More important for the future, however, was the obsession with over-the-top grandeur that *The Black Crook* initiated. Such displays would remain a characteristic of American musical theater through the *Ziegfeld Follies* of the 1920s.

Parodies of Irish and British cultures were also popular. In 1871, actors Edward (Ned) Harrigan (1845–1911) and Tony Hart (1855–1891) teamed up to create a series of comic works based on the experiences of the Irish in New York City. The best remembered of these was *The Mulligan Guard Ball* (1879). The British team of Gilbert and Sullivan would premiere *The Pirates of Penzance* in New York's Fifth Avenue Theater that same year.

CONCERT MUSIC

Musical life in New Orleans, the opera capital of North America in the years preceding the Civil War, had crumbled in 1862. With the war's conclusion, however, entrepreneurs were determined to reestablish the tradition. A February 29, 1868, report published in *Dwight's Journal of Music* suggests that this task was quickly accomplished:

> Amid all the financial, civil, social distress of this city, amid all the breaking up and general dilapidation and positive ruin of its grand career of wealth and prosperity in times past, there is still left to New Orleans a native treasure which no other city in the Union can boast.
>
> "Art is long!" I never felt the force of this adage as I did last night, while I sat at the French Opera witnessing the production of [Giacomo Meyerbeer's 1849] "Le Prophète." Here in the midst of a city groaning under a financial and political depression never felt before, where care, and anxiety, and dreary forebodings cast their gloom over the out-door world—here is this temple of musical art, beautiful to the eye, and ever ready to lift the mind up

to the fair, fresh and peaceful world of poesy and harmony. And here the people come; come as of old; come because they love Art, and look to it in times of outward depression as a sure and blessed means of relief and refreshment. It is not as a new sensation, or as the fashion of the hour, that the public, that is, the old musical public of New Orleans, now patronize their Opera. It is their old friend, their friend of balmy, bright days gone by, their friend now.

Theodore Thomas, a central figure in the New York City music scene since the early 1850s, would serve as music director of the Brooklyn Philharmonic on three occasions: 1862–1863, 1866–1868, and 1873–1878. He also would go on to lead the Theodore Thomas Orchestra to great artistic and financial success in cross-country tours from 1865 to 1890. His long-term impact was decisive. In 1873, Thomas co-founded the biennial Cincinnati May Festival, which continues today. In 1891, he took over the conducting duties for the newly formed Chicago Symphony Orchestra and directed the ensemble until his death in January of 1905.

Female instrumentalists had to be at least as accomplished, and perhaps more resolute, than their male counterparts. Indeed, even praise was undermined by irrelevant comparisons, as when the March 16, 1867, volume of *Dwight's Journal of Music* published a testimony from composer John Knowles Paine and other Boston music luminaries regarding a Harvard Music Association performance by French-born violinist Camilla Urso (1842–1902). "It is not enough to say it was a wonderful performance for a woman; it was a consummate rendering, which probably few men living could improve upon," they wrote. Urso retired in 1895 after a varied career that took her to four continents.

African-American contributors would also enrich the world of concert music. In New Orleans, Creole violinist and composer Edmund Dede (1827–1903) would have his *Quasimodo Symphony* performed in May 1865 at the Orleans Theatre by a black orchestra led by Samuel Snaer, Jr. The pianist Blind Tom made his London debut to great acclaim in 1866 and later toured South America. Vocalist sisters Anna Madah and Emma Louise Hyers of Sacramento, California, made their debut recital in 1867, toured the country in 1871, and were well received at Patrick Gilmore's 1872 World Peace Jubilee in Boston. Composer and concert violinist John Thomas Douglass (1847–1886) premiered his opera *Virginia's Ball* at the Stuyvesant Institute in New York City in 1868.

A surge of Northern interest in traditional African-American music encouraged the Fisk Jubilee Singers to set out in 1871 to present spirituals and other repertoire to a white public. The material was polished and packaged in neat European-style arrangements that must have sounded little like the original rough-hewn source material. No matter. The group's reputation was secured after a performance at the World Peace Jubilee. Using Boston as a springboard, the choir went on to sing across Europe while raising money for Fisk University.

This was just one of numerous vocal enterprises developing. Washington's Colored American Opera Company presented Julius Eichberg's the *Doctor of Alcantra* in 1873. New England Conservatory–trained soprano Nellie Brown Mitchell (1845–1924) made successful concert debuts in Boston, New York, and Washington in 1874. Coloratura soprano and possible ex-slave Marie Selika (ca. 1849–1937), who was known as the "Queen of Staccato," made her debut in San Francisco in 1876 and gave a command performance for Queen Victoria in 1882.

THE PEACE JUBILEES

Band music, so important for soldier morale during the war, continued to thrive in peacetime. Gilmore opened the first of his peace jubilees, the Boston-based National Peace Jubilee and Music Festival, on June 15, 1869. Modeling the event on the Handel festivals of London that had begun in 1859, Gilmore sought to present over the course of five days "the greatest musical festival and the grandest celebration ever witnessed in the world." He may have succeeded. Gilmore solicited singers from across the country, offering them no more than reduced travel and lodging expenses as well as copies of the music. That was enough. Ten thousand were engaged. Violin virtuoso Ole Bull served as concertmaster for an orchestra of 1,000. Soprano Euphrosyne Parepa-Rosa, who was famed for the size of her voice, was hired as soloist. E. and G. G. Hook and Company constructed the world's largest organ and Noble and Cooley built the world's largest bass drum, with heads eight feet in diameter. The opening concert on June 15 began with the Lutheran chorale "A Mighty Fortress Is Our God" and continued with music of Mozart, Rossini, Meyerbeer, and others. The biggest success of the weekend came when 100 members of the Boston Fire Department marched to the stage and pounded away in the "Anvil" chorus from Verdi's opera *Il trovatore*. The opening day's attendance was approximately 15,000. Events later in the week attracted 50,000. Dignitaries in attendance included President Grant.

The extravaganza impressed even John Sullivan Dwight, who had once blasted Gottschalk's music as too insubstantial. The festival, he wrote:

> has given a new impulse, a new consciousness of strength, a new taste of joy of unity of effort, a new love of cooperation, and a deeper sense of the divine significance and power of music than they ever had. [It has given Americans] a new belief in Music; a new conviction of its social worth; above all, of its importance as a pervading educational and fusing element in our whole democratic life. . . . Public opinion, henceforth, will count [music] among the essentials of that "liberal education" which is the birthright of a free American, and no longer as a superfluous refinement of an over-delicate and fashionable few.[4]

Such was the Jubilee's success that Gilmore decided to stage a second, bigger version. This was the eighteen-day World Peace Jubilee of 1872, which was linked to the end of the Franco-Prussian War. To fit the international flavor, foreign bands were invited to perform, including: Johann Strauss and his orchestra from Austria; military bands from England, France, and Prussia; as well as the U.S. Marine Band. The resident orchestra had 2,000 members; the chorus was 20,000; there was seating for 100,000. Gilmore was paid $50,000 for his efforts.

That was the highpoint of Gilmore's musical gigantisms. A final extravaganza of sorts took place in Chicago in June 1873, but it was a sorry affair. Arranged to celebrate the rebuilding of the city in the wake of the Great Chicago Fire of 1871, the event was held in the newly constructed and cavernous downtown train depot. Echoing acoustics made mush of the music, and the three-day event was mostly a fiasco. Later that year, Gilmore moved to New York where he took over the 22nd Regimental Band. Over the next nineteen years he toured with the ensemble across the United States and much of Europe. At his death in 1892, directorship of the band was passed to Victor Herbert.

THE BAND LEGACY

John Philip Sousa (1854–1932) started his own band that same year. Sousa, the son of a U.S. Marine Band trombonist, had led the Marine Band for twelve years beginning in 1880. Now on his own, he would create America's most famous band. Sousa was a composer as well. His marches include *The Thunderer*, *Stars and Stripes Forever*, and *El Capitan*, which was part of an operetta by the same name. Other operettas included *The Smugglers* (1882), *Desiree* (1883), and *The Charlatan* (1898).

Coming much later onto the scene, but deeply woven into Civil War band culture was Charles Ives (1874–1954). The son of George Ives, who at seventeen had organized and led a band attached to the 1st Connecticut Heavy Artillery, Charles would become one of America's most innovative composers. Quotations from Revolutionary War and Civil War–period music are common in his work. So too are experiments with layering in which different rhythmic and melodic ideas are played simultaneously, one atop the other. The effect, which Ives might have first noticed as a child at parades, is not unlike the experience of listening to two bands playing different music simultaneously. Most important, however, was that Ives composed with an unabashedly American voice. Gone were the uncomfortable imitations and echoes of German instrumental music and Italian opera that had weakened the music of Fry, Bristow, and many other Civil War–period art music composers. In its stead was music forcefully modern in character yet rustically gentle, music of complexity built from everyday ideas. Ives was one of the first to truly capture within the confines of the concert hall the cultural breadth of the American experience that was the legacy of the Civil War.

CLOSING

With the war's end, American life and music turned towards new opportunities and situations. But those who lived through America's bloodiest war would never forget those four years of terror and glory. To assist Union veterans, Dr. B. F. Stephenson founded the Grand Army of the Republic (GAR) on April 6, 1866, in Decatur, Illinois. The organization would serve the needs of former Union soldiers and their families for more than eighty years, until it was closed by surviving members in 1949. During the course of its run, and particularly in the last decades of the nineteenth century, the organization was hugely powerful. In 1890, membership reached a total of over 400,000 in some 7,000 posts established across the country. A great many Northern politicians–including presidents Grant, Hayes, Garfield, Harrison, and McKinley—were GAR members. Under the organization's political influence, pensions were established for veterans and the date of May 30 was established as Decoration Day, the day in which war survivors placed flowers on the graves of the dead. (After WWI the holiday's name was changed to Memorial Day.) The United Confederate Veterans organization was formed in 1889, led by John B. Gordon, and reached a membership of approximately 80,000 in the first years of the twentieth century.

As during the war, music continued to be a focus for these former soldiers. Men sang and bands played at massive GAR National Encampments on former battlefields as well as at smaller activities in towns or meeting houses. The fiftieth anniversary of the battle of Gettysburg drew over 50,000 veterans. Songsters were published well into the twentieth century.

These remembrances continue on today. From the comical "Goober Peas" to the evangelical "Battle Hymn of the Republic," from the rousing patriotic songs of New Englander George Frederick Root to the eclectic mix of materials that made up Gottschalk's concerts, the Civil War's music and the remarkable men who composed, sang, and performed it have been incorporated into the American psyche. We are all richer for those imprints.

The last authenticated Confederate survivor was Pleasant Crump of the 10th Alabama, who died in 1951. There are no records to confirm the service claims of John B. Salling of the 25th Virginia Infantry, who died in 1959 at the age of 113. For the Union, former drummer boy Albert Woolson of the 1st Minnesota Heavy Artillery was the last survivor. He passed away in 1956 at the age of 109.

To the Leaven'd Soil They Trod

To the leaven'd soil they trod, calling, I sing, for the last;
(Not cities, nor man alone, nor war, nor the dead,
But forth from my tent emerging for good—loosing, untying the tent-
    ropes;)
In the freshness, the forenoon air, in the far-stretching circuits and
    vistas,
again to peace restored,
To the fiery fields emanative, and the endless vistas beyond—to the
    south and the north;
To the leaven'd soil of the general western world, to attest my songs,
(To the average earth, the wordless earth, witness of war and peace,)
To the Alleghanian hills, and the tireless Mississippi,
To the rocks I, calling, sing, and all the trees in the woods,
To the plain of the poems of heroes, to the prairie spreading wide,
To the far-off sea, and the unseen winds, and the same impalpable air;
. . . And responding, they answer all, (but not in words.)
The average earth, the witness of war and peace, acknowledges mutely;
The prairie draws me close, as the father, to bosom broad, the son;
The Northern ice and rain, that began me, nourish me to the end;
But the hot sun of the South is to ripen my songs.

Walt Whitman, *Sequel to Drum-Taps*

Musicians of the Civil War Era

TERESA CARREÑO (1853–1917)

Women pianists were attempting to establish a niche on America's concert stage. In 1856, Eugenie de Rhoade became the first woman to perform with the New York Philharmonic Society. That opening quickly shut, however. The Philharmonic invited no female soloists during the war. Mary Fay (1844–1928), a student of Franz Liszt, became in 1860 the first woman to perform with the Boston Philharmonic Society. She performed with the ensemble again in 1862.

Making her New York debut in 1862 was the brilliant eight-year-old Venezuelan piano prodigy Teresa Carreño. The grandniece of Simon Bolívar, Carreño made her highly successful debut at Irving Hall on November 25, 1862, in a program she shared with violinist Theodore Thomas. Carreño became a beloved, but infrequent student of Gottschalk, who taught her when his own performance schedule would allow. She made her Boston debut on January 2, 1863, and followed that with a series of concerts that culminated in a performance with the Boston Philharmonic Society of Mendelssohn's *Capriccio brillante*, a work she learned in three days.

In the fall of 1863 Carreño appeared at the White House where she performed for President Lincoln. The event made a deep impression on the child, but not in the way one might expect. Recalling the event years later she wrote:

> The President and his family received us so informally, they were all so very nice to me that I almost forgot to be cranky under the spell of their friendly welcome. My self-consciousness all returned, however, when Mrs. Lincoln asked me if I would like to try the White House grand piano. At once I assumed the most critical attitude toward everything—the stool was unsuitable, the pedals were beyond reach, and when I had run my fingers over the key-board, the action was too hard. My poor father suggested a Bach Invention would make me more familiar with the action.
>
> That was quite enough to inspire me to instant rebellion. With-out another word, I struck out into Gottschalk's funeral *Marche de Nuit*, and after I had finished modulated into *The Last Hope*, and ended with *The Dying Poet*. I knew my father was in despair and it stimulated me to extra effort. I think I never played with more sentiment. Then what do you think I did? I jumped off the piano stool and declared that I would play no more—that the piano was too badly out of tune to be used.
>
> My unhappy father looked as if he would swoon. But Mr. Lincoln patted me on the cheek and asked me if I could play *The Mocking Bird* with variations. The whim to do it seized me and I returned to the piano, gave out the theme, and then went off in a series of impromptu variations that threatened to go on forever. When I stopped it was from sheer exhaustion.
>
> Mr. Lincoln declared that it was excellent, but my father thought I had disgraced myself, and he never ceased to apologize in his broken English until we were out of hearing.[1]

At age twelve, Carreño went to Paris where she studied with Anton Rubenstein and others. Fiery in performance and spirit, the enormously gifted musician had an extensive career throughout Europe as a pianist, vocalist, conductor, and composer.

STEPHEN FOSTER (1826–1864)

Stephen Foster died young, with just thirty-eight cents in his pocket. But he made America rich with song. The ninth of ten children, the youngest of which died in infancy, Foster was the gifted and often-indulged son of William B. and Eliza T. Foster. The extent of his formal musical training is unknown. To be sure, however, he was a melodist with the rare ability to set words to music in a natural, organic fashion. His music was accessible, yet sophisticated; easy to sing, yet invariably colorful. It remains popular today. "Old Folks at Home ('The Swanee River')" (1851) is the state song of Florida. "My Old Kentucky Home" (1853) is the state song of Kentucky.

Foster's output can be divided into two genres: parlor and minstrel. The former were built around time-honored notions of love and longing, home and hearth; the latter drew from popular minstrel conventions. His first two publications, the fervent "Open Try Lattice, Love" (1844) and the bouncy "Oh! Susanna" (1848), represent these two paths.

In its various published forms—sheet music and songsters—Foster's music sold millions of copies. Yet, as Hewitt had already discovered, it was the publisher, not the composer, who would most likely reap the profits from a successful song. Foster saw little of the revenue that his songs earned. This was because copyright laws were weak (the Confederacy would not respect Union copyrights at all) and there was minimal infrastructure for monitoring sheet music sales. Composers rarely knew how well their music was selling. They had to rely on publishers' honesty.

For Foster, that would not be enough. The Civil War found him in New York City where, financially destitute and estranged from wife and child, he fought losing battles against depression and alcoholism. A broken man, he composed sporadically. With the exception of "Beautiful Dreamer" and a few war-related songs (including the 1863 songs "My Boy Is Coming from the War" and "A Soldier in the Colored Brigade"), he produced little of consequence in these last years.

LOUIS MOREAU GOTTSCHALK (1829–1869)

Born in the sophisticated and ethnically diverse city of New Orleans to parents of Jewish and French Creole heritage, Gottschalk was both America's first great virtuoso and the first American composer to write material that remains today in the standard piano repertoire. Elegant, witty, and deeply gifted, Gottschalk found things of interest almost everywhere he looked. His greatest contribution as a composer was the manner in which he assimilated the many different strands of musical culture. During a time when most American art music composers were taking Germanic composers as their model, Gottschalk combined the light elegance of the French with both Caribbean rhythms and a sensibility that was melting-pot American.

No doubt, his peripatetic life contributed to this breadth and flexibility. Gottschalk left New Orleans at the age of twelve in order to study in France, where he stayed for nearly a decade. His American debut took place in New York City in 1853. After concertizing throughout the country until 1857, he set off for the Caribbean. In 1861, Gottschalk was financially destitute in Cuba, but fortune smiled in December when entrepreneur Max Strakosch offered him a contract for a series of stateside performances. He readily accepted. Gottschalk returned to New York in February to find the city still vibrant and hungry for entertainment. So too, as Gottschalk would happily discover, was the rest of the North.

Over the next three years the pianist traveled widely, giving recitals in burgeoning centers like St. Louis and Chicago, as well as out-of-the-way towns like Rutland, Vermont, and Adrian, Michigan. His audiences ran the gamut of American society from farmers and frontiersmen to President Lincoln. Indeed, Gottschalk probably reached as great a cross section of the American public as any artist performing during the Civil War.[2] His recitals were as varied in ingredients as a New Orleans bouillabaisse, including opera transcriptions, his own compositions, patriotic favorites, and spontaneous improvisations on tunes named or whistled by audience members.

Gottschalk's programs invariably contained one or more patriotic medleys. Perhaps the most popular of these was *The Union*, an 1863 virtuoso collage built on themes from "The Star Spangled Banner," "Yankee Doodle," and "Hail, Columbia." The piece won the praise of Republican newspapers whose editors correctly saw in it evidence of Gottschalk's pro-war, pro-reunification stance. Written somewhat later was a transcription, complete with a set of pyrotechnic variations, on "The Battle Cry of Freedom."

Not all of his music was so red, white, and blue. Gottschalk and lyricist Henry C. Watson worked together to write a number of sentimental art songs during the war. Most popular were "Slumber On, Baby Dear" (1863), "My Only Love, Goodbye!" (1863), and "The Shepherdess and the Knight" (1864). Solo piano works written during these years included *The Dying Poet* (1863), *Radieuse* (1863), *Orfa*, (1864), and *La Brise* waltzes (1865).

Throughout his career, Gottschalk was criticized for the superficiality of

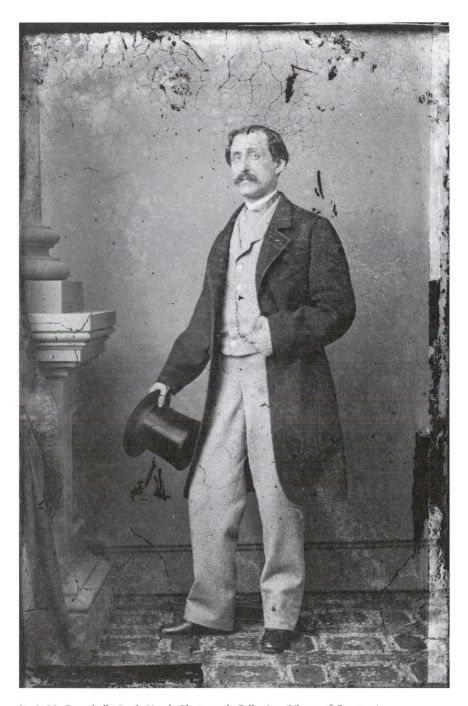

Louis M. Gottschalk. Brady-Handy Photograph Collection (Library of Congress).

his repertoire. Of Gottschalk's detractors, the stiff-necked but influential John Sullivan Dwight was the most vocal. In October 1853 he had groused:

> Who, that admired such execution as a power worth having, could not feel melancholy to see the power so thrown away? and who that went there eager to hail and praise a young native artist, could but be mortified to see an artist so little in earnest with his Art, and to find the dilettante public still so ready to extol as Art what properly is little more than sleight of hand!

In light of Dwight's hostility, it is not surprising that Gottschalk was worried about his return to Boston nine years later. Determined to win the city, he prepared a series of stratagems more sophisticated than any being applied by the hapless Union generals of the time. Writing under the pseudonym "Jem Baggs," Gottschalk began submitting positive reviews of his own concerts to *Dwight's Journal of Music*. Second, while avoiding Boston itself, he performed recitals all across New England, thereby winning new supporters at every stop. By October, Gottschalk and his admirers had the city pretty well surrounded. Dwight himself was under siege, pressured by the pro-Gottschalk surge. The ensuing sold-out concert in Boston's Chickering's Hall ended in what the *Boston Daily Courier* called "a perfect storm of applause."[3]

Whatever one thought of Gottschalk's "Art" there was no doubt of his continued popularity. During the Civil War he performed over 1,000 public recitals throughout the North as well as Canada. Competition for audiences was invariably fierce. On any given night, Gottschalk's box office rivals might have included the likes of the Booth family of actors (of which the infamous assassin John Wilkes Booth was a member), minstrel shows, circuses, magicians, and ventriloquists. On one occasion, he had to compete for an audience against the diminutive actor General Tom Thumb (Charles Sherwood Stratton). Gottschalk and his producers knew that a piano recital, even one as populist in flavor as this musician's could be, could hardly stand on its own against these other acts. So, Gottschalk spiced up his performances. He traveled with a changing array of instrumentalists and singers ranging from a seven-year-old trumpet player to famed soprano Carlotta Patti and her violinist brother Carlo. When the pianist traveled with Jacob Grau's tiny Italian Opera Company, concertgoers were entertained with excerpts from Donizetti's *Lucia de Lamermoor* or Verdi's *Il trovatore*. In between acts was sandwiched a piano recital.

Louis M. Gottschalk's farewell concerts in America. Library of Congress, Prints & Photographs Division.

The schedule was grueling, trips hardly idyllic. For weeks at a time Gottschalk would shuttle by train from one venue to the next. He often shared space with wounded or drunken soldiers, prisoners of war, caskets, widows, and screaming children. Train schedules were erratic; any given concert could be delayed or cancelled because of mechanical failures. Entire trains were sometimes commandeered for military use. Bad experiences contributed to exhaustion, occasionally depression. "The devil take the poets who dare to sing the pleasures of an artist's life," Gottschalk penned after a fifteen-hour ride to Philadelphia.[4]

Yet, the endless travel also seems to have given this observant musician considerable insight into the American people. He was often aghast at their boorish manners, lack of sophistication, and prudish ways. But he was also impressed by their independence and inventiveness. An avid diarist, Gottschalk recorded memories of both the concert stage and contemporary culture in general. After a performance in Montreal in April 1864 he wrote of the British soldiers whose fractious behavior had been "disagreeably interrupted from time to time by my piano."[5] In tiny Clyde, Ohio, Gottschalk and a "poor farmer" discussed poetry. Musing on this experience, Gottschalk noted that:

> The United States presents to strangers this remarkable condition
> of things, that it is impossible for them to conjecture from ap-
> pearances the rank or position of those they meet on their travels.
> If they meet some who sparkle with diamonds and blow their
> noses with their fingers, they will meet, just as well, superior and
> cultivated minds concealed under the fur-skin greatcoat of the pi-
> oneer of the Far West. My companion is well versed in the liter-
> ature of the Bible. He loves poetry and evidently understands it.[6]

Gottschalk's observations suggest that it was he, rather than Dwight, who
most clearly represented the American taste. Surely, this is significant. Gottschalk found a way to speak to a nation in its darkest hours. Both from the
keyboard and with his nearly indomitable spirit, Gottschalk won over devo-
tees of virtually every level of musical sophistication, from the apparently
myopic Indianapolis listener who mistook his piano for a giant accordion to
sophisticates in New York City.

Gottschalk left the United States in 1865 and never returned. Four years
later he collapsed during a recital in Rio de Janeiro. He died of pneumonia
shortly afterward.

JOHN HILL HEWITT (1801–1890)

Known as the "Bard of the Confederacy," John Hill Hewitt's musical roots
ran deep. His father, James Hewitt, was a successful songwriter and musician who, in 1790 at age 20, had been appointed to lead the court orchestra
of England's King George III. James immigrated to New York City in 1792
and had an active career in America. Son John was broadly talented and led
a peripatetic life punctuated by great successes and punishing failures. His
literary output included forty plays, two volumes of poetry, three books, and
other works. Hewitt had reservations about a career in music because of the
inevitable "mortification a master is subjected to in consideration of his being *number two* in the scale of society." Mortified or not, Hewitt composed
some 300 songs, cantatas, operettas, a variety of minor pieces, and is credited
with writing the first American oratorio, *Jeptha* (1846).[7] At various times
Hewitt also managed a theater and a publishing business. During the Civil
War he wrote nineteen songs, of which "All Quiet Along the Potomac To-
night" would be one of the period's most memorable.

It was an image of war that first brought Hewitt fame in 1825 when, while living in Greenville, South Carolina, he composed "The Minstrel's Return'd from the War." Admitting the song was "crude" in its structure, Hewitt considered it a minor accomplishment.[8] Not so minor, however, that he did not want to see it in print. He convinced his New York City–based brother James to publish it. To their mutual surprise—they had not even bothered to secure a copyright—"Minstrel" became extremely popular. It remained so throughout the Civil War.

When the war broke out, Hewitt was in Richmond, where he unsuccessfully attempted to get commissions in the Confederate government and army. Instead, he was given charge of the Richmond Broad Street Theatre. That job proved short-lived when the structure burned to the ground in the early hours of New Year's Day 1862. Hewitt was lucky to escape with his life; over three decades worth of manuscripts were lost in the conflagration. Hewitt then moved to Augusta, Georgia, where he worked as stage manager at the Concert Hall. There he wrote for the Queen Sisters Company and contributed to a number of stage productions, including: the operettas *The Artist's Wife* and *The Vivandiere*, as well as the musical plays *King Linkum the First*, *The Roll of the Drum*, and *The Veteran*.[9]

Written in blackface-minstrel style, *King Linkum the First* is worth examining for its extreme Southern viewpoint, if not its artistic worth. Contemporary sources record only two performances of this "musical burletta." Both were in Augusta's Concert Hall in late February of 1863. Hewitt wrote no new music, but attached new words to old songs. Featured along with Linkum (President Lincoln) were other prominent Yankees, including: General Fuss and Feathers (General Winfield Scott) Steward (Secretary of State William H. Seward), and General Bottler (General Benjamin F. Butler). As the sketchy plot unfolds these characters tackle the continuing ineptitudes of leadership displayed by Union generals McClellan, Pope, and Burnside at the Peninsular Campaign, 2nd Manassas, and Fredericksburg respectively. Lampooning Shakespearian language and dramatic devices while following the most hackneyed of Victorian theatrical conventions, the play is replete with bad puns, visitations of ghosts, and other gambits. The finale comes when a cannonball sails across the stage and strikes King Linkum, at which point the entire cast seems to die in sympathy. Then they all rise as Linkum says "I'm not dead—it was a hum." The play closes with the ensemble singing to the chorus of "Yankee Doodle":

> Yankee Doodle, you're no go,
> Racked by feuds and cables;
> Tho' you rant and sputter so,
> You can't put down the rebels!

With the end of the war, the South's fragile music publishing industry gradually collapsed. And with that business, so did Hewitt's fortunes. In the ensuing years Hewitt took editorial positions in Savannah and Virginia before settling in Baltimore in about 1874.

GEORGE FREDERICK ROOT (1820–1895)

To be successful, composers had to write "music for the people, having always a particular need in view," wrote George Frederick Root in his autobiography. There was no mystery in this sort of work, said Root. It was a thing that "a person may do with some success," without cause to genius, musical or otherwise.[10] Perhaps this is true, but few songwriters have been as successful as Root. Time and again he wrote music that caught the imagination of those who listened.

Root came from humble origins. He was raised on a farm in North Reading, a small town north of Boston. Although he had no formal music lessons, Root learned to play a variety of instruments. At eighteen he left home for Boston where, despite a lack of skills, he managed to find a job while beginning formal musical training with A. N. Johnson. Root progressed quickly: Within weeks Johnson made him an assistant and assigned him to teach others. Root soon began to play at Johnson's Wednesday night prayer meetings. Within two years Root was working as a voice coach for the great singing master and educator Lowell Mason.

Root moved to New York City in 1844 where he taught voice at various institutions. After a nine-month stay in Paris, he returned to New York in the late summer of 1851. Deciding that he wanted "something new" for his classes, he wrote the cantata *The Flower Queen*, which he had printed by Mason Brothers publishers. Since the music was already in the presses, the firm decided to make copies available to the general public. Thus, almost by accident, Root published his first composition. It became unexpectedly popular. Other successes followed with a series of sentimental songs that included the widely admired, if somewhat mundane, "The Hazel Dell" (1853).

Early on, Root worried that such everyday fare was below his calling as an educator. Wishing to remain anonymous, he published under a pseudonym:

> I am ashamed to say, I shared the feeling that was around me in regard to that grade of music. When Stephen C. Foster's wonderful melodies (as I now see them) began to appear, and the famous Christy's Minstrels began to make them known, I "took a hand in" and wrote a few, but put "G. Friederich Wurzel" (the German for Root) to them instead of my own name. "Hazel Dell" and "Rosalie, the Prairie Flower" [1855] were the best known of those so written. It was not until I imbibed more of Dr. Mason's spirit, and went more among the people of the country, that I saw these things in a truer light, and respected myself, and was thankful when I could write something that all the people would sing.[11]

Root moved to Chicago in 1860 where he joined the publishing firm of Root & Cady. He would go on to compose and publish over 500 songs and a variety of educational materials. Always thinking of the layman, Root kept his music simple and accessible. His autobiography, *Story of a Musical Life* (1891), provides an excellent view into the times. Root's most successful Civil War songs include "The Battle Cry of Freedom" (1862), "Just Before the Battle, Mother" (1862), and "Tramp! Tramp! Tramp!" (1864). "The Battle Cry of Freedom," would be nearly as popular at the dawn of the twentieth century as it had been during the war itself.

Dictionary of Civil War–Era Music

Ballad

> In the nineteenth century the term referred to both narrative strophic folk songs of British or American origin, and to popular songs.

Ballad Opera

> Opera in which spoken dialogue alternates with lyrics set to traditional or popular songs. Often ballad operas were written to parody traditional operas.

Blackmar, Armand Edward (1826–1888)

> A. E. Blackmar and brother Henry Clay (1831–1909) owned the Confederacy's most prolific publishing house. The company, based first in New Orleans and later in Augusta, Georgia, published some 232 compositions, including: "Dixie" (1861), "The Bonnie Blue Flag" (1861), and "Maryland, My Maryland!" (1962). A. E. Blackmar sometimes published under the pseudonym A. Noir.

Bristow, George Frederick (1825–1898)

> New York City–based violinist, conductor, and composer.

Broadside

> Sheet of paper onto which song lyrics were printed. Readers were expected to already know the melodies.

Burlesque

Up until the Civil War the term referred to theatrical spoofs on operas and plays. Shortly after the war, however, the term became associated with women in various states of undress. An example of the earlier style was John Brougham's *Po-ca-han-tas* (1855); examples of the latter can be found in *The Black Crook* (1866).

Contraband

Captured arms and munitions of war. In 1861, Union General Benjamin F. Butler applied the term to escaped slaves under Union protection.

Dodworth family

An important musician family consisting of Thomas Dodworth (1790–1876) and his sons Allen (1817–1896), Harvey (1822–1891), Charles (1826–1894), and Thomas (1830–1896). The Dodworth Band was formed under Allen's leadership in 1836, though Harvey took over a couple years later. During the Civil War the band was attached to the 71st National Guard Regiment of New York. Both Harvey and Thomas served. The Dodworths were also innovators and educators. Around 1838 they introduced the idea of valve brass instruments with bells that faced backwards so those marching behind might better hear. These instruments were popular during the Civil War. Allen's influential *Dodworth's Brass Band School* (1853) was an important wartime text.

Douglass, Frederick (1817–1895)

Former slave and abolitionist. His autobiography, *Narrative of the Life of Frederick Douglass*, was published in 1845. His abolitionist newspaper, *North Star* (later *Frederick Douglass' Paper*), was published from 1847 to 1863.

Dwight, John Sullivan (1813–1893)

Editor and principal contributor to the Boston-based *Dwight's Journal of Music* (1852–1881), an early and influential source for American music criticism.

Ellsworth, Elmer Ephraim (1837–1861)

A lawyer by profession, in 1859 Ellsworth popularized the military drill team tradition when he took command of the National Guard Cadets, dressed them in the style of French Foreign Legion soldiers (also known as Zouaves), and transformed them into the nation's finest drill team. The group inspired many imitators, including the 114th Pennsylvania Volunteers (known as the Collis Zouaves) of the Army of the Potomac. Ellsworth was the first Union officer to be killed in the war.

Emmett, Daniel Decatur (1815–1904)

Military drummer, renowned blackface minstrel composer, and performer with the Virginia Minstrels and later Bryant's Minstrels. His most famous songs include "Old Dan Tucker" (1843) and "I Wish I Was in Dixie's Land" (1859). Emmett was also co-author (with George B. Bruce) of *The Drummers and Fifers Guide*, which served as the Union army's primary training guide from 1862 to 1869.

Folksong

A common, but vague, term used to describe anonymous music of a rural class that has been handed down by oral tradition.

Field Musicians

Army fifers, buglers, and drummers whose duty it was to transmit basic daily orders and field commands to the troops.

Foster, Stephen Collins (1826–1864)

A composer known equally for his minstrel and parlor songs. Important works include "Old Folks At Home" (1851), "My Old Kentucky Home" (1853), and "Beautiful Dreamer" (1864).

Fry, William Henry (1813–1864)

New York–based composer and journalist known best as an indefatigable champion of American music. His opera *Notre Dame de Paris* was premiered in Philadelphia in 1864.

Gilmore, Patrick (1829–1892)

Irish-American cornet virtuoso and bandmaster who in 1859 organized the Boston-based Gilmore Band which served briefly with the 24th Massachusetts Infantry. He was the author of *Gilmore's Brass Band Music* (1859) and claimed to have written "When Johnny Comes Marching Home" (1863 under the pseudonym Louis Lambert). Gilmore is also remembered for his various musical extravaganzas, particularly, the National Peace Jubilee (1869) and the World Peace Jubilee (1872).

Gottschalk, Louis Moreau (1829–1869)

American pianist and composer and one of the first art music composers to successfully incorporate ethnic American styles into his music. Though he spent much of his life abroad, Gottschalk concertized extensively in the North between 1862 and 1865. His autobiography, *Notes of a Pianist*, is an important document of the era.

Grafulla, Claudio S. (1810–1880)

Spanish-born composer and band director who led the 7th New York Infantry Band from 1859 to 1880. Popular compositions include *Nightingale Waltzes* and *Washington Greys*.

Greeley, Horace (1811–1872)

New York editor, abolitionist, and supporter of temperance.

Grobe, Charles (ca. 1817–1879)

German-born composer of popular piano works who published nearly 2,000 pieces, as well as the *New Method for Pianoforte* (1859).

Hays, William Shakespeare (1837–1907)

Journalist and untutored song composer whose music sold some twenty million copies. His best-known Civil War–period work was "The Drummer Boy of Shiloh."

Hewitt, John Hill (1801–1890)

Author, journalist, and composer of cantatas, ballad operas, and some 300 songs, of which "All Quiet Along the Potomac To-night" (1862) was the best known.

Higginson, Thomas Wentworth (1823–1911)

Harvard Divinity School–educated minister, abolitionist, and author who served as the colonel of the 1st South Carolina Volunteers, the first African-American regiment. Higginson's remembrances of his time in service include many important references to music.

Hutchinson Family Singers

Popular New Hampshire vocal ensemble known for its support of abolition, women's suffrage, temperance, and other social causes.

Keyed brass instruments

Keys attached to brass instruments allowed musicians to play a broader array of pitches than they could with fixed tube length natural horns. The first such instrument was a five-key bugle invented by Irishman Joseph Haliday in 1810. Haliday's design ushered in the modern era in brass instruments.

Mason, Lowell (1792–1872)

Composer, music educator, organist, and conductor.

Minstrel show

A term used to refer to blackface entertainment from the early 1830s until the turn of the twentieth century and beyond. Minstrel shows were one of the most popular entertainment genres in the years preceding, during, and following the Civil War.

Pastiche

Music in which new words have been set to an already existing melody.

Root, George Frederick (1820–1895)

American educator, publisher, and composer of such favorites as "The Battle Cry of Freedom" (1862), "Just Before the Battle, Mother" (1862), and "Tramp, Tramp, Tramp" (1864). Root attributed the key to his success to his ability to write songs that would be appreciated by the common person. He occasionally wrote under the pseudonym G. Friederich Wurzel.

Sax, Adolphe (1814–1894)

Belgian instrument maker who designed for military use the Saxhorn, a complete family of valve instruments with similar bores, pitch characteristics, and tone color. The instruments became popular across America by the mid-1850s and were used throughout the war.

Scala, Francis (ca. 1819–1903)

Naples-born clarinetist who in 1855 became leader of the U.S. Marine Band, a position he held until 1871. John Philip Sousa was one of his bandsmen.

Songsters

> Books of song collections that included lyrics, but no musical notation. Songsters were immensely popular with Civil War soldiers.

Spirituals

> Religious songs popular throughout the nineteenth century. Southern African-American spirituals were often code songs in which images of spiritual salvation stood for freedom in the North.

Stonewall Brigade Band

> The band was formed in 1855 as the Mountain Saxhorn Band of Staunton, Virginia, and was attached to Confederate General Jackson's First Brigade, Army of the Shenandoah. The band remained active after the war, including a performance at Grant's funeral in 1885. As late as 1900, six members of the Civil War–era configuration continued to play in the band, which still performs today. Current members claim to have in their possession the only complete, unbroken set of Confederate band instruments in existence.

Strophic

> A song that sets each stanza of a poem to the same music.

Stowe, Harriet Beecher (1811–1896)

> Northern abolitionist whose novel *Uncle Tom's Cabin* (1852) set off a storm of protest in the South.

Strong, George Templeton (1820–1875)

> New York lawyer and diarist actively involved in New York's music scene.

United States Marine Band

> The Marine Band, originally a group of field musicians, was formed in 1798 under the direction of Drum Major William Farr. In 1862 it reached a membership of thirty-two and Congress raised its status to that of concert band. The band frequently performed in Washington throughout the war.

Winner, Septimus (1827–1902)

> A prolific composer of over 200 volumes of popular and minstrel songs, and arranger of some 2,000 works for violin and piano. Many of his

works appear under the pseudonym Alice Hawthorne. Songs include "Listen to the Mocking Bird" (1854) and "Down upon the Rappahannock" (1863).

Work, Henry Clay (1832–1884)

A self-taught composer whose Civil War songs include two of the most memorable: "Kingdom Coming" (1862) and "Marching Through Georgia" (1865).

Zouave

A term used to refer to the French Foreign Legion. These troops' discipline was much admired in Civil War–era America.

Notes

PREFACE

1. James M. McPherson, *For Cause & Comrades: Why Men Fought in the Civil War* (New York: Oxford University Press, 1997), 11.

2. "American Memory" can be found at http://memory.loc.gov/; the "Lester S. Levy Collection of Sheet Music" at http://levysheetmusic.mse.jhu.edu/index.html; "Historic American Sheet Music" at http://scriptorium.lib.duke.edu/sheetmusic/; and "North American Slave Narratives" at http://docsouth.unc.edu/neh/neh.html [cited March 12, 2004].

3. Louis Moreau Gottschalk, *Notes of a Pianist*, ed. Jeanne Behrend (New York: Alfred A. Knopf, 1964), 131.

4. Joshua Lawrence Chamberlain, *The Passing of the Armies: An Account of the Final Campaign of the Army of the Potomac, Based upon Personal Reminiscences of the Fifth Army Corps* (Lincoln: University of Nebraska Press, 1998), 260–61.

CHAPTER 1

1. Alexis de Tocqueville, *Democracy in America*, with a critical appraisal of each volume by John Stuart Mill, trans. Henry Reeve (New York: Schocken Books, 1961).

2. Early on, those owning 20 slaves or more were exempt from the draft. By 1863 a "$500 commutation fee" was required. Northerners could hire substitutes or pay a $300 fee. Michael J. Varhola, *Everyday Life during the Civil War: A Guide for Writers, Students, and Historians* (Cincinnati: Writer's Digest Books, 1999), 123.

3. Names of lyricists and composers are given as listed on sheet music publications. Many are untraceable, some may be pseudonyms.

4. Harriet Beecher Stowe, *Uncle Tom's Cabin* (Pleasantville, NY: The Reader's Digest Association, 1991), 316.

5. Edgar Allan Poe, *The Works of the Late Edgar Allan Poe, Volume III: The Literati* (New York: J. S. Redfield, 1850), 255.

6. Elise K. Kirk, *Music at the White House: A History of the American Spirit* (Urbana: University of Illinois Press, 1986), 78.

7. Charles A. L. Lamar's ship *Wanderer*, for example, brought 400 slaves to Georgia in 1858. Caught in the act, Lamar and members of the crew were arrested but later acquitted by a Savannah jury.

8. Dee Brown, *Bury My Heart at Wounded Knee: An Indian History of the American West* (New York: Bantam Books, 1972), 87.

9. Porter W. Ware and Thaddeus C. Lockard, Jr., *P. T. Barnum Presents Jenny Lind: The American Tour of the Swedish Nightingale* (Baton Rouge: Louisiana State University Press, 1908), 7, 31.

10. Gottschalk, *Notes*, 44–45.

11. From Douglass's Introduction to John Wallace Hutchinson, *Story of the Hutchinsons, Volume I* (Boston: Lee and Shepard, 1896), xvi.

12. Robert C. Toll, *Blacking Up: The Minstrel Show in Nineteenth Century America* (New York: Oxford University Press, 1974), 17–18.

13. Richard Crawford, *America's Musical Life* (New York: W. W. Norton & Company, 2001), 232.

14. Richard Barksdale Harwell, *Confederate Music* (Chapel Hill: University of North Carolina Press, 1950), 10–11.

15. Ibid., 10–11.

16. Ibid., 16–17.

17. Ibid., 17.

18. Dena J. Epstein, *Music Publishing in Chicago before 1871: The Firm of Root and Cady* (Detroit: Information Coordinators, 1969), 44–49.

19. Ibid., 52.

20. George Frederick Root, *The Story of a Musical Life, An Autobiography* (New York: Da Capo Press, 1970), 155.

21. Thomas W. Marrocco and Mark Jacobs, "Ditson, Oliver," in *Music Printing and Publishing*, ed. D. W. Krummel and Stanley Sadie (New York: W. W. Norton & Company, 1990), 217–18.

22. Arthur Loesser, *Men, Women and Pianos: A Social History* (New York: Simon and Schuster, 1954), 511.

23. Ibid., 505–6.

24. Cyril Ehrlich, *The Piano: A History* (Oxford: Clarendon Press, 1990), 49.

CHAPTER 2

1. Katherine Little Bakeless, *Glory, Hallelujah! The Story of* The Battle Hymn of the Republic (Philadelphia: J. B. Lippincott Company, 1944), 95–99.

2. Willard A. Heaps and Porter W. Heaps, *The Singing Sixties: The Spirit of Civil War Days Drawn from the Music of the Times* (Norman: University of Oklahoma Press, 1960), 50–51.

3. Vicki Eaklor, *American Antislavery Songs: A Collection and Analysis* (Westport, CT: Greenwood Press, 1988), 504. These words appeared in the *Liberator*, January 23, 1863.

4. Eileen Southern, *The Music of Black Americans: A History*, 2nd ed. (New York: W. W. Norton & Company, 1983), 209.

5. Thomas Wentworth Higginson, *Army Life in a Black Regiment* (Boston: Beacon Press, 1962), 22.

6. Christopher Looby ed., *The Complete Civil War Journal and Selected Letters of Thomas Wentworth Higginson* (Chicago: University of Chicago Press, 2000), 190.

7. Sherrill V. Martin, "Music of Black Americans during the War Years," in *Feel the Spirit: Studies in Nineteenth-Century Afro-American Music*, ed. George R. Keck and Sherrill V. Martin (Westport, CT: Greenwood Press, 1988), 8.

8. Web site of Jerry Ernst [cited May 14, 2003], http://www.gtg1848.de/sngbk. htm#Blenker. The date 1848 refers to the European revolutions of that year.

9. Julia Ward Howe, "The Battle Hymn of the Republic" [cited March 14, 2004], http://www.theatlantic.com/issues/1862feb/batthym.htm.

10. According to Gilbert Chase, the name Dixie probably comes from an 1850 blackface minstrel skit portraying a black postboy named Dixie. See Gilbert Chase, *America's Music from the Pilgrims to the Present* (New York: McGraw-Hill Book Company, 1955), 241–42.

11. Rev. Louis Albert Banks, D.D., *Immortal Songs of Camp and Field* (Cleveland: Imperial Press, 1898), 114–5.

12. Heaps and Heaps, *Singing Sixties*, 46.

13. Zouave was another name for the French Foreign Legion.

14. Harwell, *Confederate Music*, 42.

15. Ibid., 46–47.

16. Ibid.

17. Howard L. Sacks and Judith R. Sacks, *Way Up North in Dixie: A Black Family's Claim to the Confederate Anthem* (Washington, DC: Smithsonian Institution Press, 1993), 3.

18. Heaps and Heaps, *Singing Sixties*, 48.

19. This quote appears in many slightly different forms in a variety of sources.

20. For different takes on the song's origin, see Heaps and Heaps, *Singing Sixties* 54–57 and Irwin Silber, *Songs of the Civil War* (New York: Columbia University Press, 1960), 52–54.

21. Heaps and Heaps, *Singing Sixties*, 57.

22. Kenneth E. Olson, *Music and Musket: Bands and Bandsmen of the American Civil War* (Westport, CT: Greenwood Press, 1981), 58.

23. Root, *Story*, 132–133.

24. William Wiley, *The Civil War Diary of a Common Soldier: William Wiley of the 77th Illinois Infantry*, ed. Terrence J. Winschel (Baton Rouge: Louisiana State University Press, 2001), 160.

25. Daniel Crotty, May 7, 1864, Third Michigan Infantry, Battle of the Wilderness, Virginia [cited March 20, 2004], http://www.sos.state.mi.us/history/museum/explore/museums/hismus/special/flags/rally.html.

26. Root, *Story*, 134–35.

27. Olson, *Music and Musket*, 250.

28. Heaps and Heaps, *Singing Sixties*, 146–47.

29. Russell Sanjek, *American Popular Music and Its Business: The First Four Hundred Years, Vol. II: From 1790 to 1909* (New York: Oxford University Press, 1988), 244–45.

30. Ibid., 245.

31. James M. McPherson, *Battle Cry of Freedom: The Civil War Era* (New York: Oxford University Press, 1988), 808–10.

32. Ibid., 810.

33. Root, *Story*, 138.

34. A balmoral is a woolen petticoat.

35. Burke Davis, *The Long Surrender* (New York: Random House, 1985), 144–45.

36. Bell Irvin Wiley, *The Life of Billy Yank: The Common Soldier of the Union* (Indianapolis: Bobbs-Merrill Company, 1951), 157.

37. Carlton McCarthy, *Detailed Minutiae of Soldier Life in the Army of Northern Virginia, 1861–1865* (Lincoln: University of Nebraska Press, 1993), 6.

38. The Maxwelton House, originally named Glancairne Castle, still stands. A "brae" is a hill or steep river bank.

39. "Mavourneen" means "my darling."

40. John Beatty, *Memoirs of a Volunteer 1861–1863* (New York: W. W. Norton & Company, 1946), 59.

41. Ibid., 63–64.

42. John D. Billings, *Hardtack & Coffee: The Unwritten Story of Army Life* (Boston: George M. Smith & Company, 1887; reprint, Lincoln: University of Nebraska Press, 1993), 335–36.

43. Beatty, *Memoirs*, 93.

44. Theodore Raph, *The American Song Treasury: 100 Favorites* (New York: Dover Publications, 1986), 26.

45. Robert Knox Sneden, *The Eye of the Storm: A Civil War Odyssey*, ed. Charles F. Bryan, Jr. and Nelson D. Lankford (New York: The Free Press, 2000), 109.

46. Augustus Meyers, *Ten Years in the Ranks, U.S. Army* (New York: The Stirling Press, 1914), 217.

47. John Overton Casler, *Four Years in the Stonewall Brigade* (Dayton, OH: Morningside Bookshop, 1971), 204–5.

48. Billings, *Hardtack*, 69–70.

49. Joyce H. Cauthen, *With Fiddle and Well-Rosined Bow: Old-Time Fiddling in Alabama* (Tuscaloosa: University of Alabama Press, 1989), 16–17. Cauthen cites Edward McMorrie, *History of the First Regiment, Alabama Volunteer Infantry, CSA* (Montgomery: Brown Printing Company, 1904), 52.

50. Burke Davis, *Jeb Stuart: The Last Cavalier* (New York: Rinehart & Company, 1957), 70.

51. Ibid., 68–69.

52. Caroline Moseley, " 'Those Songs Which So Much Remind Me of You': The Musical Taste of General J.E.B. Stuart," *American Music* 9, no. 4 (1991): 399. Moseley quotes Lieutenant Colonel William W. Blackford's *War Years with Jeb Stuart* (New York: C. Scribner's Sons, 1945).

53. Ibid., 385.

54. Edwin O. Kimberley Papers, State Historical Society of Wisconsin Archive.

55. Heaps and Heaps, *Singing Sixties*, 345.

56. Martin, *Music*, 8.

57. Dudley Tayler Cornish, *The Sable Arm: Black Troops in the Union Army, 1861–1865* (1956; reprint, Lawrence: University of Kansas, 1987), 229–31.

58. Edwin O. Kimberley set the words to new music and published it in 1899. Kimberley Papers. More information can be found at http://www.1stbrigadeband.org/Band_History.html#Hamilton.

59. Francis Adams Donaldson, *Inside the Army of the Potomac: The Civil War Experience of Captain Francis Adams Donaldson*, ed. Gregory J. Acken (Mechanicsburg, PA: Stackpole Books, 1998), 118.

60. Billings, *Hardtack*, 215.

61. James A. Connolly, *Three Years in the Army of the Cumberland: The Letters and Diary of Major James A. Connolly*, ed. Paul M. Angle (Bloomington: Indiana University Press, 1959), 306–8.

62. Elizabeth R. Baer, ed., *Shadows on My Heart: The Civil War Diary of Lucy Rebecca Buck* (Athens: University of Georgia Press, 1997), 107–8.

63. Root, *Story*, 136.

64. David Holt, *A Mississippi Rebel in the Army of Northern Virginia*, ed. Thomas D. Cockrell and Michael B. Ballard (Baton Rouge: Louisiana State University Press, 1995), 233.

65. Fannie A. Beers, *Memories: A Record of Personal Experience and Adventure During Four Years of War* (1888; reprint, Alexandria, VA: Time-Life Books, 1985), 150.

66. Beatty, *Memoirs*, 150.

67. Ibid., 66–67.

68. Ibid., 67–68.

69. Walter Clark, *Histories of the Several Regiments and Battalions from North Carolina in the Great War 1861–'65. Volume 1* (Wendell, NC: Avera Press, 1982), 320.

70. Donaldson, *Inside the Army*, 161.

71. Ibid., 334–36.

72. The "war is hell" statement was supposedly made at the 1880 Ohio State Fair.

73. William H. Bentley, *History of the 77th Illinois Volunteer Infantry* (Peoria, IL: Edward Hine, Printer, 1883) [cited March 20, 2004]. http://77illinois.homestead.com/files/77il/77ch15.html.

74. Sneden, *Eye of the Storm*, 171.

75. Ibid., 178.

76. Ibid., 246–47.

77. Ibid., 239–41. The entry is listed as July 4, 1864. In fact, however, Confederate General Howell Cobb actually arrived at Andersonville Prison the week after July 4.

78. John McElroy, *Andersonville: A Story of Rebel Military Prisons, Fifteen Months as a Guest of the So-Called Southern Confederacy* (Toledo, OH: D. R. Locke, 1879), 262.

79. Root, *Story*, 214–15.

CHAPTER 3

1. Southern, *Music*, 162.

2. Vodun is a Fon word meaning "spirit" or "power." The religion's roots can be found in the Bight of Benin region of West Africa. For a discussion of the religion's roots see Gerdès Fleurant, *Folk Songs and Drum Rhythms of Haiti* (Cambridge, MA: Gawou Ginou Publication, 1994).

3. Anti-slavery publications began in 1821 with Benjamin Lundy's newspaper, *Genius of Universal Emancipation*. Other anti-slavery papers included, among numerous others, editor William Lloyd Garrison's *The Liberator*, Frederick Douglass's *North*

Star, Julia Ward Howe and Samuel Gridley Howe's *Commonwealth*, Elijah P. Lovejoy's *St. Louis Observer*, Lydia Maria Child's *National Anti-Slavery Standard*, and John Greenleaf Whittier's *Pennsylvania Freeman*.

4. Martin, "Music," 2–3.

5. Eileen Southern, *Readings in Black American Music*, 2nd ed. (New York: W. W. Norton & Company, 1983), 87.

6. Southern, *Music*, 101. Southern notes that historian Gilbert Chase described parlor music in much the same fashion in his 1966 *America's Music*. Projecting an aesthetic hierarchy onto musical practice is obviously problematic.

7. Ibid., 103–4.

8. Ibid., 133.

9. Ibid., 107. Southern is quoting James Trotter, *Music and Some Highly Musical People* (Boston: Lee and Shepard, 1878).

10. Elizabeth Hyde Botume, *First Days amongst the Contrabands* (New York: Arno Press, 1968), 79.

11. The Port Royal Gideonites consisted of volunteers from Boston, New York, and Philadelphia. The men served mostly as agriculture overseers, the women as teachers.

12. Sara Dalmas Jonsberg, "Yankee Schoolmarms in the South: Models or Monsters?" *English Journal, National Council of Teachers of English*, 91, no. 4 (2002), 77. Also see Willie Lee Nichols Rose, *Rehearsal for Reconstruction: The Port Royal Experiment* (Indianapolis: Bobbs-Merrill, 1964).

13. Charlotte L. Forten, "Life on the Sea Island," in *Work of Teachers in America: A Social History Through Stories*, ed. Rosetta Marantz Cohen and Samuel Scheer (Mahwah, NJ: Lawrence Erlbaum Associates, 1997), 128. The article draws from Forten's daily journal, which has been published as: *The Journal of Charlotte Forten: A Free Negro in the Slave Era*, ed. Ray Allen Billington (New York: Collier Books, 1953). Haitian patriot Toussaint L'Ouverture was a former slave who fought against the French until his death in 1803.

14. Forten, "Life," 128.

15. Ibid., 127.

16. Ibid., 129.

17. Botume, *First Days*, 74.

18. Higginson was a lifelong supporter of women's suffrage, an ardent member of the Boston abolition movement, and a supporter for John Brown in his raid on Harpers Ferry. Higginson's remembrances of his time as a Union officer in South Carolina were published in 1867 in *The Atlantic Monthly* and more fully in his *Army Life*.

19. Shaw led the regiment in the bold but unsuccessful July 18, 1864, assault on Fort Wagner. He was killed in the action. The 54th Massachusetts was brought to contemporary attention through the 1989 Tri-Star Pictures film *Glory*. Casualties and

missing from the engagement amounted to well over half the regiment. While the assault was unsuccessful, the battle did much to establish the reputation of African-American soldiers as hard fighters.

20. Higginson, *Army Life*, 11–13.

21. In the introduction to *Army Life in a Black Regiment*, John Hope Franklin notes that the author "regarded these attributes as the result of circumstances and limited opportunities [imposed by slavery] rather than as innate, insuperable qualities." Ibid., xvi.

22. Ibid., 16–17.

23. Looby, *Higginson*, 220.

24. Higginson, *Army Life*, 17–18.

25. Ibid., 253.

26. Neither Higginson nor the collaborative authors William Francis Allen, Lucy McKim Garrison, and Charles Pickard Ware, who wrote *Slave Songs of the United States* (1867, reprint, New York: Peter Smith, 1929), define the term spiritual. This was a sign, suggests Southern, that the term had been "in common usage by the 1860s." Southern identifies spirituals "for singing in the worship service, for singing while 'jes' sittin' around,' and for singing to accompany the shout," and suggests there were other categories as well. Southern, *Music*, 168.

27. Higginson, *Army Life*, 198–99.

28. Ibid., 199.

29. Ibid., 197.

30. Allen et al., *Slave Songs*, iv.

31. Ibid., 22–23.

32. Higginson, *Army Life*, 197–98.

33. Allen, et al. *Slave Songs*, iv–v.

34. Ibid., x.

35. Higginson, *Army Life*, 203.

36. Allen et al., *Slave Songs*, xxiii.

37. Higginson, *Army Life*, 219.

38. Ibid., xliii. Higginson gives three different versions of the song "The Ship of Zion," 214–15.

39. Charles Carleton Coffin, "Contrabands" (1866), in *The Romance of the Civil War*, ed. Albert Bushnell Hart (New York: Macmillan, 1903; reprint, Charlottesville: Electronic Text Center, University of Virginia Library, 2000), 110–12.

40. Narrative of Mrs. Fannie Berry as recorded in *Born in Slavery: Slave Narratives from the Federal Writers' Project, 1936–1938, Virginia Narratives, Volume 17* (Federal Writers' Project, United States Work Projects Administration; Manuscript Division, Library of Congress. Digital ID#: mesn 170/004001), 6 [cited September 1, 2003], http://memory.loc.gov/ammem/snhtml/snhome.html.

41. The Federal Writers' Project was administered under the auspices of the President Franklin D. Roosevelt's 1935-initiated Works Project Administration.

42. Narrative of "Parson" Rezin Williams as recorded in *Born in Slavery: Slave Narratives from the Federal Writers' Project, 1936–1938, Maryland Narratives, Volume 8* (Federal Writers' Project, United States Work Projects Administration; Manuscript Division, Library of Congress. Digital ID#: mesn 080/071068), 72 [cited September 1, 2003], http://memory.loc.gov/ammem/snhtml/snhome.html.

43. Narrative of James Calhart James as recorded in *Born in Slavery: Slave Narratives from the Federal Writers' Project, 1936–1938, Maryland Narratives, Volume 8* (Federal Writers' Project, United States Work Projects Administration; Manuscript Division, Library of Congress. Digital ID#: mesn 080/037034), 35–36 [cited September 1, 2003], http://memory.loc.gov/ammem/snhtml/snhome.html.

44. Martin, "Music," 4.

45. Kevin Bales notes that slavery persists into the twenty-first century in part because the institution "brings about a psychological degradation that often renders victims unable to function in the outside world," in, "The Social Psychology of Modern Slavery," *Scientific American* (April 24, 2002), 80–88.

46. Narrative of James Lucas as recorded in *Born in Slavery: Slave Narratives from the Federal Writers' Project, 1936–1938, Mississippi Narratives, Volume 9* (Federal Writers' Project, United States Work Projects Administration; Manuscript Division, Library of Congress. Digital ID#: mesn 090/095091), 94–95 [cited September 1, 2003], http://memory.loc.gov/ammem/snhtml/snhome.html.

47. Narrative of Maria Sutton Clements as recorded in *Born in Slavery: Slave Narratives from the Federal Writers' Project, 1936–1938, Arkansas Narratives, Volume 2, Part 2* (Federal Writers' Project, United States Work Projects Administration; Manuscript Division, Library of Congress. Digital ID#: mesn 022/031027), 27 [cited September 1, 2003], http://memory.loc.gov/ammem/snhtml/snhome.html.

48. Narrative of Charley Williams as recorded in *Born in Slavery: Slave Narratives from the Federal Writers' Project, 1936–1938, Oklahoma Narratives, Volume 13* (Federal Writers' Project, United States Work Projects Administration; Manuscript Division, Library of Congress. Digital ID#: mesn 130/337330), 337–38 [cited September 1, 2003], http://memory.loc.gov/ammem/snhtml/snhome.html.

49. Narrative of Margaret Thornton as recorded in *Born in Slavery: Slave Narratives from the Federal Writers' Project, 1936–1938, North Carolina Narratives, Volume 11, Part 2* (Federal Writers' Project, United States Work Projects Administration; Manuscript Division, Library of Congress. Digital ID#: mesn 112/356352), 353 [cited September 1, 2003], http://memory.loc.gov/ammem/snhtml/snhome.html.

50. Narrative of Martha King as recorded in *Born in Slavery: Slave Narratives from the Federal Writers' Project, 1936–1938, Oklahoma Narratives, Volume 13* (Federal Writers' Project, United States Work Projects Administration; Manuscript Division,

Library of Congress. Digital ID#: mesn 130/174169), 169 [cited September 1, 2003], http://memory.loc.gov/ammem/snhtml/snhome.html.

51. Narrative of Lewis Bonner as recorded in *Born in Slavery: Slave Narratives from the Federal Writers' Project, 1936–1938, Oklahoma Narratives, Volume 13* (Federal Writers' Project, United States Work Projects Administration; Manuscript Division, Library of Congress. Digital ID#: mesn 130/021017), 18 [cited September 1, 2003], http://memory.loc.gov/ammem/snhtml/snhome.html.

52. There was nothing "Ethiopian" about this type of entertainment, or the people whom the entertainers were parodying. Almost all African Americans traced their heritage to West, not East, Africa. Perhaps the moniker was used because it sounded suitably ostentatious.

53. Toll, *Minstrel Show*, 30. The quote is from a Virginia Minstrels 1844 program presented in Dublin, Ireland.

54. William J. Mahar, *Behind the Burnt Cork Mask: Early Blackface Minstrelsy and Antebellum American Popular Culture* (Urbana: University of Illinois Press, 1999), 1.

55. Also published in 1862 was "Song of the Negro boatman, at Port Royal" with words by John G. Whittier and music by E. W. Kellogg.

56. Strictly speaking, the term "contraband" refers to captured arms and munitions of war. In 1861, the Union's General Benjamin Butler applied the term to escaped slaves.

57. The year of jubilee is described in Leviticus 25:8 of the Old Testament. On every fiftieth year, the slaves were to be set free.

58. Rembert W. Patrick, *The Fall of Richmond* (Baton Rouge: Louisiana State University Press, 1960), 15. Patrick calls the piece "a Negro song borrowed from the Yankees."

59. Toll, *Minstrel Show*, 117.

60. The Chamber of Commerce of Elbert County, Georgia, claims the song originated with the slaves of Reverend Daniel Tucker (1740–1818). Historical Sites [cited March 25, 2004], http://www.elbertga.com/attractions/dan_tucker.html.

61. Other abolitionist song collections included *Hymns and Songs for the Friends of Freedom* (1842), *Anti-Slavery Melodies: for the Friends of Freedom* (1843), *Hartley Wood's Anniversary Book of Music, for the Fourth of July, Temperance, and Anti-Slavery Occasions* (1843), *The Anti-Slavery Harp* (1848), and *The Emancipation Car* (1854). Periodicals that published abolitionist songs included *The African Repository and Colonial Journal*, *Douglass' Monthly*, *The Liberty Bell*, *National Anti-Slavery Standard*, and *Anti-Slavery Tracts*.

62. Vera Brodsky Lawrence, *Music for Patriots, Politicians, and Presidents* (New York: Macmillan Publishing Company, 1975), 326. In fact, these lyrics turned out to be uncomfortably accurate. After emancipation, the government (and even the abolitionists) did little to nothing to help the former slaves dig out of the economic and educational hole in which they had been held.

63. McPherson, *Battle Cry of Freedom*, 121.

64. Eaklor, *American Antislavery Songs*, 468. Lawrence, Kansas, was sacked on May 21, 1856, by some 800 pro-slavery deputies. Just two days after making his anti-slavery "The Crime against Kansas" speech of May 19–20, Massachusetts Senator Charles Sumner was cane whipped at his desk in the senate chamber by South Carolina Congressman Preston Brooks.

65. "Fence rails" refers to "Honest Abe's" penchant for honest hard labor. "Tippecanoe" was William Henry Harrison who built his 1840 campaign on the image that he was an Ohio backwoodsman.

66. Irwin Silber, *Songs America Voted By* (Harrisburg, PA: Stackpole Books, 1971), 80.

CHAPTER 4

1. Gottschalk, *Notes*, 50.

2. Vera Brodsky Lawrence, *Strong on Music: The New York Scene in the Days of George Templeton Strong, Volume 3: Repercussions 1857–1862* (Chicago: University of Chicago Press, 1999), 425.

3. Ibid.

4. Ibid., 426.

5. Mary Sue Morrow, "Somewhere between Beer and Wagner: The Cultural and Musical Impact of German Männerchöre in New York and New Orleans," in *Music and Culture in America, 1861–1918*, ed. Michael Saffle (New York: Garland Publishing, 1998), 85.

6. Edwin M. Good, "William Steinway and Music in New York, 1861–1871," in *Music and Culture in America, 1861–1918*, ed. Michael Saffle (New York: Garland Publishing, 1998), 10–11.

7. Lawrence, *Strong on Music*, 422.

8. Ibid.

9. Ibid., 436.

10. Ibid., 437.

11. Howard Shanet, *Philharmonic: A History of New York's Orchestra* (Garden City, NY: Doubleday & Company, 1975), 88.

12. Chase, *America's Music*, 308.

13. William Treat Upton, *William Henry Fry: American Journalist and Composer-Critic* (New York: Thomas Y. Crowell, 1954), 264.

14. Ibid., 265.

15. Ibid., 272–73.

16. Ibid.

17. Ibid., 274–75.

18. Delmer D. Rogers, "Bristow, George Frederick," in *Grove Music Online*, ed. L. Macy [accessed March 20, 2004], http://www.grovemusic.com.

19. Upton, 166.

20. Fry would not outlive the war. He died in the West Indies of tuberculosis on December 21, 1864, just nine days after completing his final composition, a mass. After his death, journalists used superlatives to describe his contributions. According to Upton, Philadelphia's *Sunday Transcript* placed his compositional skill alongside Meyerbeer and above that of Verdi, while the New York paper the *Independent* characterized Fry as an "orator, a writer, a politician, a conversationalist, he was one of the most versatile of men—a rare wit, a self-poised gentleman, a true friend, a charming playmate of children, and one of the most unselfish of human beings." Ibid., 170–73.

21. Ibid., 280.

22. Lawrence, *Strong on Music*, 466.

23. Ibid., 547.

24. Varhola, *Everyday Life during the Civil War*, 110; Jay Winik, *April 1865: The Month That Saved America* (New York: HarperCollins, 2001), 383–87; Angel Price, "Whitman's Drum Taps and Washington's Civil War Hospitals" [cited March 28, 2004], http://xroads.virginia.edu/~CAP/hospital/whitman.htm.

25. Kenneth A. Bernard, *Lincoln and the Music of the Civil War* (Caldwell, ID: Caxton Printers, 1966), 13.

26. Ibid., 28.

27. Ibid., 22–23.

28. Ibid., 16.

29. Kirk, *Music*, 84.

30. Hutchinson, *Story*, 381–91.

31. Gottschalk, *Notes*, 171.

32. Ibid.

33. Henry A. Kmen, *Music in New Orleans: The Formative Years 1791–1841* (Baton Rouge: Louisiana State University Press, 1966), 5.

34. Ibid., 52.

35. Ibid., 58.

36. F. H. Buffum, *A Memorial of the Great Rebellion: Being a History of the Fourteenth Regiment New-Hampshire Volunteers* (Boston: Franklin Press: Rand, Avery, & Company, 1882), 130–32.

37. Francis Alfred Lord and Arthur Wise, *Bands and Drummer Boys of the Civil War* (New York: Thomas Yoseloff, 1966), 30.

38. For a more extended analysis, see William A. Bufkin, *Union Bands of the Civil War (1861–1865): Instrumentation and Score Analysis, Volume I* (Ann Arbor, MI: University Microfilms International, 1982), 27–29.

39. Lord and Wise, *Bands*, 28–30.

40. Bufkin, *Union Bands*, 165.

41. Margaret Hindle Hazen and Robert M. Hazen, *The Music Men: An Illustrated History of Brass Bands in America, 1800–1920* (Washington DC: Smithsonian Institution Press, 1987), 7–8; Robert Garafalo and Mark Elrod, *A Pictorial History of Civil War Era Musical Instruments & Military Bands* (Charleston, WV: Pictorial Histories Publishing Company, 1985), 1.

42. Garafalo and Elrod, *Pictorial History*, 2.

43. Allen Dodworth, *Dodworth's Brass Band School* (New York: H. B. Dodworth & Company, 1853), 12.

44. This material was taken from a variety of sources, including Hazen and Hazen, *Music Men*, 134–35; Garofalo and Elrod, *Pictorial History*, 4–14; and Robert Eliason, *Early American Brass Makers* (Nashville, TN: The Brass Press, 1979).

45. Hazen and Hazen, *Music Men*, 136; Garofalo and Elrod, *Pictorial History*, 15–29.

46. George B. Bruce and Daniel D. Emmett, *The Drummer's and Fifer's Guide* (New York: Firth, Pond & Company, 1862), 16.

47. Garofalo and Elrod, *Pictorial History*, 36.

48. Frank Rauscher, *Music on the March: 1862–'65* (Philadelphia: Wm. F. Fell & Company, 1892), 69.

49. Buffum, *A Memorial*, 300–01.

50. Lord and Wise, *Bands*, 82–84. Extended descriptions of camp life can be found in Rauscher, *Music*, 68–72 and in Billings, *Hardtack*, 164–97.

51. Wiley, *Billy Yank*, 247.

52. Meyers gives a detailed description of his experiences at the School of Practice. He entered in 1854 at age twelve and was discharged on March 24, 1865. Meyers, *Ten Years*, 1–17.

53. Charles Stewart Ashworth was Drum Major, The United States Marine Corps Band. His book contains fife melodies as well as drum rhythms.

54. Kenneth E. Olson, *Music and Musket: Bands and Bandsmen of the American Civil War* (Westport, CT: Greenwood Press, 1981), 93.

55. The Company of Fifers and Drummers Music Committee, *The Camp Duty* (The Company of Fifers and Drummers, 1980), Introduction.

56. Ibid., 28–36.

57. John Pullen, *The Twentieth Maine* (Philadelphia: J. B. Lippincott, 1957), 2.

58. Charles William Bardeen, *A Little Fifer's War Diary* (Syracuse, NY: C. W. Bardeen, 1910), 18.

59. Ibid., 20.

60. Benjamin A. Botkin, *A Civil War Treasury of Tales, Legends, and Folklore* (New York: Random House, 1960), 64–65.

61. Buffum, *A Memorial*, 302.

62. Delavan S. Miller, *Drum Taps in Dixie: Memories of a Drummer Boy 1861–1865* (Watertown, NY: Hungerford-Holbrook Company 1905), 19.

63. Ibid., 28–29.

64. Lord and Wise, *Bands*, 111.

65. Meyers, *Ten Years*, 130–132.

66. Wiley, *Billy Yank*, 297–98.

67. Pullen, *Twentieth Maine*, 20–21.

68. Major Fredrick C. Winkler. *Civil War Letters of Major Frederick C. Winkler, 1864,* Home page of the 26th Wisconsin Infantry [cited March 20, 2004], http://www. russscott.com/~rscott/26thwis/26pgwk64.htm.

69. Harry H. Hall, *A Johnny Reb Band from Salem: The Pride of Tarheelia.* (Raleigh, NC: The North Carolina Confederate Centennial Commission, 1963), 64–65. Hall reports that the original Leinbach diary has been lost (p. 1).

70. There has been much controversy over the origin of "Taps." Norton's remembrances can be found in Oliver Wilcox Norton, *Army Letters, 1861–1865: Being Extracts from Private Letters to Relatives and Friends from a Soldier in the Field during the Civil War* (Chicago: O. L. Deming, 1903). Jari A. Villanueva, who served as curator for the "Taps Bugle Exhibit" that ran from 1999–2002 at Arlington National Cemetery, has posted detailed histories of "Taps." See "24 Notes That Tap Deep Emotions" [cited September 18, 2003], http://www.west-point.org/taps/Taps.html.

71. Bufkin, *Union Bands*, 38.

72. Ibid., 46.

73. Ibid., 65.

74. Ibid., 68.

75. Ibid., 77.

76. Donald L. Smith, *The Twenty-Fourth Michigan of the Iron Brigade* (Harrisburg, PA: The Stackpole Company, 1962), 200.

77. Bufkin, *Union Bands*, 137.

78. Ibid., 49–50.

79. Edward King Wightman, *From Antietam to Fort Fisher: The Civil War Letters of Edward King Wightman, 1862–1865*, ed. by Edward G. Longacre (Rutherford, NJ: Fairleigh Dickson University Press, Inc., 1985), 47.

80. Bufkin, *Union Bands*, 75.

81. Rauscher, *Music*, 121.

82. Bufkin, *Union Bands*, 301.

83. *Dwight's Journal of Music* 19, no. 26 (September 28, 1861), 207.

84. Wiley, *Billy Yank*, 158.

85. Luis F. Emilio, *History of the Fifty-Fourth Regiment of Massachusetts Volunteer Infantry, 1863–1865* (Boston: The Boston Book Company, 1894), 31 and 318.

86. Three months was the amount of time Unionists generally thought would

be needed to quell the rebellion. After the thrashing at 1st Bull Run they realized that they were mistaken. Confederates called that same battle 1st Manassas.

87. Today Ellsworth is best remembered for the fact that as colonel of the 11th New York Infantry ("Ellsworth's Zouaves") he became on May 24, 1861, the first federal officer to be killed in action. His death caused mourning across the North, inspired songs and poems, as well as the formation of a New York military unit known as Ellsworth's Avengers.

88. Meade, wrote Rauscher, was charmed by any "pretty flowing melody, smoothly arranged, whether operatic or ballad." Rauscher, *Music*, 145.

89. Stonewall Brigade Band Web site [cited March 28, 2004], http//stonewallbrigadeband.com/History/history.html.

90. Dodworth, *Band School*, 11–12.

91. Bufkin, *Union Bands*, 158.

92. Bell Irvin Wiley, *The Life of Johnny Reb: The Common Soldier of the Confederacy* (Indianapolis: Bobbs-Merrill Company, 1943), 157. The quote was taken from the diary manuscript of James J. Kirkpatrick.

93. Bufkin, *Union Bands*, 83.

94. S. Millett Thompson, *Thirteenth Regiment of New Hampshire Volunteer Infantry in the War of the Rebellion, 1861–1865: A Diary Covering Three Years and a Day* (Boston: Houghton, Mifflin and Company, 1888), 223. Entry dated December 22, 1863.

95. Wiley, *Diary*, 101.

96. Sneden, *Storm*, 106.

97. Charles Monroe Chase, Diary, July 22, 1861, Charles Monroe Chase Papers 1861, Western Historical Manuscript Collection, Columbia, MO.

98. Ibid.

99. Francis Alfred Lord, *They Fought for the Union* (Westport, CT: Greenwood Press, 1960), 48.

100. Edwin O. Kimberley to his parents, January 14, 1862. Kimberley Papers.

101. Sir Arthur James Lyon Fremantle, *The Fremantle Diary: Being the Journal of Lieutenant Colonel James Arthur Lyon Freemantle, Coldstream Guards, on His Three Months in the Southern States*, ed. Walter Lord (Boston: Little, Brown and Company, 1954), 297.

102. General Horace Porter, *Campaigning with Grant* (New York: The Century Company, 1897), 234–235.

103. Bruce Catton, *A Stillness at Appomattox* (Garden City, NY: Doubleday & Company 1953), 36.

104. Bernard, *Lincoln*, 47–48. Interestingly, it was listening to soldiers sing in the aftermath of this event that inspired Julia Ward Howe to write, in the early morning hours of November 21, the words to "Battle Hymn of the Republic."

105. Buffum, *A Memorial*, 305.

106. Charles D. Page, *History of the Fourteenth Regiment, Connecticut Volunteer Infantry* (Meriden, CT: The Horton Printing Company, 1906), 60–61.

107. James I. Robertson, Jr., *The Stonewall Brigade* (Baton Rouge: Louisiana State University Press, 1963), 34.

108. Sneden, *Storm*, 103.

109. Catton, *Appomattox*, 347.

110. Page, *Fourteenth*, 120–21.

111. Unpublished diary of Daniel B. Harris as cited by both Bufkin, *Union Bands*, 89–90, and Olson, *Music*, 207.

112. William J. K. Beaudot and Lance J. Herdegen, eds. *An Irishman in the Iron Brigade: the Civil War memoirs of James P. Sullivan, Sergt., Company K, 6th Wisconsin Volunteers* (New York: Fordham University Press, 1993), 93–94.

113. Fremantle, *Diary*, 208.

114. Julius Leinbach, *Regiment Band of the Twenty-Sixth North Carolina*, ed. Donald M. McCorkle (Winston-Salem, NC: The Moravian Music Foundation, 1958), 229. The 26th North Carolina suffered nearly 90 percent casualties at Gettysburg.

115. Quote taken from Diary of D. S. Redding, typescript, Georgia Archives, cited in Wiley, *Johnny Reb*, 156.

116. Bufkin, *Union Bands*, 98. From the diary of L. D. Young, "Reminiscences of a Soldier of the Orphan Brigade" (Paris, KY: Chickamauga National Military Park, n.d.).

117. Patrick, *Richmond*, 36.

118. James Cooper Nisbet, *Four Years on the Firing Line* (Wilmington, NC: Broadfoot Publishing Company, 1991), 204.

119. Bruce Catton, *Mr. Lincoln's Army* (Garden City, NY: Doubleday and Company, 1962), 178.

120. Asbury L. Kerwood, *Annals of the Fifty-Seventh Regiment Indiana Volunteers* (Dayton, OH: W. J. Shuey, 1868), 216, cited in Bufkin, *Union Bands*, 100.

121. Thompson, *A Diary*, 369.

122. George A. Bruce's, *The Twentieth Regiment of Massachusetts Volunteer Infantry, 1861–1865* (Boston: Houghton, Mifflin and Company 1906), 396, cited in Bufkin, *Union Bands*, 100.

123. Ibid., 183.

124. Buck, *Shadows*, 74, 77.

125. Edwin Kimberley, letter, September 1864, Kimberley Papers.

126. Rauscher, *Music*, 160.

127. Ibid., 192.

128. Page, *Fourteenth*, 58.

129. Rauscher, *Music*, 145.

130. Ibid., 265.

131. Olson, *Music*, 48.

132. Pullen, *Twentieth Maine*, 21.

CHAPTER 5

1. Hall, *Johnny Reb Band*, 106. Hall quotes from the Leinbach diary.

2. John Lomax and Alan Lomax, *American Ballads and Folk Songs* (New York: The Macmillan Company, 1934), 5.

3. Hutchinson, *Story*, 453–54.

4. *Dwight's Journal of Music* 29, no. 8 (July 3, 1869), 63–64.

CHAPTER 6

1. Kirk, *White House*, 84–85. In the years that followed, Carreño led a life as varied and explosive as her temperament. A risk taker and perfectionist, she performed as a pianist, vocalist, and opera conductor, and also composed. Her career took her across Europe and the Americas. Carreño studied piano with Anton Rubinstein and was a mentor to Edward MacDowell, who was seven years her junior. Carreño married four times.

2. S. Frederick Starr, *Bamboula! The Life and Times of Louis Moreau Gottschalk* (New York: Oxford University Press, 1995), 330.

3. Ibid., 329. Quoted from the *Boston Daily Courier* of October 12, 1862.

4. Ibid., 346.

5. Ibid., 201.

6. Ibid., 241.

7. John Hill Hewitt, *Shadows on the Wall* (1877; reprint, New York: AMS Press, 1971), 93.

8. Charles Hamm, *Yesterdays: Popular Song in America* (New York: W. W. Norton & Company, 1979), 103. Hamm notes Hewitt's "transparent" modeling of songs by earlier writers, including his own father, James.

9. For a complete list of theatrical productions, see Harwell, *Confederate Music* 34.

10. Root, *Story*, 97–98.

11. Ibid., 83.

Bibliography

Abrahams, Roger D. *Singing the Master: The Emergence of African American Culture in the Plantation South.* New York: Pantheon Books, 1992.

Alexander, John H. *Mosby's Men.* New York: The Neale Publishing Company, 1907.

Allen, William Francis, Lucy McKim Garrison, and Charles Pickard Ware. *Slave Songs of the United States.* 1867. Reprint, New York: Peter Smith, 1929.

Ammer, Christine. *Unsung: A History of Women in American Music.* Portland, OR: Amadeus Press, 2001.

Ashworth, Charles Stewart. *A New, Useful and Complete System of Drumbeating.* 1812. Revised, Supplemented and Interpreted in Modern Notation by Drum Major George P. Carroll. Williamsburg, VA: George P. Carroll, 1966.

Austin, William W. *"Susanna," "Jeanie," and "The Old Folks at Home": The Songs of Stephen C. Foster from His Time to Ours.* Urbana: University of Illinois Press, 1987.

Baer, Elizabeth R., ed. *Shadows on My Heart: The Civil War Diary of Lucy Rebecca Buck of Virginia.* Athens: University of Georgia Press, 1997.

Bakeless, Katherine Little. *Glory, Hallelujah! The Story of* The Battle Hymn of the Republic. Philadelphia: J. B. Lippincott Company, 1944.

Bales, Kevin. "The Social Psychology of Modern Slavery." *Scientific American,* April 24, 2002, 80–88.

Banks, Rev. Louis Albert, D.D. *Immortal Songs of Camp and Field.* Cleveland: Imperial Press, 1898.

Barber, Flavel C. *Holding the Line: The Third Tennessee Infantry, 1861–1864.* Kent, OH: Kent State University Press, 1994.

Bardeen, Charles William. *A Little Fifer's War Diary.* Syracuse, NY: C. W. Bardeen, 1910.

Beatty, John. *Memoires of a Volunteer, 1861–1863*. New York: W. W. Norton & Company, 1946.

Beaudot, William J. K., and Lance J. Herdegen, eds. *An Irishman in the Iron Brigade: The Civil War Memoirs of James P. Sullivan, Sergt., Company K, 6th Wisconsin Volunteers*. New York: Fordham University Press, 1993.

Beers, Fannie A. *Memories: A Record of Personal Experience and Adventure during Four Years of War*. 1888. Reprint, Alexandria, VA: Time-Life Books, 1985.

Bentley, William H. *History of the 77th Illinois Volunteer Infantry*. Peoria, IL: Edward Hine, Printer, 1883 [cited March 20, 2004]. http://77illinois.homestead.com/files/77il/77ch15.html.

Bernard, Kenneth A. *Lincoln and the Music of the Civil War*. Caldwell, ID: Caxton Printers, 1966.

Bever, Joseph. *The Christian Songster: A Collection of Hymns and Spiritual Songs, Usually Sung at Camp, Prayer, and Social Meetings, and Revivals of Religion. Designed for All Denominations*. Dayton, OH: United Brethren in Christ, 1858.

Bierce, Ambrose. *The Ambrose Bierce Satanic Reader: Selections from the Invective Journalism of the Great Satirist*. Edited by Ernest Jerome Hopkins. Garden City, NY: Doubleday, 1968.

———. *Ambrose Bierce's Civil War*. Edited by William McCann. Washington, DC: Regnery Gateway, 1988.

Bilby, Joseph G. *Remember Fontenoy! The 69th New York and the Irish Brigade in the Civil War*. Hightstown, NJ: Longstreet House, 1995.

Billings, John D. *Hardtack & Coffee: The Unwritten Story of Army Life*. Boston: George M. Smith & Company, 1887. Reprint, Lincoln: University of Nebraska Press, 1993.

Birdoff, Harry. *The World's Greatest Hit—Uncle Tom's Cabin*. New York: S. F. Vanni, 1947.

Blackford, William W. *War Years with Jeb Stuart*. New York: C. Scribner's Sons, 1945.

Blassingame, John W. *The Slave Community: Plantation Life in the Antebellum South*. New York: Oxford University Press, 1979.

Bolton, Dorothy G., and H. T. Burleigh. *Old Songs Hymnal*. New York: Century Company, 1929.

Born in Slavery: Slave Narratives from the Federal Writers' Project, 1936–1938. Manuscript Division, Library of Congress and Prints and Photographs Division, Library of Congress. Washington, DC: Library of Congress, 2001 [cited September 1, 2003]. http://memory.loc.gov/ammem/snhtml/snhome.html.

Botkin, Benjamin A. *A Civil War Treasury of Tales, Legends, and Folklore*. New York: Random House, 1960.

Botume, Elizabeth Hyde. *First Days amongst the Contrabands*. New York: Arno Press, 1968.

A Brief History of the 1st Brigade Band. [cited March 28, 2004]. http://www.1stbrigadeband.org/Band_History.html#Hamilton.

Brown, Dee. *Bury My Heart at Wounded Knee: An Indian History of the American West*. New York: Bantam Books, 1972.

Brown, William Wells. *Clotel, or, The President's Daughter: A Narrative of Slave Life in the United States*. Edited by Robert S. Levine. Boston: Bedford/St. Martin's, 2000.

Bruce, George A. *The Twentieth Regiment of Massachusetts Volunteer Infantry, 1861–1865.* Boston: Houghton, Mifflin & Company, 1906.

Bruce, George B., and Daniel D. Emmett. *The Drummer's and Fifer's Guide.* New York: Firth, Pond & Company, 1862.

Bryant, Carolyn. *And the Band Played On: 1776–1976.* Washington, DC: Smithsonian Institution Press, 1975.

Buffum, F. H. *A Memorial of the Great Rebellion: Being a History of the Fourteenth Regiment New-Hampshire Volunteers.* Boston: Franklin Press: Rand, Avery, & Company, 1882.

Bufkin, William A. *Union Bands of the Civil War (1862–1865): Instrumentation and Score Analysis.* Ann Arbor, MI: University Microfilms International, 1973.

Burgess, Phillipa. "Popular Opera and Bands in the American Civil War." In *Opera and the Golden West: The Past, Present, and Future of Opera in the U.S.A.* Edited by John L. DiGaetani and Josef P. Sirefman. Rutherford, NJ: Fairleigh Dickinson University Press, 1994.

Casler, John Overton. *Four Years in the Stonewall Brigade.* Dayton, OH: Morningside Bookshop, 1971.

Catton, Bruce. *Mr. Lincoln's Army.* Garden City, NY: Doubleday and Company, 1962.

———. *A Stillness at Appomattox.* Garden City, NY: Doubleday and Company, 1953.

Cauthen, Joyce H. *With Fiddle and Well-Rosined Bow: Old-Time Fiddling in Alabama.* Tuscaloosa: University of Alabama Press, 1989.

Chamberlain, Joshua Lawrence. *The Passing of the Armies: An Account of the Final Campaign of the Army of the Potomac, Based upon Personal Reminiscences of the Fifth Army Corps.* Lincoln: University of Nebraska Press, 1998.

Chase, Charles Monroe. Diary. Charles Monroe Chase Papers 1861. Western Historical Manuscript Collection, Columbia, MO.

Chase, Gilbert. *America's Music from the Pilgrims to the Present.* New York: McGraw-Hill Book Company, 1955.

Clark, Walter. *Histories of the Several Regiments and Battalions from North Carolina in the Great War 1861–'65, Volume 1.* Wendell, NC: Avera Press, 1982.

Coffin, Charles Carleton. "Contrabands" (1866). In *The Romance of the Civil War.* Edited by Albert Bushnell Hart. New York: Macmillan, 1903. Reprint, Charlottesville: Electronic Text Center, University of Virginia Library, 2000.

Cohen, Norm. *Long Steel Rail: The Railroad in American Folksong.* Urbana: University of Illinois Press, 1981.

Cohen, Rosetta Marantz, and Samuel Scheer, eds. *The Work of Teachers in America: A Social History through Stories.* Mahwah, NJ: Lawrence Erlbaum Associates, 1997.

Commange, Henry Steele, ed. *The Blue and the Gray: The Story of the Civil War as Told by Participants.* New York: The Fairfax Press, 1982.

The Company of Fifers and Drummers Music Committee. *The Camp Duty.* The Company of Fifers and Drummers, 1980.

Connolly, James A. *Three Years in the Army of the Cumberland: The Letters and Diary of Major James A. Connolly.* Edited by Paul M. Angle. Bloomington: Indiana University Press, 1959.

Cooke, John Esten. *Wearing of the Gray; Personal Portraits, Scenes and Adventures of the War.* New York: E. B. Treat & Company, 1867.

Cornish, Dudley Taylor. *The Sable Arm: Negro Troops in the Union Army, 1861–1865.* 1956. Reprint, Lawrence: University Press of Kansas, 1987.

Courlander, Harold. *Negro Folk Music, U.S.A.* New York: Columbia University Press, 1963.

Crawford, David E. "The Jesuit Relations and Allied Documents, Early Sources for an Ethnography of Music among American Indians," *Ethnomusicology* 11, no. 2 (1967): 199–201.

Crawford, Richard. *The American Musical Landscape.* Berkeley: University of California Press, 1993.

———. *America's Musical Life.* New York: W. W. Norton & Company, 2001.

Crotty, Daniel. "Rally Round the Flags." Web site of the Michigan Historical Museum [cited March 20, 2004]. http://www.sos.state.mi.us/history/museum/explore/museums/hismus/special/flags/rally.html.

Davis, Burke. *Jeb Stuart: The Last Cavalier.* New York: Rinehart & Company, 1957.

———. *The Long Surrender.* New York: Random House, 1985.

Davis, Ronald L. *A History of Music in American Life. Volume I: The Formative Years, 1620–1865.* Malabar, FL: Robert Krieger Publishing Company, 1982.

Dichter, Harry, and Elliott Shapiro. *Handbook of Early American Sheet Music 1768–1889.* New York: Dover Publications, 1977.

DiGaetani, John L., and Josef P. Sirefman. *Opera and the Golden West: The Past, Present, and Future of Opera in the U.S.A.* Rutherford, NJ: Fairleigh Dickinson University Press, 1994.

The Dixie Land Songster. Augusta, GA: Blackmar & Bro.; Macon, GA: Burke, Boykin, & Co., 1863.

Dizikes, John. *Opera in America: A Cultural History.* New Haven, CT: Yale University Press, 1993.

Dobie, J. Frank, ed. *Follow de Drinkn' Gou'd.* Austin: Texas Folklore Society, 1928.

Dodworth, Allen. *Dodworth's Brass Band School.* New York: H. B. Dodworth & Company, 1853.

Dolge, Alfred. *Pianos and Their Makers: A Comprehensive History of the Development of the Piano.* 1911. Reprint, New York: Dover Publication, 1972.

Donaldson, Francis Adams. *Inside the Army of the Potomac: The Civil War Experience of Captain Francis Adams Donaldson.* Edited by Gregory J. Acken. Mechanicsburg, PA: Stackpole Books, 1998.

Douglass, Frederick. *My Bondage and My Freedom.* Edited and with an introduction by William L. Andrews. Urbana: University of Illinois Press, 1987.

———. *Narrative of the Life of Frederick Douglass, An American Slave.* Boston: Anti-Slavery Office, 1845.

Dwight, John Sullivan. *Dwight's Journal of Music: A Paper of Art and Literature.* Boston, 1852–1881.

Eaklor, Vicki L. *American Antislavery Songs: A Collection and Analysis.* Westport, CT: Greenwood Press, 1988.

Eggleston, George Cary. *A Rebel's Recollections.* New York: Hurd and Houghton, 1875.

Ehrlich, Cyril. *The Piano: A History.* Oxford: Clarendon Press, 1990.

Eliason, Robert. *Early American Brass Makers.* Nashville, TN: The Brass Press, 1979.

Emerson, Ken. *Doo-dah! Stephen Foster and the Rise of American Popular Culture.* New York: Simon & Schuster, 1997.

Emilio, Luis F. *History of the Fifty-Fourth Regiment of Massachusetts Volunteer Infantry, 1863–1865*. Boston: The Boston Book Company, 1894.

Epstein, Dena J. *Music Publishing in Chicago before 1871: The Firm of Root and Cady*. Detroit: Information Coordinators, 1969.

———. *Sinful Tunes and Spirituals: Black Folk Music to the Civil War*. Urbana: University of Illinois Press, 1977.

Ernst, Jerry. "The German-American Songbook of the American Civil War" [cited May 14, 2003]. http://www.gtg1848.de/sngbk.htm#Blenker.

Felts, Jack. "Some Aspects of the Rise and Development of the Wind Band during the Civil War." *Journal of Band Research* 3, no. 2 (Spring 1967): 15.

Fennell, Frederick. "The Civil War: Its Music and its Sounds." *Journal of Band Research* 4, no. 2 (Spring 1968), 36–44; and 5, no. 1 (Fall 1968): 8–14.

Fisher, Miles Mark. *Negro Slave Song in the United States*. Ithaca, NY: Cornell University Press, 1953.

Fisher, William Arms. *One Hundred and Fifty Years of Music Publishing in the United States; An Historical Sketch with Special Reference to the Pioneer Publisher, Oliver Ditson Company, Inc.* Boston: Oliver Ditson Company, 1933.

Fleurant, Gerdès. *Folk Songs and Drum Rhythms of Haiti*. Cambridge, MA: Gawou Ginou Publication, 1994.

Foote, Shelby. *Stars in Their Courses: The Gettysburg Campaign, June–July 1863*. New York: Modern Library, 1994.

Forten, Charlotte L. *The Journal of Charlotte Forten: A Free Negro in the Slave Era*. Edited by Ray Allen Billington. New York: Collier Books, 1953.

———. "Life on the Sea Island." In *Work of Teachers in America: A Social History Through Stories*. Edited by Rosetta Marantz Cohen and Samuel Scheer. Mahwah, NJ: Lawrence Erlbaum Associates, 1997.

Fremantle, Sir James Arthur Lyon. *The Fremantle Diary: Being the Journal of Lieutenant Colonel James Arthur Lyon Fremantle, Coldstream Guards, on His Three Months in the Southern States*. Edited by Walter Lord. Boston: Little, Brown and Company, 1954.

Garofalo, Robert, and Mark Elrod. *A Pictorial History of Civil War Era Musical Instruments & Military Bands*. Charleston, WV: Pictorial Histories Publishing Company, 1985.

The Gen. Lee Songster: Being a Collection of the Most Popular Sentimental, Patriotic and Comic Songs. Macon, GA and Savannah, GA: John C. Schreiner and Son, 1864.

Good, Edwin M. "William Steinway and Music in New York, 1861–1871." In *Music and Culture in America, 1861–1918*. Edited by Michael Saffle. New York: Garland Publishing, 1998.

Gordon, John B. *Reminiscences of the Civil War*. Baton Rouge: Louisiana State University Press. 1993.

Gottschalk, Louis Moreau. *Notes of a Pianist*. Edited by Jeanne Behrend. New York: Alfred A. Knopf, 1964.

Hall, Harry H. *A Johnny Reb Band from Salem: The Pride of Tarheelia*. Raleigh: The North Carolina Confederate Centennial Commission, 1963.

Hamm, Charles. *Yesterdays: Popular Song in America*. New York: W. W. Norton & Company, 1979.

Hart, Albert Bushnell. *The Romance of the Civil War*. 1903. Reprint, Charlottesville: Electronic Text Center, University of Virginia Library, 2000.

Harwell, Richard Barksdale.*Confederate Music*. Chapel Hill: University of North Carolina Press, 1950.

Hauptman, Laurence M. *Between Two Fires: American Indians in the Civil War*. New York: Free Press, 1995.

Hazen, Margaret Hindle, and Robert M. Hazen. *The Music Men: An Illustrated History of Brass Bands in America, 1800–1920*. Washington, DC: Smithsonian Institution Press, 1987.

Heaps, Willard A., and Porter W. Heaps. *The Singing Sixties: The Spirit of Civil War Days Drawn from the Music of the Times*. Norman: University of Oklahoma Press, 1960.

Hewitt, John Hill. *King Linkum The First*. Atlanta: Emory University, 1947.

———. *Shadows on the Wall*. 1877. Reprint, New York: AMS Press, 1971.

Higginson, Thomas Wentworth. *Army Life in a Black Regiment*. Boston: Beacon Press, 1962.

Hitchcock, H. Wiley. *Music in the United States: A Historical Introduction*. Englewood Cliffs, NJ: Prentice-Hall, 1988.

Holt, David. *A Mississippi Rebel in the Army of Northern Virginia*. Edited by Thomas D. Cockrell and Michael B. Ballard. Baton Rouge: Louisiana State University Press, 1995.

Horwitz, Tony. *Confederates in the Attic: Dispatches from the Unfinished Civil War*. New York: Pantheon Books. 1998.

Howe, Elias, Jr. *Howe's School for the Fife*. Boston: Oliver Ditson & Co., 1851.

Howe, Julia Ward. "The Battle Hymn of the Republic" [cited March 14, 2004]. http://www.theatlantic.com/issues/1862feb/batthym.htm.

Hutchinson, John Wallace. *Story of the Hutchinsons*. Boston: Lee and Shepard, 1896.

Jackson, George Pullen. *White and Negro Spirituals*. New York: J. J. Augustin, 1943.

———. *White Spirituals in the Southern Uplands*. Chapel Hill: The University of North Carolina Press, 1933.

Jackson, Irene V., ed. *More Than Dancing*. Westport, CT: Greenwood Press, 1985.

Jonsberg, Sara Dalmas. "Yankee Schoolmarms in the South: Models or Monsters?" *English Journal, National Council of Teachers of English* 91, no. 4 (2002): 75–81.

Keck, George R., and Sherrill V. Martin, eds. *Feel the Spirit: Studies in Nineteenth-Century Afro-American Music*. Westport, CT: Greenwood Press, 1988.

Kerwood, Asbury L. *Annals of the Fifty-Seventh Regiment Indiana Volunteers*. Dayton, OH: W. J. Shuey, 1868.

Kimberley, Edwin O. Edwin O. Kimberley Papers, State Historical Society of Wisconsin Archive.

Kirk, Elise K. *Music at the White House: A History of the American Spirit*. Urbana: University of Illinois Press, 1986.

Kmen, Henry A. *Music in New Orleans: The Formative Years 1791–1841*. Baton Rouge: Louisiana State University Press, 1966.

Lawrence, Vera Brodsky. *Music for Patriots, Politicians, and Presidents*. New York: Macmillan Publishing Company, 1975.

———. *Strong on Music: The New York Scene in the Days of George Templeton Strong, Volume 3: Repercussions 1857–1862*. Chicago: University of Chicago Press, 1999.

Leinbach, Julius. *Regiment Band of the Twenty-Sixth North Carolina*. Edited by Donald M. McCorkle. Winston-Salem, NC: The Moravian Music Foundation, 1958.

Loesser, Arthur. *Men, Women and Pianos: A Social History.* New York: Simon and Schuster, 1954.

Lomax, John, and Alan Lomax. *American Ballads and Folk Songs.* New York: The Macmillan Company, 1934.

Longstreet, James. "Our March against Pope." In *Battles and Leaders of the Civil War, Volume II.* Edited by Robert Underwood Johnson and Clarence Clough Buel. New York: Century Company, 1884–1887.

Looby, Christopher, ed. *The Complete Civil War Journal and Selected Letters of Thomas Wentworth Higginson.* Chicago: University of Chicago Press, 2000.

Lord, Francis Alfred. *They Fought for the Union.* Westport, CT: Greenwood Press, 1960.

Lord, Francis Alfred, and Arthur Wise. *Bands and Drummer Boys of the Civil War.* New York: Thomas Yoseloff, 1966.

Lott, R. Allen. "Bernard Ullman: Nineteenth-Century American Impresario." *A Celebration of American Music: Words and Music in Honor of H. Wiley Hitchcock.* Edited by Richard Crawford, R. Allen Lott, and Carol J. Oja. Ann Arbor: University of Michigan Press, 1990.

Mahar, William J. *Behind the Burnt Cork Mask: Early Blackface Minstrelsy and Antebellum American Popular Culture.* Urbana: University of Illinois Press, 1999.

Marrocco, Thomas W. and Mark Jacobs. "Ditson, Oliver." In *Music Printing and Publishing.* Edited by D. W. Krummel and Stanley Sadie. New York: W. W. Norton & Company, 1990.

Martin, Sherrill V. "Music of Black Americans during the War Years." In *Feel the Spirit: Studies in Nineteenth-Century Afro-American Music.* Edited by George R. Keck and Sherrill V. Martin. Westport, CT: Greenwood Press, 1988.

Mattfeld, Julius. *A Hundred Years of Grand Opera in New York.* New York: New York Public Library, 1927.

McCarter, William. *My Life in the Irish Brigade, The Civil War Memoirs of Private William McCarter, 116th Pennsylvania Infantry.* Edited by Kevin O'Brien. Campbell, CA: Savas Publishing Company, 1996.

McCarthy, Carlton. *Detailed Minutiae of Soldier Life in the Army of Northern Virginia, 1861–1865.* Lincoln: University of Nebraska Press, 1993.

McElroy, John. *Andersonville: A Story of Rebel Military Prisons, Fifteen Months as a Guest of the So-Called Southern Confederacy.* Toledo, OH: D. R. Locke, 1879.

McMorrie, Edward. *History of the First Regiment, Alabama Volunteer Infantry, CSA.* Montgomery: Brown Printing Company, 1904.

McPherson, James M. *Battle Cry of Freedom: The Civil War Era.* New York: Ballantine Books, 1988.

———. *For Cause and Comrades: Why Men Fought in the Civil War.* New York: Oxford University Press, 1997.

———. *The Negro's Civil War: How American Negroes Felt and Acted during the War for the Union.* New York: Vintage, 1965.

Meyers, Augustus. *Ten Years in the Ranks, U.S. Army.* New York: The Stirling Press, 1914.

Miller, Delavan S. *Drum Taps in Dixie: Memories of a Drummer Boy 1861–1865.* Watertown, NY: Hungerford-Holbrook Company, 1905.

Moore, Frank. *The Civil War in Song and Story 1860–1865.* New York: Peter Fenelon Collier, 1889.

Morrow, Mary Sue. "Somewhere between Beer and Wagner: The Cultural and Musical Impact of German Männerchöre in New York and New Orleans." In *Music and Culture in America, 1861–1918*. Edited by Michael Saffle. New York: Garland Publishing, 1998.

Moseley, Caroline. " 'Those Songs Which So Much Remind Me of You': The Musical Taste of General J.E.B. Stuart." *American Music* 9, no. 4 (1991): 384–404.

———. " 'When Will Dis Cruel War BE Ober?' Attitudes Toward Blacks in Popular Song of the Civil War." *American Music* 2, no. 3 (1984): 1–26.

Mueller, John. *The American Symphony Orchestra*. Bloomington: Indiana University Press, 1951.

Nash, Roderick. *Wilderness and the American Mind*. New Haven, CT: Yale University Press, 1973.

Nathan, Hans. *Dan Emmett and the Rise of Early Negro Minstrelsy*. Norman: University of Oklahoma Press, 1962.

Nisbet, James Cooper. *Four Years on the Firing Line*. Wilmington, NC: Broadfoot Publishing Company, 1991.

Norton, Oliver Wilcox. *Army Letters, 1861–1865: Being Extracts from Private Letters to Relatives and Friends from a Soldier in the Field during the Civil War*. Chicago: O. L. Deming, 1903.

Olson, Kenneth E. *Music and Musket: Bands and Bandsmen of the American Civil War*. Westport, CT: Greenwood Press, 1981.

Orr, N. Lee, and Lynn Wood Bertrand. *Nineteenth-Century American Musical Theater: The Collected Works of John Hill Hewitt*. New York: Garland Publishing, 1994.

Ottenberg, June C. *Opera Odyssey: Toward a History of Opera in Nineteenth-Century America*. Westport, CT: Greenwood Press, 1994.

Page, Charles D. *History of the Fourteenth Regiment, Connecticut Volunteer Infantry*. Meriden, CT: The Horton Printing Company, 1906.

Patrick, Rembert W. *The Fall of Richmond*. Baton Rouge: Louisiana State University Press, 1960.

Pisani, Michael V. "Longfellow, Robert Stoepel, and an Early Music Setting of *Hiawatha* (1859)." *American Music* 16, no. 1 (1998): 45–85.

Poe, Edgar Allan. *The Works of the Late Edgar Allan Poe, Volume III: The Literati*. New York: J. S. Redfield, 1850.

Porter, General Horace. *Campaigning with Grant*. New York: The Century Company, 1897.

Price, Angel. "Whitman's Drum Taps and Washington's Civil War Hospitals" [cited March 28, 2004]. http://xroads.virginia.edu/~CAP/hospital/whitman.htm.

Pullen, John. *The Twentieth Maine*. Philadelphia: J. B. Lippincott, 1957.

Quarles, Benjamin. *The Negro in the Making of America*. New York: Collier Books, 1987.

Raph, Theodore. *The American Song Treasury: 100 Favorites*. New York: Dover Publications, 1986.

Rauscher, Frank. *Music on the March: 1862–'65*. Philadelphia: Wm. F. Fell & Company, 1892.

Rawick, George P., ed. *The American Slave: A Composite Autobiography*. Westport, CT: Greenwood Press, 1972–1979.

Rhodes, Elisha Hunt. *All for the Union: The Civil War Diary and Letters of Elisha Hunt Rhodes*. Edited by Robert Hunt Rhodes. New York: Orion Books, 1991.

Robbins, Charles. *The Drum and Fife Instructor.* Exeter, New Hampshire: C. Norris & Co. 1812.

Robertson, James I., Jr. *The Stonewall Brigade.* Baton Rouge: Louisiana State University Press, 1963.

Rogers, Delmer D. "Bristow, George Frederick." In *Grove Music* Online. Edited by L. Macy [accessed March 20, 2004]. http://www.grovemusic.com.

Root, George Frederick. *The Story of a Musical Life, An Autobiography.* New York: Da Capo Press, 1970.

Rose, Willie Lee Nichols. *Rehearsal for Reconstruction: The Port Royal Experiment.* Indianapolis: Bobbs-Merrill, 1964.

Sablosky, Irving. *What They Heard: Music in America, 1852–1881, From the Pages of Dwight's Journal of Music.* Baton Rouge: Louisiana State University Press, 1986.

Sacks, Howard L., and Judith R. Sacks. *Way Up North in Dixie: A Black Family's Claim to the Confederate Anthem.* Washington, DC: Smithsonian Institution Press, 1993.

Sanjek, Russell. *American Popular Music and Its Business: The First Four Hundred Years. Volume II: From 1790 to 1909.* New York: Oxford University Press, 1988.

Schwartz, H. W. *Bands of America.* Garden City, NY: Doubleday & Company, 1957.

Sedgwick, Ellery. *The Atlantic Monthly, 1857–1909: Yankee Humanism at High Tide and Ebb.* Amherst: University of Massachusetts Press, 1994.

Shanet, Howard. *Philharmonic: A History of New York's Orchestra.* Garden City, NY: Doubleday & Company, 1975.

Silber, Irwin. *Songs America Voted By.* Harrisburg, PA: Stackpole Books, 1971.

———. *Songs of the Civil War.* New York: Columbia University Press, 1960.

A Sketch of the Life of Thomas Greene Bethune (Blind Tom). Philadelphia: Ledger Book and Job Printing Establishment, 1865. Text transcribed by Apex Data Services, Inc. Text encoded by Apex Data Services, Inc., Elizabeth S. Wright and Natalia Smith. First edition, 2001. Academic Affairs Library, UNC-CH, University of North Carolina at Chapel Hill, 2001 [cited September 1, 2003]. Available from World Wide Web: http://docsouth.unc.edu/neh/bethune/bethune.html.

Smith, Donald L. *The Twenty-Fourth Michigan of the Iron Brigade.* Harrisburg, PA: The Stackpole Company, 1962.

Sneden, Robert Knox. *The Eye of the Storm: A Civil War Odyssey.* Edited by Charles F. Bryan, Jr. and Nelson D. Lankford. New York: The Free Press, 2000.

Solomon, Clara. *The Civil War Diary of Clara Solomon: Growing up in New Orleans, 1861–1862.* Edited by Elliott Ashkenazi. Baton Rouge: Louisiana State University Press, 1995.

Sorrel, G. Moxley. *Recollections of a Confederate Staff Officer.* New York: Neale Publishing Company, 1905.

Southern, Eileen. *The Music of Black Americans: A History.* 2nd ed. New York: W. W. Norton & Company, 1983.

———. *Readings in Black American Music.* 2nd ed. New York: W. W. Norton & Company, 1983.

The Spiritual Songster: Containing a Variety of Camp-Meeting, and Other Hymns. Frederick-Town, MD: George Kolb, 1819.

Starr, S. Frederick. *Bamboula! The Life and Times of Louis Moreau Gottschalk.* New York: Oxford University Press, 1995.

Stonewall Brigade Band Web site [cited March 28, 2004]. http://stonewall brigadeband.com/History/history.html.

Stowe, Harriet Beecher. *Uncle Tom's Cabin*. Pleasantville, NY: The Reader's Digest Association, 1991.

Strube, Gardiner A. *Strube's Drum and Fife Instructor*. New York: D. Appleton & Co., 1869.

Stuckey, Sterling. *Slave Culture*. Oxford: Oxford University Press, 1987.

Sullivan, Lester, "Composers of Color of Nineteenth-Century New Orleans: The History behind the Music." In *Creole: The History and Legacy of Louisiana's Free People of Color*. Edited by Sybil Kein. Baton Rouge: Louisiana State University Press, 2000.

Tawa, Nicholas, E. *High-Minded and Low-Down: Music in the Lives of Americans, 1800–1861*. Boston: Northeastern University Press, 2000.

———. *A Music for the Millions: Antebellum Democratic Attitudes and the Birth of American Popular Music*. New York: Pendragon Press, 1984.

Thompson, S. Millett. *Thirteenth Regiment of New Hampshire Volunteer Infantry in the War of the Rebellion, 1861–1865: A Diary Covering Three Years and a Day*. Boston: Houghton, Mifflin and Company, 1888.

Tocqueville, Alexis de. *Democracy in America*. With a critical appraisal of each volume by John Stuart Mill. Translated by Henry Reeve. New York: Schocken Books. 1961.

Toll, Robert C. *Blacking Up: The Minstrel Show in Nineteenth Century America*. New York: Oxford University Press, 1974.

Trotter, James. *Music and Some Highly Musical People*. Boston: Lee and Shepard, 1878.

Upton, William Treat. *Willian Henry Fry: American Journalist and Composer-Critic*. New York: Thomas Y. Crowell, 1954.

Varhola, Michael J. *Everyday Life during the Civil War: A Guide for Writers, Students and Historians*. Cincinnati: Writer's Digest Books, 1999.

Vennum, Thomas, Jr. *The Ojibwa Dance Drum: Its History and Construction*. Washington, DC: Smithsonian Folklife Studies, Number 2, 1982.

Villanueva, Jari A. "24 Notes That Tap Deep Emotions" [cited September 18, 2003]. http://www.west-point.org/taps/Taps.html.

Ware, Porter W., and Thaddeus C. Lockard, Jr. *P. T. Barnum Presents Jenny Lind: The American Tour of the Swedish Nightingale*. Baton Rouge: Louisiana State University Press, 1908.

Werly, Stephen. Diary 1862–1864, Stephen Werly Papers. Western Historical Manuscript Collection, Columbia, MO.

White, William Carter. *A History of Military Music in America*. New York: The Exposition Press, 1944.

Whitman, Walt. *Drum-Taps and Sequel to Drum-Taps*. Edited by F. DeWolfe Miller. Gainesville, FL: Scholars' Facsimiles & Reprints, 1959.

Wightman, Edward King. *From Antietam to Fort Fisher: The Civil War Letters of Edward King Wightman, 1862–1865*. Edited by Edward G. Longacre. Rutherford, NJ: Fairleigh Dickinson University Press, 1985.

Wiley, Bell Irvin. *The Life of Billy Yank: The Common Soldier of the Union*. Indianapolis: Bobbs-Merrill Company, 1951.

———. *The Life of Johnny Reb: The Common Soldier of the Confederacy*. Indianapolis: Bobbs-Merrill Company, 1943.

Wiley, William. *The Civil War Diary of a Common Soldier: William Wiley of the 77th Illinois Infantry.* Edited by Terrence J. Winschel. Baton Rouge: Louisiana State University Press, 2001.

Winik, Jay. *April 1865: The Month That Saved America.* New York: HarperCollins, 2001.

Winkler, Major Frederick C. *Civil War Letters of Major Frederick C. Winkler, 1864. Home page of the 26th Wisconsin Infantry* [cited March 20, 2004]. http://www.russscott.com/~rscott/26thwis/26pgwk64.htm.

Wise, Arthur, and Francis A. Lord. *Bands and Drummer Boys of the Civil War.* South Brunswick, NJ: Thomas Yoseloff, 1966.

Yetman, Norman R. *Life under the "Peculiar Institution": Selections from the Slave Narratives.* New York: Holt, Rinehart and Winston, 1970.

Young, L. D. "Reminiscenses of a Soldier of the Orphan Brigade." Paris, KY: Chickamauga National Military Park, n.d.

Zinn, Howard. *A People's History of the United States: 1492–Present.* New York: Harper & Row, 1980.

Song Index

Subject Index

About the Author

STEVEN H. CORNELIUS is Associate Professor of Music at Bowling Green University, with a specialization in African music. He also teaches courses on nineteenth-century American music.